THE LAST PRINCIPALITY: POLITICS, RELIGION AND SOCIETY IN THE BISHOPRIC OF DURHAM, 1494–1660

Studies in Regional and Local History No 1

Editor

DAVID MARCOMBE

University of Nottingham
Department of Adult Education
1987

ISBN 1 85041 016 X

Printed by ECHO PRESS (1983) LTD., LOUGHBOROUGH

TABLE OF CONTENTS

EDITORIAL NOTE

In editing the contributions for this volume I have attempted to maintain a reasonable consistency in the use of punctuation and capitals and the modes of description employed in the footnotes. Spelling has been modernised throughout and new style dating has been employed.

The papers were submitted for publication in 1982, since when various administrative delays have held up the production of the volume. The editor and contributors would therefore like to stress that no account has been taken of books and articles published after the submission date.

David Marcombe
University of Nottingham
June 1985.

PREFACE

This volume sets out to commemorate an unusually fertile period of research into the history of the North of England, a period in which government grants were more generous than they are today and during which Professor David Loades was Senior Lecturer and later Reader in Modern History at the University of Durham.

Between 1968 and 1980 David Loades's reputation and enthusiasm attracted an unprecedented number of research students to the Durham Department where they worked on a wide range of topics, many of them relevant to the Tudor North. But Loades was more than simply an instigator and supervisor of research. His own active interests in Northern England in the broader context of the Tudor state made his advice all the more meaningful and relevant and he was always available as a sounding board, not only to his own students, but also to a wider circle of scholars and researchers whose work brought them to the North. The establishing of the Durham Research Seminar by him did much to draw together what had hitherto been a diverse and somewhat unco-ordinated series of efforts. When he left Durham to take up the Chair of History at the University College of North Wales in 1980, Northern history lost one of its great patrons and promoters.

The present collection is an attempt to mark David Loades's years at Durham by those who either knew him or worked with him as research students. All of the contributors owe him a greater or a lesser debt of gratitude. In some senses the volume represents merely the tip of an iceberg, because a wealth of important regional data still remains submerged in unpublished theses. Nevertheless, it is hoped that this book will at least provide a flavour of those pioneer years and perhaps encourage some to look further into the problems and possibilities posed by 'the last Principality'.

David Marcombe

NOTES ON CONTRIBUTORS

Louise Stevens Benham, A.B. (Smith College, Northampton, Massachusetts), M.A. (Durham) was Reader in History at Smith College from 1981–82 and is now a teacher/aide at a treatment centre for emotionally disturbed children in Saco, Maine.

Susan Keeling (née Goodliffe), B.A., Ph.D. (Durham) worked as Assistant to the General Editor of the Victoria County History from 1974–82. She is a contributor to the V.C.H. for Sussex and Cambridgeshire and to *Northern History*.

Christopher Kitching B.A., Ph.D. (Durham) is Assistant Secretary to the Royal Commission on Historical Manuscripts. Between 1970 and 1982 he was an Assistant Keeper of Public Records and in 1973 winner of the Royal Historical Society's Alexander Prize. His publications include *The Royal Visitation of 1559* (Surtees Society) and *The Chantry Certificate for London and Middlesex* (London Record Society).

J. Linda Drury (née Proom), M.A. (St. Andrews) is Assistant Keeper in the Department of Palaeography and Diplomatic, University of Durham. She has undertaken research on fourteenth century naval history and is a contributor to a range of local journals.

David Loades, B.A., M.A., Ph.D., Litt. D. (Cambridge) is Professor of History at the University College of North Wales, Bangor. Prior to that he was Reader in History at the University of Durham. He has written extensively on Tudor history and his works include *Two Tudor Conspiracies*, *The Oxford Martyrs*, *Politics and the Nation, 1450–1660* and *The Reign of Mary Tudor*.

David Marcombe, B.A. (York), Ph.D. (Durham), is Director of the Centre for Local History, Department of Adult Education, University of Nottingham. Between 1975 and 1980 he was Lecturer and Senior Lecturer in History at the College of St. Hild and St. Bede, University of Durham. He has published articles on Tudor and Stuart religious history.

Jane Freeman B.A., Ph.D. (Durham) is Assistant Editor of the Victoria County History of Wiltshire. She is a contributor to the V.C.H. for Wiltshire and is also preparing a volume for the Wiltshire Record Society.

Andrew Foster, B.A., D.Phil (Oxford) is Lecturer in History at the West Sussex College of Higher Education. His thesis comprises a biography of Bishop Richard Neile and he has published papers on related themes.

Michael Tillbrook, B.A., Ph.D. (Liverpool) is Lecturer in History at Collyer's Sixth Form College, Horsham. His thesis 'Some aspects of the government and society of County Durham, 1558–1642' covers a vast span of Palatinate history.

Bill Dumble, B.A. (London), M.Litt (Durham) is Head of the Department of English at a South Tyneside Comprehensive School. He is an occasional contributor to the *Times Educational Supplement.*

Standard Abbreviations used in Footnotes

A.A.	Archaeologia Aeliana.
A.C.	Alnwick Castle Manuscripts.
A.P.C.	Acts of the Privy Council.
B.I.	Borthwick Institute, University of York.
B.L.	British Library.
B.L.O.	Bodleian Library, Oxford.
C.B.P.	Calendar of Border Papers.
C.J.	Commons Journal.
C.P.R.	Calendar of Patent Rolls.
C.S.P.	Calendar of State Papers, Domestic.
C.S.P. For	Calendar of State Papers, Foreign.
C.S.P.Scot	Calendar of State Papers, Scottish.
C.S.P.Span	Calendar of State Papers, Spanish.
D.C.L.	Durham Cathedral Library.
D.C.R.	Durham Chapter Records, Priors Kitchen, Durham University, Department of Palaeography and Diplomatic.
D.C.R.O.	Durham County Record Office.
D.D.R.	Durham Diocesan Records, South Road, Durham University Department of Palaeography and Diplomatic.
D.U.L.	Durham University Library.
H.M.C.	Historical Manuscripts Commission.
L.J.	Lords Journal.
L.P.	Letters and Papers of Henry VIII.
N.C.H.	Northumberland County History.
N.H.	Northern History.
P.R.O.	Public Record Office.
S.S.	Surtees Society.

INTRODUCTION
DAVID LOADES

By the sixteenth century the County Palatine of Durham was unique in England. Its nearest counterpart, the County Palatine of Chester, had been in the hands of the Crown since 1301; so that although writs there ran in the name of the Earl, and were issued by the Earl's Chancery, the fact that the Earl and the King were the same person reduced that ancient liberty to the status of a convenience.[1] Other ecclesiastical franchises existed, notably in Hexhamshire (belonging to the Archbishopric of York) and in the Isle of Ely (belonging to the Bishop of Ely), but these lacked both the scope and the importance of Durham. Only in the Marches of Wales did any lay subjects of the English Crown enjoy comparable jurisdiction, and individually those Lordships were small.[2] The Principality of Wales itself was comparable, both in size and in organisation, but, like the Earldom of Chester, was in the hands of the Crown except for those comparatively brief interludes when there was a duly invested Prince.[3]

The Palatinate of Durham had been instituted in the aftermath of the Conquest; a deliberate attempt to strengthen the defences of England against the Scots by creating an autonomous power in the North, without running the risk of it turning into an independent dynastic principality. Since then the Border had stabilised further to the North and the Bishop's tenants and retainers no longer occupied the front line, but they were still very much involved in Border defence. Occasionally Scottish raids still penetrated as far south as Derwentdale; many tenures were by 'border service'; and no direct taxes were paid to the Crown, in consideration of the upkeep and garrisoning of the Bishop's castles and other warlike duties.

The Bishop in consequence was a great feudal magnate, but since his appointment was in practice always controlled by the Crown, he was seldom tempted, even during troubled periods like the mid-fifteenth century, to display the independence of his lay counterparts. His great revenues were only derived to a very small extent from his functions as a Count Palatine and his estates did not correspond, even approximately, with the boundaries of his jurisdiction. The Bishop held manors and other lands all over his vast diocese, and outside it, including a splendid London residence at Durham Place in what is now the Strand. At the same time, many other great landholders, including the Crown itself, held estates within the Palatinate; the great castles of Raby and Brancepeth, principal seats of the Nevilles, lay close to the Bishop's own residences at Durham and Bishop Auckland. The important manor of Barnard Castle belonged to the Duchy of York and the castle itself, guarding the crossing of the Tees, was in the hands of the Crown. To make the situation more complex, there were outlying parts of the Palatinate; Howdenshire, geographically in North Yorkshire, and Norhamshire along the Tweed. Norham castle, in the Bishop's hands, was a key border fortress. Also, within the Bishopric but outside the Palatinate, lay those other distinctive franchises, the Liberties of Tynedale and Redesdale, presenting all sorts of problems to outside authority, both secular and ecclesiastical.

The Bishopric of Durham was thus an exceedingly complex institution. Its ordinary ecclesiastical jurisdiction extended from the Scottish border to the Tees and from the coast to the high Pennines on the border of Cumbria, embracing the whole of the East and Middle Marches, the shires of Northumberland and Durham and the great town of Newcastle-upon-Tyne. The Palatinate was much more restricted in scope, covering County Durham itself, Howdenshire and Norhamshire. From the spiritual revenues of his see, from the profits of his Palatinate jurisdiction and from his numerous estates, the Bishop derived an income which was assessed in 1535 at £2,821, placing him among the wealthiest peers in the kingdom and second only to Winchester among the bishops.[4] Alongside the Bishopric lay the almost equally wealthy Cathedral monastery, a great Benedictine foundation reformed after the Conquest, but founded as a house of secular canons in the tenth century. The monastery also held extensive estates largely, but not entirely, within the Bishopric and the Prior was a powerful man.

This complex of wealth and power has not lacked its historians; Lapsley for the Palatinate, Storey for the late Mediaeval Bishopric and Dobson for the later days of the Priory, to name but a few.[5] There has, however, been no comprehensive study, investigating simultaneously a whole range of topics in a manner which can enable the reader to grasp the richness of this strange amalgam of secular and clerical jurisdiction. That is the objective of this collection of essays, produced by a group of scholars, most of whom have past or present connections with the University of Durham. The period chosen – roughly from the middle of the fifteenth century to the middle of the seventeenth – was a period of crisis and rapid change in the Bishopric and a period of rich and varied documentation. This was the period which saw the disappearance of the Border as an international frontier and its replacement with the 'middle shires'. It also saw the Protestant Reformation, so long resisted and so slowly absorbed in Northern England; the conversion of the Cathedral monastery into a secular Chapter (with roughly the same endowment); and two attempts to abolish the ancient Bishopric altogether. The later, and better known, of these removed both the Bishopric and the Palatinate from the jurisdictional map for nearly fifteen years (1646–1660) and saw the temporary establishment of a University[6] and normal Parliamentary representation. The former, a brief and insignificant interlude by comparison, took place a century earlier and is more interesting in the context of national politics than it is of regional history.

This was also the period which saw the first and most important stage in the permanent reduction of the Palatinate from its high Mediaeval autonomy to that lingering shadow which finally departed with the abolition of the Chancery Court in 1975. The great Franchise Act of 1536 did not (as is sometimes claimed) do away with the Palatinate; indeed, most people living in the area continued to plead in the Bishop's courts and would scarcely have noticed any difference. The Bishop's Chancery continued to issue writs and processes and the Bishops themselves to lay successful claim to regalian rights within their boundaries. Nevertheless a fundamental change had taken place. Justice was now administered in the name of the King and it was by virtue of the King's commission that the Sessions of the Peace were held. Although the full effects of the Henrician statute were only very slowly realised, they nevertheless represented the biggest single change in the status of the Palatinate between its formation and its virtual abolition in the 1830s.

A similar observation could be made concerning the dissolution of the monastery in 1540 and the erection of the Chapter a year later. The continuity was very great. Most of the endowments were simply transferred; the last Prior, Hugh Whitehead, became the first Dean and most of the former monks found places as canons or minor canons of the new foundation, to remain a subject of scandal and concern to zealous reformers for another thirty years. In a way the history of the Bishopric in these troubled years is encapsulated in the personal history of Cuthbert Tunstall, Bishop from 1530 to 1559[7]. A man of the New Learning in his youth, by the time he came to Durham Tunstall was a cautious, but tough and resilient conservative. Suspect for supporting Catherine of Aragon and less than energetic in combatting the Pilgrimage of Grace, he never dissented from the Royal Supremacy while Henry lived, and supported it to the limit of his legal obligation. Deprived for his persistent obstruction of the Protestant establishment under Edward VI, he quietly reverted to the Papal allegiance and emerged in 1553 as a strong supporter of Mary. A persecutor neither by instinct nor compulsion, he continued to be a much respected figure in the North and in spite of his great age Elizabeth made strenuous efforts to enlist his support for her new regime. In this she was unsuccessful, and in 1559 Tunstall was deprived a second time, to die shortly after in honourable confinement. Like his Bishopric, Cuthbert Tunstall was a survivor and under his rule the Church in the North East of England began to cross the watershed from Mediaeval Catholicism to Elizabethan Anglicanism with much less disruption than might have been expected. The fact that Tunstall's successors did not match up to his moderation only reflected the wisdom of the Queen in at least attempting to procure his co-operation.

Various aspects of this transition, as well as the fortunes of the Palatinate and the secular politics and administration of the area, form the subject matter of the essays which follow; a tribute to a remarkably durable set of institutions and to a period of endless variety and fascination.

NOTES

1. The even greater franchise of the Duchy of Lancaster had been in the hands of the Crown since 1399, but that was slightly different in that it lacked the geographical coherence of Durham and Chester.
2. There were nine of those Marcher Lordships, Monmouth, Ruthin, Denbigh, Bromfield and Yale, Kerry and Cydewain, Whittington, Cemaes, Chirk, and Powys. Several of these were also in the hands of the Crown by 1536. J. G. Edwards, *The Principality of Wales, 1267–1967*, pp. 15–21.
3. There was a Prince of Wales in the following periods:
   1301–1307 (Edward of Caernarfon)
   1343–1376 (Edward the Black Prince)
   1376–1377 (Richard, later Richard II)
   1399–1413 (Henry, later Henry V)
   1454–1471 (Edward, son of Henry VI)
   1471–1483 (Edward, later Edward V)
   1483–1484 (Edward, son of Richard III)
   1489–1502 (Arthur, son of Henry VII)
   1504–1509 (Henry, later Henry VIII)
   There was then no Prince of Wales until Henry, son of James I was so created in 1610. T. G. Edwards, *The Principality of Wales, 1267–1967*, pp. 30–31.
4. Winchester was valued at £3,385 in the *Valor* and the Archbishopric of Canterbury at £3,223.
5. G. T. Lapsley *The County Palatine of Durham*, (1900). R. L. Storey *Thomas Langley and the Bishopric of Durham, 1406–1537*, (1961). R. B. Dobson *Durham Priory 1400–1450*, (1973).
6. All bishoprics were abolished on October 9 1646; *Acts and Ordinances of the Interregnum*, I, pp. 879–883. C. E. Whiting *A History of Durham University*, (1932).
7. C. Sturge, *Cuthbert Tunstall*, (1938).

The Durham Clergy, 1494–1540: a study of continuity and mediocrity among the unbeneficed.

L. M. Stevens Benham

'England North of the Trent': to any student of English history the phrase conjures up romantic visions of a wild and sparsely populated countryside beyond the pale of monarchical control, the last bastion of feudalism and the 'overmighty subject' in the England of the 'new monarchy', staunchly entrenched in the time-honoured traditions and beliefs of Roman Catholicism, the church universal. Such is the traditional picture given by historians when describing the problems in enforcing monarchical authority faced by the early Tudors. Life itself was precarious in the sixteenth century, a fact to which the Pastons in East Anglia,[1] a mere hundred miles distance from the capital, could attest. How much more insecure did life become as one proceeded progressively North to the region of the Borders and Durham County?

Certainly there were elements in Northern society upon whose existence one could pretty well depend. Plague, famine and raids by border thieves were common occurrences, as a letter of the Archdeacon of Durham proves:

> I assure your Lordship your Bishopric men be very joyous and glad . . . even now to do the King's Grace and your Lordship the best pleasure and service that lieth in their power. How be it, they be not so able now by as much as they were within these three years . . . past by reason of the great death that was lately here, for within these two years there is dead within the Bishopric above the number of four thousand people, whereof in Durham town and Darlington parish only there died three thousand. And also they be very loath to have any meddling with that country . . . about Bewcastle Dale and Carlisle, by cause they did as much or more noyance to Englishmen than in manner was done unto them by the Scots at the last field . . . And besides that there is much harness lying in houses infected with sickness, where with no man dare or will meddle . . .[2]

Proximity to the Border engendered a general hatred of the Scots, pervasive to the point that if one wished to discredit a colleague, as William Franklyn wished to do in 1523, one need only voice some vague mutterings about the offending party's descent:

> albeit the . . . Dean (of Auckland) deserved great punishment for his misdemeanour (delaying the collection of a subsidy) . . . yet his act and dealing was not far discrepant from his own nature and kind, for his father's grandsire and all other of his progeny were Scotsmen born and whether he be so or not I stand in doubt.[3]

Regular indeed were these attitudes and incidents; stabilising they were not. Other forces were necessary to ensure some degree of continuity in the North. The Yorkists and later the Tudors had attempted to ensure good order through the establishment of successive councils of the North[4], thereby recognising the separate nature of the region. Society's unspoken organization according to the principle of 'good lordship', defined by Professor Loades[5] as a reciprocal relationship in which those of lesser estate recognised their obligation to serve those who had offered them protection and advice, also worked to good effect. There were certain natural leaders in sixteenth century society, a fact expressed in practical terms by Thomas Tempest in 1537, during the Pilgrimage of Grace:

> My Lord, your coming to these North parts is much comfort to all good subjects for never was so much need as now. The absence of the Bishop of Durham and of the Earl of Westmorland set all this country of Durham out of good order . . . My Lady of Westmorland with such counsel as she taketh to her stayeth the country here for a time. I assure your Lordship she rather playeth the part of a Knight than of a Lady . . .[6]

Durham County itself could offer its almost unique status as a Palatinate, a 'murus lapideus contra Scottos',[7] in which its leader was both Bishop and 'Lord Palatine' of this administrative seat to deal with the Borders. The presence of the incorruptible body of St. Cuthbert, entombed in Durham Cathedral and watched over by the Benedictine monks of that institution, offered a further aura of mysticism. Indeed, if one is looking for sources of stability and continuity in sixteenth century rural society, then one must not only consider those administrative councils or the 'body politic' which the monarchy was so careful to maintain, but the pervasive influence of the Church as well. Operating at that most basic level of society – the parish – were the vast majority of its representatives, the rectors and vicars in whose charge lay the cure of souls, and more particularly, the unbeneficed clergy, chantry priests and chaplains whose main occupation was the singing of mass for the souls of the dead. As members of the clerical estate, these men stood at once both apart from and above the normal social strata. In effect, they were 'leaders', yet their existence within the county was by any account more at one with the laity than that of most beneficed clergymen or diocesan administrators. Through them, the parishioners gained their closest experience of the day to day ministrations of the pre-Reformed Church. The complaint against the pre-Reformation clergy has tradionally been that they were too accessible and if this means that, despite their clerical status, they still shared many experiences and characteristics with the laity, then that complaint has some basis in fact for Durham County. Far from being a focus for discontent, the unbeneficed clergy were a source of continuity and stability.

William Franklyn's above allusion to the Dean of Auckland's ancestry demonstrates that there were certain traits which a man brought to the priesthood, characteristics about himself from which he could not escape. Birth, family background and educational opportunities lost or taken: these were all factors which might influence the closeness of clergy/lay relations. The conclusions of other historians working on regional studies for the sixteenth century reflect this as well. Haigh compared the anticlericalism noted by Dickens for York diocese with its apparent lack in Lancashire and observed that the Lancashire clergy were 'usually local men working in the parishes of their birth and there was no marked antipathy towards them.'[8] Bowker concluded that a priest's ability to get along with his parishioners was probably of more concern to those people than the amount of education he had.[9]

Polemical literature of the Henrician Reformation referred to the clergy as 'ruinous wolves' who had crept in and 'are now increased . . . not only into a great number, but also into a kingdom.'[10] In Simon Fish's opinion he saw the clergy as a group apart, having little in common with those to whom they ministered. The beneficed clergy (and Fish's opinion) can be briefly dispensed with, for the majority came from Durham diocese and the Northern parts of the realm. Whether they came from Westmorland, Lancashire, Yorkshire, or the diocese itself, they shared the common experience of a rural society in shires far distant from the hub of the capital.

In considering the unbeneficed, it is even difficult to give a final total of their numbers for the period. Some men appear only obscurely as witnesses in wills and then disappear entirely from the records. It has been pointed out, however, that the higher the salary of the priest, the more likely he was to have been non-resident.[11] To take this a little further, the relatively poor stipend of a chantry priest or chaplain argues for the strong likelihood that a large majority of the unbeneficed clergy were local men. Perhaps the true test of origins for the unbeneficed would be longevity of tenure. If a man had education and the right contacts, he would certainly only travel far afield to take on more than a poor chantry. Perhaps it is fair to postulate that the longer a priest held a particular chantry and remained bound to a particular area, the more likely he was to have come from that very area.

TABLE 1
The unbenificed Clergy, 1494–1540

Total	250
Appear only once in the records	153
Appear over a one to five year period	27
Appear over a five to ten year period	12
Appear over a ten to fifteen year period	19
Appear for more than fifteen years	39

Table I gives a breakdown of the unbeneficed clergy according to the time span over which each man occurs in the records. The total number of men considered is the minimum possible for the period. It does not include those men among the ordination lists, both diocesan and archiepiscopal, who do not appear as serving in some capacity after their ordination. Nor does it include those curates and chaplains named in wills and documents dated after 1540, who do not appear in any of the records of the period itself. Moreover, the time spans are calculated from a curate's first appearance as serving in some official capacity, such as acting as a proctor in the Consistory Court or witnessing a will, not from the date of his ordination.

The figures are deceiving. One would initially conclude that the unbeneficed were a fairly mobile group of men. After all, more than half of the total make a solitary showing. It is essential to understand the state of the evidence upon which these figures are based and at whose mercy the historian remains. The bulk of these one hundred and fifty-three men are mentioned in the Visitation of 1501, conducted by the Archbishop of York during a vacancy in the see of Durham.[12] Although some information can be gleaned from the registers of Durham Priory and from the records now housed in the Public Record Office, there is no other collaborative evidence available for the early sixteenth century. Fox's episcopate ended with his translation to the see of Winchester in 1501. After that date, there are no episcopal registers extant until that of Tunstall for 1530–59. No doubt quite a few of the one hundred and fifty-three men in this first category served at various chantries and curacies for several years. Ordination lists, although not conclusive, are helpful. For example, Thomas Curwen, who appeared at the Visitation as a chaplain at St. Nicholas, Durham, and for whom there is no further reference in the Durham diocesan records, appeared at York in 1493 bearing letters dimissory and was ordained to the orders of acolyte, subdeacon and deacon.[13] The case is similar for Simon Hetherington.[14] He had been issued letters dimissory by Fox and had received his final orders at York during 1499–1500. Clearly, some men's association with Durham diocese went further back than the figures in Table I show.

Similarly, the sum of the last two categories reflects the abundant evidence available at the latter end of the period, in particular for the 1530s. Perhaps the most systematic record of incumbents during that decade occurs incidentally in the *Valor Ecclesiasticus*. A comparison of these unbeneficed clergy with the chantry returns for 1548 reveals that almost 50% of the men appearing in the 1535 records recur in 1548.[15] Almost all of them were still serving at the same chantries and chapels. The case of Thomas Saunderson is not atypical. In 1535, he appeared as 'Thomas Saundersun cap'nus cantarista' at the Chantry of the Twelve Apostles in the Chapel within Barnard Castle. He was still there in 1548. Further research shows that he was present in the diocese somewhat longer than those thirteen years. He had been ordained priest by Tunstall in 1532, prior to which, in 1530, he had received the afore-named chantry as a grant from the King on the death of the previous incumbent, Christopher Appulby.[16]. Evidence over the longer period is sparce but not lacking. In 1501 German Creighton appeared as a priest at Gateshead. Thirty-four years later he was still serving as a priest at Gateshead. Thirty-four years later he was still serving in the same parish at the Chapel of the Holy Trinity.[17] Other evidence, although limited, supports the argument for local origins. Extremely few wills survive for this group of men, yet most individuals named relatives resident within the county as their beneficiaries. William Blenkinsopp and William Blunt both left bequests to their brothers.[18] Richard Towgall of Gateshead[19] established his relationship to another unbeneficed priest called John Huchenson by referring to him as 'my sister's son', and Edward Adthe[20] named what seems like a legion of men of the same surname, some of whom were based in Long Newton and who seem to have been nephews rather than siblings.

In brief, 38.7% of the two hundred and fifty unbeneficed clergy spent varying amounts of time in their chantries and of that number 64.5% remained for what seem like exceedingly long periods of time. Vicars and rectors might come and go, but the unbeneficed clergyman, the local parish priest, tended to be a rather well-established fixture in the parish. For the unbeneficed clergy in particular, their parishioners were frequently the neighbours and relatives among whom they had grown up. In many an instance, these men were an integral part of the region well before ordination.

Educationally, the experience of the future chantry priest was therefore much the same as that afforded to the layman: attendance at grammer schools maintained by chantry priests. A. F. Leach[21] regarded the grammer schools, and in particular those taught by chantry priests, as the panacea to the educational ills of the fifteenth and sixteenth centuries on the sheer strength of numbers alone. The Durham evidence argues against him in a two-fold way. Leaving aside population figures,[22] there is the matter of geographical distribution of those schools which did exist in Durham diocese. To put it mildly, they were not sprinkled at convenient intervals, but occurred in a string along the Eastern half of the diocese, the only exception being the twin schools of grammar and song at Barnard Castle in the Guild of the Trinity, located six miles from the parish church. Young boys in the North Western part of Durham County, in the areas surrounding Stanhope, Middleton-in-Teesdale and Wolsingham, would have had a fair distance to travel to attend these schools. The town of Stanhope, for example, was twenty miles from Barnard Castle, fifteen from Bishop Auckland, and twenty miles West of Durham City.[23] John Hamsterley, Rector of St. Mary in the South Bailey in 1537[24] and a local man to judge from his surname and the proximity of his patron the Earl of Westmorland, probably attended the Barnard Castle school, unless Neville had taken sufficient interest in him at an early enough age to have sent him to one of the other schools in the Eastern half of the county. Open to him were the Chantry of All Saints in Darlington which maintained 'a free school of Grammar for all manner of children thither resorting.'[25]

Durham City itself offered a wider selection, including the grammar and song schools founded in the fifteenth century by Bishop Langley[26] and taught by Robert Hertburn and William Cockey, priests at the Chantry of our Lady and St. Cuthbert in the Galilee Chapel of Durham Cathedral, and the schools maintained by the monastery for poor secular scholars. Perhaps the educational picture in Durham County would not look so grim had more of the records of the five collegiate churches survived.[27] Across the border in Northumberland only two schools come to light in the chantry certificates of Henry VIII and Edward VI. Northernmost was Alnwick, in which 'Lands and possessions belonging to the use and stipend of two priests, the one master of a grammar school and the other master of a song school . . .' were set aside.[28] In 1547, the two priests were accounted 'well learned, of honest conversation and qualities.' The other school, this time only a grammar school, was located in Morpeth[29] and was maintained by the Chantry of All Saints within the same town. The real question educationally is one of accessability, particularly relevant for the Western half of this diocese.

The education received by the future unbeneficed clergy within Durham diocese was distinctly limited, but no more so than that available to the laymen in the region. To what extent did these same men offer education after their ordination? Leach again emphasised the role played by chantry priests. Fortified by his published evidence from the chantry certificates, he not only maintained that at least two hundred chantry priests were involved in teaching but that, owing to the fitful survival of documents, many more were as well.[30] Wood-Legh and Dickens in their respective studies dispute this[31] and the Durham records support their contention that teaching was not the widespread duty among the cantarists which Leach represented it to be. Of the two hundred and fifty unbeneficed clergy known to be active in Durham County from 1494–1540, only seven men were involved actively in education.[32] One is forced to the conclusion that, just as few opportunities for learning were available to would-be clerics in the remoter areas of the diocese, so these men, when they finally obtained a chantry, would be similarly able to offer little in the way of education.

Upon his entry at Durham College in Oxford Robert Hertburn had transcended a line of demarcation which in the vast majority of cases separated the beneficed from the unbeneficed clergy. Few chantry priests ever aspired beyond the grammar schools. William Cockey, B.A. 1516 from Oxford,[33] a frequent proctor in the Durham Consistory Court and a school master in Durham, and Henry Tailboys, B.A. and a chaplain of the Chantry in Dinsdale from 1513 to 1515,[34] were two of the few men who did. Little additional evidence survives to show the results of whatever educational process the members of the Durham clergy had undergone. Many chantry certificates state, in addition to the age of the incumbent, the commissioners' general estimation of educational abilities. While the Durham documents are extraordinarily silent on this matter, the Northumberland certificates feature four chantry priests ordained under Fox and Tunstall. John Cowper, Matthew Swane, and Cuthbert Bayliff, of the ages of seventy-six, fifty, and thirty-four years respectively, were all accounted 'meanly learned' but 'of good and honest conversation and qualities.'[35] Roland Pratt, forty-eight years of age and ordained priest by Tunstall in September 1533, was alone to be considered 'well learned, of honest conversation and qualities.'[36] His will and inventory of 1565 make no mention, however, of either books owned or any bequests for educational purposes.[37]

Latinity is similarly inconclusive. Palliser has suggested that the majority of wills, because they employed the same phraseology in the opening bequests, were probably written by the priests whose names are subscribed as witnesses.[38] One fact should be noted. The majority of Durham wills, clerical in addition to lay, are in English and the only exceptions are those testaments extant for the very early part of the sixteenth century, covering the period from April through to September of 1507. These are preserved in the archives of the Dean and Chapter of Durham. The diocesan see was vacant on the death of Bishop Sever in 1505 and continued so until Bainbridge attained the post in 1507. He did not receive the temporalities until November 17 1507.[39] The Priory obviously continued some of the routine business of the Bishopric in lieu of the Archbishop of York, its traditional rival whenever the see of Durham was vacant. The urgency of the moment may well have precluded the rendering of many wills into Latin, particularly if the priest's fluency in the language made it an obviously time consuming chore. The brethren of the Priory, however, had mastered the language to such an extent as to be able to use it, not only in their official and sometimes highly legalized registers, but in such mundane matters as the 'do et lego' of last wills and testaments.

The possession of books was not only an indication of surplus wealth but the mark of an educated man. A study of the Yorkshire clergy disclosed that liturgical works predominated prior to 1540 and gradually disappeared after that date to be replaced by Renaissance writings. 1560 proved to be another watershed in terms of clerical reading material, for after that date theological works, particularly by Calvin and Beza, became common.[40] Only six of the Durham wills mention books, either generally or by name. William Blenkinsopp, successively chantry priest in Durham Castle (1534), at St. Nicholas Church, Durham (1535) and at Gateshead (1548), made provision that 'my books shall be given and distributed as . . . William Smyth, clerk, . . . shall think good.'[41] Only Humphrey Gascoigne, Master of Greatham Hospital in 1522 and Canon and Prebendary of Chester, and Richard Towgall became more detailed. Gascoigne had several books but only chose to describe 'one book of Latin of a large volume named *Sermones Discipuli*'.[42] Towgall enumerated

> a massbook . . . a manual . . . all his books . . . a dirige book . . . to Sir Stephan Tomson *Sermonis Discipuli*, Sir Thomas Childon *Sermones Parati* . . . Sir Thomas Huchinson *Assencius*, Sir Robert Bakar *Gulernus*.[43]

Clement Cockson, priest at St. John's, Newcastle-upon-Tyne, at the end of the sixteenth century bequeathed books of an intellectually more rigorous nature. Ordained in the 1530s under Tunstall, in 1598 he listed among his possessions a

> book of Cupper's *Sermons of the Visitation* . . . Calvin's *Institutions* . . . a book of *Precedents* . . . Mr. Udall his *Sermons* and Beza his *Questions* . . . the *Bible* . . . Cupper's *Dictionary* . . . a book called *The Golden Epistles*.[44]

For the early part of the century, however, the reading material of the unbeneficed was limited to liturgical tracts. Even that of the beneficed clergy, one third of whom held university degrees, was by no means mentally exacting, as Gascoigne's will shows. It is only when one considers the reading material available at such places as Auckland Collegiate Church that one encounters the humanist authors and theological works.[45] The unbeneficed clergy, to steal a phrase from their Archdeacon, were thus 'not far discrepant', at least in origins, education and social standing, from the mass of the laity whom they would serve.

In establishing a chantry, most founders went to great lengths to prescribe the exact duties they expected their cantarist to perform. The Chantry of Farnacres, in Whickham parish, founded in 1429, provides just one example of this:

> Une Chanterie d'un Maistre Chapellain et un autre Chapellain a luy associer, chauntantz divines en la Chapell de Fernacres checun jour a l'autre de St. Jean Baptiste et St. Jean L'Evaneliste, pour le bon estat de noz (Langley) et les . . . Robert Umfravile, Chivaler, et Isabelle sa feme, tancome viverons, et pour noz almes apres notre decesse, et pour les almes de Henry Quart et Henry Quint nadguirs Roys d'Engleterre, et pour toute cristens ames au merci de Dieu.[46]

The chantry statutes went on to stipulate the duties incumbent upon the chaplains. In the 1530s these men were, successively, Richard Greathead and Robert Claxton.[47] They were to celebrate regularly the canonical hours and special services of placebo, dirige and mass were to be held on every anniversary of the founder's obit.[48] It was also specifically stated that the chaplains were not to take on any form of secular employment, 'quia frequenter dum colitur Martha expellitur Maria.'[49] There is no evidence that Claxton or Greathead contravened this particular requirement. In addition they were to live continually within the quarters provided with the chantry. They were also not to consort with females, not even as servants, and were allowed two months absence every year from the chantry. After all of the qualifications were made as to their mode of living, their prime purpose remained one of intercession, of offering up services to the Saints John the Baptist and John the Evangelist for the souls of the founders and their kin.

This belief in the efficacy of the intercession of the Saints continued unabated to within years of the ultimate dissolution of the chantries. John Jackson set forth instructions in his will of 1526[50] for the foundation of a chantry in Easington parish church, worth £3 per annum to its incumbent. He awarded the patronage of the chantry to the Prior of Durham. The endowment was not only to benefit the souls of Jackson and his wife, with sundry relatives, but also a former Archdeacon of Durham, Thomas Hobbes; the then Archdeacon, William Frankleyn; Hugh Whitehead, the Prior; and one John Bentley. Although Jackson was writing almost a century after Langley and Umfravile, his provisions differed little from the fifteenth century regulations for Farnacres. The incumbent was to be continally resident, although he might have forty days absence each year for the purpose of pilgrimage or to visit friends. Matins, mass and evensong were to be his particular duties, as well as attendance at all festival days within the parish church of Easington. Jackson did not trouble himself unduly about the company which his chantry priest might keep, but he did issue the warning that if the incumbent paid too much attention to farming and the selling of grain and cattle, to the detriment of his intercessory duties, he would risk replacement by the Prior of Durham.

The incumbent of the parish was himself usually involved in choosing priests for the chaplaincies and chantries. A few such examples survive for Durham, in particular for the chantries not in the gift of the Prior and Convent. In 1531 William Stephenson was presented to the chantry in the chapel of the Blessed Virgin Mary in Gainford. His patron was William Fulthorpe, the Vicar there, who had himself been nominated for this task by the commons and burgesses of Barnard Castle in Gainford parish.[51] Just as easily the new Vicar might not have been allowed a part at all. Richard Gregg was promoted to the two chantries of St. Helen without the walls of Hartlepool and St. Nicholas within the chapel of Hartlepool, not by an ecclesiastical body or patron, but by the Mayor, Richard Lasynby and the community.[52] There is no evidence of a chantry priest actually approaching the patron himself in search of preferment. Such men always seem to have been represented by a third party, as Towgall did with his cousin, John Huchenson:

> Item: I give my chalice unto the church of this condition. And if it please God that there fall a chantry within this foresaid church being at the parishioners gift and the parishioners to be so good unto my cousin Sir John as to give and promise him before another . . . then this chalice to stand as gift. And if he be not promised and sped by those foresaid parishioners then this chalice stand as no gift but only to go unto my executors . . .[53]

Just as often, a third party was necessary to protect the rights of the cantarist once he had been appointed. George Lawson of Sheriff Hutton in North Yorkshire, for example, had to write to Cromwell in 1528 for aid in defending his chaplain's rights to an annual service in St. Edmund's chapel in Gateshead:

> So it is that the Prioress of the nuns of Newcastle who pretendeth to be patroness of the said chapel will not suffer my said chaplain to enjoy the profits and commodities of his said grant . . .[54]

Upon admittance to a benefice or chantry, the local parish priest was by no means left to his own devices in the performance of his duties. Archidiaconal visitations were meant to take place every year, episcopal visitations every three. The Prior and Convent of Durham might also decide to hold visitations of the clergy attached to their appropriated livings. There are a number of citations for such events recorded in the Priory records, but no record of the actual procedure. Upon the death of Bishop William Sever in 1505 a synod of the clergy was held in the nave of Durham Cathedral, with a list made up of the clergy attending,[55] but this in no way approached the actual examinations which were attendant upon an episcopal visitation. On such an occasion the entire body of the clergy from each parish church and chapelry would be required to gather at certain churches, chosen as centres for the visitation, where letters of ordination would be examined, oaths of obedience received, non-residency and vacancies noted and the grievances of the laity taken down.

On November 12 and 13 1501,[56] the clergy of various churches, together with representatives from the laity of each parish, gathered at

St. Nicholas Church in Durham City for the first day's proceedings in the Visitation conducted by the Archbishop of York. On November 12 the chantry priest of St. James, St. Nicholas parish, Nicholas Rowlyn, was reported to be 'infirmiter.'[57] John Hackforth, Rector of St. Mary in the South Bailey, was declared non-resident, as was Edward Strangeways, Rector of Brancepeth; four unbeneficed priests who did not appear but whose names were recorded were suspended.[58] For all seventeen parishes and chapelries examined on that day, the reports from the parishioners were a unanimous 'omnia bene', and it was much the same for the fifteen parishes on the 13th. On November 15 the venue was changed to Chester-le-Street,[59] with much the same results. The parishioners had no grievances of which to speak. The Rector of Washington, Edmund Cowper, and the Rector of Whickham, Robert Walker, failed to appear, as did two chaplains, Roger Herington of Whickham parish and Thomas Huchinson of Boldon. All four were marked 'non comparuit ideo suspensus est'. Auckland and Darlington were examined on, respectively, November 18 and 29 and on these dates the predominant concern was the state of the church fabric.[60]

There is always the question of whether greater neglect resulted in the parishes where the incumbent was non-resident. There are no court books extant for this early period so that it is impossible to discover whether the chaplains left in charge of the benefices and commonly believed to be more troublesome did, in fact, consume vast amounts of the court's time with their indiscretions. Haigh reported very few problems with the unbeneficed clergy of Lancashire.[61] The tendency of the Lancashire parishes to have two or three cantarists was repeated in Durham County. This was certainly true of such outlying parishes as Middleton-in-Teesdale with its three chaplains and Stanhope with its two.[62] St. Nicholas parish, within Durham City, had the extreme number of thirteen priests, five of whom were attached to various chantries.[63] As one proceeded further East into the smaller parishes, however, the number of these assistants dwindled. John Feld of Dalton had only one assistant while Thomas Dobson had no help whatever.[64] In the cases of the seven absentees of 1501, all of the men had coverage in their parishes to varying degrees except for John Surtees of Dinsdale, for whose parish the following was noted: '. . . Thomas Surtes, parochianus ibidem, non comparuit, qui solus est parochianus ibidem et non plures infra eandem parochiam.'[65] Dinsdale had all the appearance of a rotten borough with none of the saving grace of a Pitt!

Of those seven parishes where the incumbents were absent, for only one did the parishioners lodge any complaints and that was for the collegiate church of Darlington where it was stated that the 'fenestrae vitriae in cancello sunt confractae . . .'[66] It was hardly a fault for which the unbeneficed clergy were solely responsible. Similar complaints were heard at Egglescliffe and Conniscliffe,[67] for both of which the rectors had not appeared, as opposed to being non-resident. Nor was this failing confined to benefices where the incumbent was permanently non-resident or simply temporarily absent. At Heighington the chancel was in poor repair,[68] and at Hurworth the graveyard was not well looked after.[69] All such deficiences fell under the general category of dilapidations for which the incumbent himself was responsible, if he could not prove that he had inherited them upon his collation. There does not seem to be any positive correlation between laxadaisical unbeneficed priests and non-resident incumbents.

It is only with the return from the parish church of Gateshead that one approaches anything near a personal attack upon an individual. These attacks were directed, however, against certain members of the laity. William Gollen, Robert Syment, Stephan Byrome and Thomas Mose declared, among other things, the following:

> Dicunt insuper quod Johannes Dawson de eadem fornicatus fuit cum quadam muliere quam secum tenet in domo sua ut uxorem suam. Vir citatus comparens negat articulum a tempore quo petiit penitentiam suam sibi pro eodem crimine per ordinarium injunctam, et habet decimam diem mensis Februarii proxime futuram ad purgandum se super eodem articulo cum sua quarta manu honestarum viciniarum, et postea submisit se correctioni judicis, et habet duas fustigationes circa ecclesiam parochialem de Gateshed predictam . . . Richardus Hed de eadem fornicatus cum Jana Hadshawe de Gateshead predicta solempnizari fecerunt matrimonium inter eosdem, et judex remisit eisdem suam penitentiam publicam.[70]

These parishioners had no compunction in declaring openly the faults of one of their own. One would have expected them to show less restraint where a man, set apart from them socially by his clerical status, was concerned. Yet no grievance was voiced which could possibly be construed as indicative of strained relations. John Turpyn was declared to have allowed dilapidations to occur in his chantry, to which he replied that the 'defectus et ruinae dictae canteriae non devenerunt nec acciderunt tempore incumbentiae suae . . .'[71] He did not deny that he had failed to maintain divine service. In terms of a chantry priest's duties these were legitimate complaints on the part of the laity.[72]

The obligation to provide hospitality was not the sole province of the beneficed clergy, but it was more amply fulfilled by them and with good reason. Valuations for the chantries are only available for 1535 and the reign of Edward VI, when a chantry priest might expect an average annual gross income of £5 2s 10d and £5 2s 9d respectively. Not surprisingly, the chantries show the greatest dependence for their revenues on land. As charitable endowments, it was not uncommon for anywhere from 85 to 100% of the chantry's income to be derived from immovable property: cottages, tenements, burgages, messuages, as well as their dwelling sites. Of the fifty five chantries surveyed in 1535, thirty three of them derived 100% of their income from landed endowments, a fact oddly at variance with the traditionally very poor stipend received by the cantarists in comparison with a beneficed man.

The endowments upon which three chantries above the average income were founded are therefore notably instructive. The Guild of St. Nicholas, attached to St. Nicholas parish church in Durham City, had an annual value of £6 8s 0d,[73] based not only upon the dwelling site for the cantarist, but including numerous tenements. Four such tenements were located next to Durham Castle, two more were in Silver Street, two more in Framwellgate and another in Sadlergate, with an enclosed area next to Durham. The Chantry of St. John[74] in St. Oswald's parish was possessed of the dwelling site and a parcel of land called Edderacres, as well as one tenement in Fleshergate and another in Elvet. This particular chantry was assessed at £11 11s 4d. Bishop Langley's chantry in Durham Cathedral[75], meant to support two priests, received annual stipends from the monastery of Jervaulx and the Bishop of Durham himself for a total of £20 12s 4d. The fact of the matter seems to be that, if a chantry were to rise above the average stipend, its revenues would have to come from a fixed stable source such as a monastery or, if it were based on land holdings, these parcels would have to be both numerous and concentrated in one area, perhaps to make up for their individual small acreage. This, at least, was the case for these three chantries in Durham City, where property values were conceivably higher.

This tendency was not so apparent in the countryside, where several chantries held lands widely scattered throughout the county and drew their revenues to a successful level. In Sedgefield, the chantry of St. Thomas[76] was only some 2s 6d below the average, yet its revenues came from rather widely disparate sources. It held lands and a tenement in Ponteland parish in Northumberland, two parcels of land in Newcastle and another parcel described as lying next to the Tyne. The parish of

Sedgefield itself was some eighteen to twenty miles South of the Tyne. It was thus impossible for the incumbent of this chantry to oversee these lands himself and at the same time fulfil his obligations at the chantry. Significantly, these Newcastle lands were once again, as with the Durham City examples, within an urban area and contributed £2 6s 8d to the total gross annual income for this particular institution. The Chantry of Jesus[77] in Brancepeth parish showed a similar assortment of dispersed lands: a tenement let to farm in Whickham parish along the Tyne, another in Staindrop parish bordering Gainford on the Tees, as well as two burgages in North Auckland to the South of Brancepeth itself. These lands totalled £3 1s 0d of the total income of £7 1s 0d. The extent of these lands and more particularly their dispersal at opposite ends of the county, necessitating the farming of them by individuals other than the chantry priests, no doubt diminished their potential value to the cantarist himself.

Farming out tenements seems to have been carried out upon a grand scale in Gateshead, where despite their apparent proximity to the priest as well as their location in an urban centre, their personal administration would have proven too much for the one cantarist they were meant to support. The Chantry within the church of Gateshead had an annual income of £6 17s 0d.[78] In 1535 Robert Golele derived his living from the 'mans' dict cantarie et ceter' fruct' eiusdem'. When itemised these other fruits turned out to be a formidable list of some eleven tenements farmed out to various individuals for various fees. Such a system, whereby many people had a stake in the support of a chantry, was not always so profitable. The Chantry of the Holy Trinity in the same city[79] brought German Creighton a stipend of only £4 14s 8d based on the contributions of some twenty-three individuals. Profitable or not, such a system was significant for the fact that it brought these unbeneficed men in contact with the laity not in a religious capacity, but in a businesslike one, in much the same way that the rectors and vicars, as farmers of their glebe and collectors of tithe, had extra-religious contact with their parishioners.

How was the economic status of the unbeneficed priest reflected in his standard of living? How comfortably did the cantarist live and into what sort of possessions had he invested his money? Chantries on occasion were endowed with a dwelling. Farnacres was endowed with the entire vill and manor of Farnacres.[80] Not infrequently, however, there was no structure assigned whatsoever, or if accommodation was provided, it amounted to no more than a mere room or chamber. The Chantry of St.

James on Elvet Bridge was one such example, as was the Chantry of the Guild of the Holy Trinity in Houghton-le-Spring.[81]

Richard Towgall was a chantry priest at Gateshead, presumably at the Chantry of the Blessed Virgin Mary, and he remained so until his death. In his will he made a bequest of 'another gown that was Sir William Gowlandes . . .'[82] A William Gollyne appeared at the same chantry in 1535, when it had an assessed value of £5 4s 8d.[83] Towgall can only have enjoyed the revenues from this post for at most the six years prior to his death in 1541. There was no mention of a separate dwelling establishment or even a room in the 1535 evaluation. After all of its official expenses had been discharged it had a net income of £3 15s 4d per annum, and was assessed, if not actually required, to pay 7s 6d of that sum toward the clerical tenth. In reality Towgall could count on £3 7s 10d for his own free use.

No inventory appears to have been made of his possessions after his death. Perhaps it was felt that he did not own much of value. Be that as it may, one is left to determine his earthly goods by means of his rather short will. His initial bequests were concerned mostly with his clothes, almost all of which he left to his relatives, the Huchensons. This was one area in which clerical wills traditionally departed from those of the laity, who seldom itemised their raiment. Towgall apparently owned some little land of his own, for he bequeathed 'unto Robert Huchinson my tenement . . .' Virtually the only furniture mentioned was his bed 'that is to know a feather bed, a bolster, two coddes (*sic*) . . . blankets, two coverlets, two sheets . . .' The bulk of his other bequests were mainly concerned with religious articles. Among other things he gave to St. Cuthbert's Guild 'two altar clothes, one towel, two candlesticks, one Antiphonal, one presessiner, a dirge book, a pax . . .' By contrast, at his death in 1565, Edward Adthe, one of the 'clericil jurati' in the Durham Consistory Court of the 1530s, was found to possess two mattresses, two featherbeds and bolsters and a 'stand bed', as well as numerous sheets and blankets. His apparent wealth, however, may have been due to the fact that he had become Vicar of Lesbury in 1556.[84]

A little extra income, as well as more contact with the laity, could be gained in the Durham Consistory Court, held in the Galilee Chapel of Durham Cathedral. Graduates in civil and canon law abounded at the top of the ecclesiastical hierarchy; they took little part in the doings of the Consistory. Leaving aside the clergy who were the actual parties to suits, the class of clergy who were most conspicuous in the courts were those members of the unbeneficed group who appeared in the capacity of proctor in the various cases, the most frequent being Ralph Todd and William Cockey.[85] A further ten men appeared on May 29 1535 under the collective description 'clerici jurati', three of whom made individual appearances as proctors.[86]

Service in the ecclesiastical courts in some instances seems to have ceased with the reception of one's first living. During the 1530s seven men – Ralph Todd, John Langhorne, John Clerke, William Cockey, Lancelot Smith, George Thompson and Edward Adthe – made identifiable appearances in various suits. Todd was the most active of these men. He held an LLB from Oxford,[87] highly unusual for an unbeneficed man. Active in the Consistory from at least July 1 1531, at which session the Act Book commences, he last appeared in March of 1533 as the proctor of Bartholomew Hardwick.[88] He next appeared in the records in 1535,[89] when he was in possession of the Chantry of the Virgin and St. Cuthbert in Durham Cathedral and its precincts. William Cockey's fairly heavy duties as proctor also abruptly ceased with the attainment of a chantry. He was active in the Consistory from October 1531 until March 1534; he appeared at the same chantry as Todd in 1535.[90] If Cockey and Todd did hold this chantry while conducting suits in the court, their frequent appearance is perhaps explained by the proximity of their holding to the Galilee Chapel itself. After taking on a chantry such participation in the church courts seems fitful at best. Edward Adthe received his full canonical orders in September 1534.[91] In 1548 he appeared as a chaplain at the Guild of St. Cuthbert in Durham Castle, a post he may well have held in May of 1535 when he made his sole appearance in the Consistory.[92] Lancelot Smith made his only appearance on this same occasion with Adthe. He was probably already in possession of the Chantry of St. James in St. Nicholas parish church and the chantry chapel of St. James and St. Andrew on Elvet Bridge, also within the same parish.[93]

Unless a cleric was especially close to the courts, it does not seem likely that he would have allowed himself to become involved in much litigation. With only two exceptions[94] all of the proctors traceable to a subsequent chantry or benefice were settled in the environs of Durham City. Proper qualifications therefore must be made as to the extent of the clergy's participation in the ecclesiastical courts. The opinion that the church had a 'tendency to be run by lawyers rather than theologians,'[95] may have been true in the upper reaches of the hierarchy, but both were conspicuously lacking at the parish level in Durham County in the 1530s. Similarly, one cannot categorise the unbeneficed clergy together as a group of 'pettifogging attorneys.'[96] Only fifteen men are known to have served as proctors in the Durham Consistory, out of a total of two hundred and fifty individuals and that participation was limited by geographical location. Such limitations prevented their becoming too closely identified with this particular forum for grievances.

More problematical in its determination is the extent to which the parish clergy exerted their theological influence over the laity in their care. Mediaeval piety in all its manifestations continued to be well-supported throughout most of the period. Indulgences, the granting of which would eventually precipitate the protest of Martin Luther, were freely announced by Fox. In all, four such entries occur in his register, all for the maintenance of chapels on bridges, hospitals or altars.[97]

Ecclesiastical fire was turned upon the particularly secular problem of the border thieves.[98] Border government was not strong enough to deal with such lawlessness; people were similarly helpless in other situations with the result that religion, or at least its ritual, was a pervasive and perhaps an imperative influence in all aspects of their lives. A heresy case came before Tunstall in November of 1531 concerning a merchant from Newcastle, Roger Dichaunte, and his abjuration is instructive no less of heretical opinion than of what was considered to be orthodox belief at the time:

> I have grievously offended and erred in divers articles contrary to the doctrine of Holy Church otherwise than a good Christian man ought to have done. And chiefly and namely in these articles, that is to say. That there is no purgatory after that a man is dead. And that it is but folly to pray for them that be dead. Also that the sacrifice of the mass is not acceptable to God but rather stirreth the ire of God and crucifieth Christ of new. Also that it is but vain to pray to Saints because Christ is only our mediator. Also that because we be justified by faith no good work neither commanded by God nor invented by man can make us acceptable to God. Also that man hath no free will but all things be done by necessity so that it is not in the power of man to do good or to eschew evil. Also that every Christian man is a priest and hath power to consecrate the body of our Lord and to do all other things which priests alone now use to do. Also that every priest might and ought to be married. And also that all life of religious men living in their cloisters is but hypocrisy and therefore all monasteries ought to be pulled down.[99]

Whether one attempts to identify Dichaunte's heresy with the old time Lollardy or the Lutheran variety of Protestantism,[100] English Catholicism in the 1530s was sufficiently orthodox to condemn this merchant.

There was no sympathy for a priesthood of all believers, justification by faith alone or predestination.

Dickens and Palliser have drawn attention to the initial bequests in York wills as a possible barometer of religious conviction. Palliser divided the people making these bequests into three different groups: traditional, semi-traditional and neutral.[101] Before 1538, most York wills were of the traditional type, leaving their souls to God, the Virgin Mary and all the holy company of heaven. After 1538, the bequest of one's soul simply to God became more common, as did the semi-traditional compromise to God, yet seeking the intercession of Mary and the Saints. Suffice to say that for Durham County prior to 1540, very few lay wills are extant, but those that are display the usual opening formula: 'do et lego animam meam deo omnipotenti beate marie et omnibus sanctis . . .'[102] So begin the wills surviving for 1507. During Tunstall's episcopate, John Sherwood used the same formula and displayed a steadfast belief in the Holy Trinity as well as the efficacy of prayer to Saints.[103] While it is evident from Dichaunte's heresy that dissenting opinions were already being bruited about as early as 1531, it is not until after the 1540s that testators began making outright bequests of their souls to God alone in any significant numbers. The opening clause of the will of Sir Thomas Hilton, knight, was still a rarity, even in 1558:

> I bequeath unto almighty the father my soul and to his son Jesus Christ who hath redeemed me and all mankind by his most glorious death and passion hoping thereby to lie resuscitate with the elect in the day of his Judgement when he shall come to judge the quick and the dead . . .[104]

The wills of the Durham clergy post 1540 can also be divided into categories.[105] None can be assigned to the semi-traditional category and at first glance it seems as though the others were evenly divided between traditional beliefs and a painstakingly contrived neutrality. On the basis of their opening bequests, five wills could be considered of the traditional type, five of an unbiased nature. Of the traditional wills, three need little comment. George Baytes,[106] Vicar of Kelloe from 1535 until his death in March 1548, left his soul to God, the Virgin Mary and the holy company of heaven, as did Richard Towgall and George Reid, the Rector of Dinsdale from 1529 until his death in 1561.[107] Baytes asked that his executor, William Cockey, 'bestow my . . . goods as he shall think good for the health of my soul.' Towgall made several pious bequests and willed that his cousin John Huchenson 'sing xv masses of requiem and other xv de quinqu vulneribus for my soul's health . . .' George Reid made the usual initial bequest and left ten shillings to be distributed among the poor of various towns.

The remaining two traditional testaments and four of the five supposedly neutral wills need some measure of qualification. Anthony Farell of Dalton-le-Dale, 1530–1560,[108] made what seems a compromise variation on the traditional style:

> 'First I commend my soul unto Almighty God the maker and redeemer of all the whole world and to his blessed mother our Lady Saint Mary and to all the blessed company of heaven . . .'

He made sure to emphasise the prime place of God as the ultimate redeemer, but seemed hesitant to dispense with the Virgin and the Saints. He still believed that intercessory prayers and acts of charity were necessary, for he went on to 'bequeath to the poor folk for Jesus Christ's sake and for that of my soul my wheat stack . . .' Among his supervisors was the same Thomas Wright mentioned by Baites. John Semer[109] emphasised the supremacy of God the father by his omission of Mary, yet the 'holy company of heaven' was retained in the rubric. He too made bequests 'for the health of my soul.' One Richard Gregg, cantarist at Hartlepool in 1535 and 1548, witnessed his testament. The predestination of Calvinism and the justification by faith alone of Lutheranism had made no inroads with these two men.

Only Clement Cockson,[110] by the time of his death in 1598 a curate at St. John's Newcastle-upon-Tyne, showed no hesitation in dispensing with Mary and the whole regiment of Saints. He began very simply, 'I give my soul to Almighty God, my maker and redeemer . . .', but in the fortieth year of Elizabeth there was probably no need to hedge one's religious bets. There is no indication elsewhere in his will that he entertained any beliefs in earthly activities which could help the soul to heaven. The answer in all probability lies in the fact that one of his bequests was a copy of Calvin's *Institutions*. Cockson, who had received his orders under Tunstall in the 1530s,[111] asked for nothing to be done for the health of his soul. His will was clearly Protestant.

For the others, Edward Adthe and Thomas Wall of Bishopton, both unbeneficed, showed their position by the description they accorded to Almighty God. For Adthe,[112] God was 'my only saviour and redeemer'; for Wall,[113] the honours were shared by God Almighty and 'his son Jesus Christ my maker and redeemer.' The two most interesting wills are those of Roland Pratt and Humphrey Gascoigne. Both appear as neutral from the initial bequests. Both were far from being completely unbiased. Roland Pratt, like Adthe and Cockson, had been ordained in the 1530s.[114] He had been, in turn, a chantry priest, then Rector of Wooler in Northumberland and finally Rector of Washington in Durham County.[115] In 1565, he made his last will and testament and began by bequeathing his soul to Almighty God.[116] No Saints, no Virgin, were mentioned. Nor did he make any provisions to promote the health of his soul. Yet Pratt's will can hardly be deemed that of a man with no preference religiously. He had at some point married. Midway through his testament he left

> 'the residue of all my goods not bequeathed my debts legacies and funeral expenses deducted and paid I give unto Katherine Whytey my daughter and to her 6 children . . . and the child in her body if it shall be baptised . . . And I make Thomas Whytey my son-in-law the supervisor of the same . . .'

Pratt's marriage, together with the fact that he made no pleas for the health of his soul, allies him squarely with Protestantism.

Humphrey Gasgoigne was Master of Greatham Hospital from 1522 until his death in 1540.[117] He made a pointblank bequeathal of his soul to God, and God alone.[118] Here, at a relatively early date, was what appeared to be a neutral will, yet internal evidence lays bare the lie of that first impression. Gasgoigne went on to stipulate that placebo, dirige and mass be sung on the day of his burial, that a candle 'burn daily at mass the space of one whole year,' that a perpetual 'tabernacle for the image of our Lady' be constructed and alms be distributed for the 'health of my soul.'[119] He stipulated further that

> Sir Robert Parkin my servant shall sing at Barnburgh church for the health of my soul one whole year next and immediately following the day of my burial . . . I will that five priests at Greatham shall sing solemnly placebo, dirige and mass and have for their labours every one singularly 8d . . .[120]

The years in which these wills were made in part explain the religious character of the opening bequest. Palliser reported that while non-traditional wills were rare before the death of Henry VIII, a definitely Protestant testament was an absolute unknown in those years.[121] Baytes, Towgall and Reid made their very traditional wills in 1548, 1541 and 1559, and Gasgoigne, whose leanings were no less conservative, did so in 1540. Semer and Fawell made theirs in 1561 and 1560. In the cases of Baytes, Towgall and Gasgoigne, no great doctrinal change had yet been demanded of them. Reid, Fawell and Semer made their testaments in the early years of Elizabeth and perhaps reflect an uncertainty as to whether this settlement would last any longer than the six years of Edward or the five of Mary. None of these beneficed men are known to have been non-resident, so it is perhaps safe to infer that the preferences expressed in their wills are in some way indicative of the thinking which they encouraged in their chantry priests. These three wills are complemented by those of Pratt, Adthe and Wall.

This uneasy balance between old and new beliefs may well have been typical of the general mass of the parish clergy and probably accounted for the vacillation exhibited by a former chantry priest, William Blenkinsopp,[122] during the Rebellion of 1569. Sixty five years old at the time, by chance he happened to hear mass in Durham Cathedral on November 30 1569. Upon hearing a 'form absolucionis in Latin', Blenkinsopp knelt down and was reconciled to the Roman Catholic faith. Other priests experienced similar lapses. At the age of seventy nine, Thomas Wright, Vicar of Seaham, was accused of having sworn 'once by God and another time by Saint John.'[123] The Curate of Chester 'ministravit communionem Domini contra jura ecclesiastica . . .'[124] and Dr. Keeling has reported several instances in which priests revived the ceremony for the churching of women.[125] Old practices died a slow and lingering death and in many cases this was no doubt the result of their being almost second nature to the men involved. They, no less than their parishioners, were products of their environment and times.

The clergy made bequests to people who were among the circle of their family and friends, people in whom they deposited their trust. In that sense, the laity were no different from the clergy and in a significant number of instances the clergy appear among the most trusted of their parishioners' acquaintances. Bequests to the church works, to high altars or the poor man's box were not unusual, but they were to the institution of the church. Legacies were a sign of a more personal relationship. The singling out of a particular cleric by a layman speaks of cordial and good natured relations between the two and, in some instances, of great mutual trust. Clergymen were generally among the witnesses to a last will and testament and while they might exhort the dying parishioner to make certain pious requests for the health of their soul, it was certainly not in their power to force a parishioner to express gratitude which was lacking in the first place. Robert Bedyke, tanner of Durham City, in 1545 made his bequests to the high altar, as well as to thirty priests to be present on the day of his burial.[126] He went further, however and singled out one priest by name:

> to Jonn Foster priest for the manifold kindness that I have found in him both toward my self and my son Robert trusting that he will continue them, one ryall in gold for a token.

Many were the priests who were asked to supervise the distribution of alms and several were given the care of the deceased's children, although these were frequently their own relatives. The real significance in these bequests to clerics lies in the class of clergy singled out. Rarely was it the parish rector, more often the vicar, but predominantly the curates and chantry priests. The John Foster mentioned by Bedyke did not hold a cure of souls. Nor did Richard Dimsforth for the parish of Chester-le-Street, but it was to him that John Hedworth left 3s 4d in 1534 and he witnessed the will as well.[127] On the whole it was to the clergymen whose presence was most constant in the community, the unbeneficed, that parishioners turned.

The unbeneficed clergy, who could not afford to be non-resident and who spent great spans of time in mundane ministrations to the same parish, should be considered apart from the great mass of ecclesiastical administrators. The men in diocesan government tended to reflect the official doctrinal line at the moment. The unbeneficed clergy did not and it was their influence which was felt most closely in the parishes. If the laity showed some hesitation and vacillation in those initial bequests of their souls, it may have been in no small part due to the fact that their priests did so as well. On the whole there appears to have been remarkably little strife between the laity and the clergy in Durham County. In short, if the unbeneficed were conspicuous for anything, it was not for any clerical abuses, riotous living or wanton squandering of their livings, not even for exemplary behaviour, but for their very mediocrity. High leadership, outstanding scholarship and great social distinction were not the qualities demanded of the Durham clergy by their laity. Quite simply, the Durham clergy satisfied the expectations of this particular lay community.

NOTES

1. H. S. Bennett, *The Pastons and their England* (1979), passim.
2. P.R.O., SP/1/26/24. Sept. 10 1522, William Frankleyn to Bishop Ruthall.
3. B.L., Cottonian Ms, Titus B I, f. 295v. William Frankleyn to Bishop Wolsey.
4. R. R. Reid, *The King's Council in the North* (1921), passim.
5. D. M. Loades, *Politics and the Nation 1450–1660* (1974), p. 11.
6. P.R.O., SP 1/115/197. 6 Feb. 1537, Thomas Tempest to the Duke of Norfolk.
7. G. T. Lapsley, *The County Palatine of Durham* (1900), p. 37.
8. Christopher Haigh, *Reformation and Resistance in Tudor Lancashire* (1975), pp. 84–85.
9. Margaret Bowker, *The Secular Clergy in the Diocese of Lincoln 1495–1520* (1968), p. 56.
10. Simon Fish, *A Supplication for the Beggars*, ed. Frederick J. Furnivall, Early English Text Society, XIII (1871), p. 1.
11. Bowker, p. 92.
12. B. I., A(rchiepiscopal) R(egister), 25, ff. 148v–155v.
13. B. I., AR, 25, fol. 148v; AR, 23, f. 196r.
14. *Ibid.*, AR, 25, f. 155r; *The Register of Richard Fox Lord Bishop of Durham 1494–1501*, ed. M. P. Howden, S.S. 147 (1932), p. 127.
15. *Valor Ecclesiasticus Temp. Henr. VIII Auctoritate Regia Institutus*, Record Commission, 1825, V, pp. 312–326 (hereafter referred to as *Valor*, V); *The Injuctions and Other Ecclesiastical Proceedings of Richard Barnes, Bishop of Durham*, ed. James Raine, S.S., 22 (1845), Appendix, pp. 59–76.
16. *Ibid.*, Appendix, p. 67; *Valor*, V, p. 321; *The Registers of Cuthbert Tunstall Bishop of Durham 1530–1559 and James Pilkington Bishop of Durham 1561–1576*, ed. Gladys Hinde, Surtees Society, 161 (1952), p. 42. (Hereafter *TR*); P.R.O., Patent Rolls, C 66/657.
17. B.I., AR, 25, f. 150r; *Valor*, V, p. 322.
18. *Wills and Inventories from the Registry at Durham, III*, Surtees Society, 112 (1906), p. 102 (Hereafter referred to as *Wills and Inventories*); D.D.R., Original Will, William Blunt, priest, Croxdale, 1558.
19. D.D.R., Orig. Will, Richard Towgall, priest, Gateshead, 1541.
20. *Ibid.*, P(robate) R(egister), II, f. 225, Edward Athey, clerk, 1565. A reference to 'Edwardo Adthe consanguindo Roberti Adthe nuper de Dunelm defuncti' appears among the Chancery Enrollments of 1536, although this individual is not in any way identified as being in orders. P.R.O., DURH 3/78/membrane 4, no. 111.
21. A. F. Leach, *English Schools at the Reformation 1546–1548* (1972), passim.
22. The chantry certificates give some population figures. Barnard Castle was credited with 1,017 'howsling people', Gainford with 900, Stanhope with 1,000, and Middleton with 440. S.S., 22, Appendix, pp. 59–76.
23. William Fordyce, *The History and Antiquities of the County Palatine of Durham* (1857), I, p. 649.
24. *Fasti Dunelmenses*, ed. D. S. Boutflower, S.S., 139 (1906), p. 55.

25. Leach, p. 61.
26. *Ibid.*, p. 60.
27. However, 'Since the majority of canons were non-resident, ancient collegiate churches, particularly those which originated as royal free chapels, often had little corporate life or local influence.' Joan Simon, *Education and Society in Tudor England* (1966), p. 35.
28. Leach, p. 156.
29. *Ibid.*, pp. 155–6.
30. *Ibid.*, p. 5.
31. A. G. Dickens, *The English Reformation* (1966), p. 211; K. L. Wood-Legh, *Perpetual Chantries in Britain* (1965), pp. 269–70.
32. At the Chantry of Our Lady and St. Cuthbert in Durham Cathedral: Robert Hertburn and William Cockey; at the Guild of the Trinity in Barnard Castle: Peter Cawerd; at Bishop Langley's school: John Hotchinson, William Dossey, Thomas Sanderson and Edward Watson. Leach, pp. 60–61; *Victoria County History of Durham* (1907), I, pp. 373–4.
33. C. W. Boase, *Register of the University of Oxford* (1885), I, p. 97.
34. D. C. R., S(mall) P(rior's) Reg(ister), IV, f. 194v; *TR*. p. 127.
35. S.S., 22, Appendix, pp. 79–86.
36. *Ibid.*, Appendix, p. 84.
37. D.D.R., Orig. Will, Roland Pratt, Washington, Parson, 1565.
38. D. M. Palliser, *The Reformation in York 1534–1553* (1971), p. 19.
39. A. B. Emden, *A Biographical Register of the University of Oxford to A.D. 1500* (1957), I, p. 92.
40. J. S. Purvis, 'The Literacy of the Later Tudor Clergy in Yorkshire', *Studies in Church History*, 5, (1969), pp. 147–165.
41. S.S., 112, p. 102.
42. B.I., AR, 28, ff. 182v–183r.
43. D.D.R., Orig. Will, Richard Towgall, priest, Gateshead, 1541.
44. *Ibid.*, Orig. Will, Clement Cockson, clerk, curate of St. John's, Newcastle-upon-Tyne, 1598.
45. *TR*, p. 93.
46. Robert Surtees, *The History and Antiquities of the County Palatine of Durham* (1816–1820), II, p. 243.
47. *Valor*, V, p. 323; *TR*, p. 72; S.S., 22, Appendix, p. 72.
48. Surtees, II, p. 243.
49. *Ibid.*
50. D.C.R., P(rior's) R(egister), V, ff. 218v–219v.
51. *TR*, p. 31.
52. *Ibid.*, p. 65.
53. D.D.R. Orig. Will, Richard Towgall, Gateshead, priest, 1541.
54. P.R.O., SP 1/50/243.
55. D.C.R., PReg, V, ff. 88r–88v. This list is not by surname, but by the 'Vicar of Heighington', etc.
56. B.I., AR, 25, ff. 148v–150v.
57. *Ibid.*, f. 148v.
58. *Ibid.*, ff. 148v–149r.
59. *Ibid.*, f. 150v.

60. *Ibid.*, ff. 154r–155v.
61. Haigh, p. 28.
62. B.I., AR, 25, f. 154r.
63. *Ibid.*, f. 148v.
64. *Ibid.*, ff. 149v–150r.
65. *Ibid.*, f. 155v.
66. *Ibid.*, f. 154r.
67. *Ibid.*, ff. 155r–v.
68. *Ibid.*, f. 155r.
69. *Ibid.*, f. 155r.
70. *Ibid.*, ff. 150r–151r.
71. *Ibid.*, f. 151r.
72. There is but one single example of a moral offence concerning an unbeneficed clerk who survived into the late 1490s. Robert Seggefeld, cantarist at the Chantry of the Blessed Virgin Mary in St. Oswald's parish church, had died by December 7 1498. In the mid fifteenth century, he appeared before the Consistory Court 'quod fornicatus est et carnaliter cognovit Margaretam Bell sororem Thomae Cornforth.' D.C.R., PReg, V, f. 45v.; *Depositions and Other Ecclesiastical Proceedings from the Courts of Durham* ed. James Raine, S.S., 21 (1845), pp. 35–36.
73. *Valor*, V, p. 318.
74. *Ibid.*, p. 324.
75. *Ibid.*
76. *Ibid.*, p. 321.
77. *Ibid.*, p. 322.
78. *Ibid.*
79. *Ibid.*, The figure given is that of the *Valor*. By my addition, it should be £4 16s 8d.
80. Surtees, II, p. 243.
81. *Valor*, V. pp. 324–325.
82. D.D.R., Orig. Will, Richard Towgall, Gateshead, priest, 1541.
83. *Valor*, V, p. 322.
84. D.D.R., C(onsistory) C(ourt) A(ct) B(ook), f. 73v; PR, II, f. 225v; *TR*, p. 107.
85. D.D.R., CCAB, see ff. 7v, 37r, 60v. 66v–67r for Cockey; for Todd, see ff. 1r–62v.
86. *Ibid.*, f 73v. They were Lancelot Smith, George Thompson, and Edward Adthe.
87. Ann Forster, 'Bishop Tunstall's Priests', *Recusant History*, 9 (1967–68), p. 201.
88. D.D.R., CCAB, f. 62v.
89. *Valor*, V, p. 324.
90. *Ibid.*
91. *TR*, p. 58.
92. S.S., 22, Appendix, p. 62; D.D.R., CCAB, f. 73v.
93. *Valor*, V, pp. 324–325.
94. The exceptions were George Thompson, a chaplain at Boldon, not only a proctor but a frequent party to suits, and John Langhorne, who appeared

in a probate case of the Rector of Sedgefield in 1531. Both of these men were located in the Eastern lowland regions of Durham County. D.D.R., CCAB, ff. 29r, 52r, 73r, 1v; Orig. Will, John Barforth, Sedgefield, 1548.

95. Bowker, p. 5.
96. H. Maynard Smith, *Pre-Reformation England* (1938), p. 82.
97. *TR*, pp. 15–19, 134–35.
98. *Ibid.*, pp. 80–84.
99. *TR*, p. 35.
100. See A. G. Dickens, *Lollards and Protestants in the Diocese of York 1509–1558* (1959), passim.
101. Palliser, p. 20.
102. D.C.R., Locellus 37, nos. 7, 8, 10–16.
103. *TR*, pp. 53–54; D.D.R., PR, I, f. 29.
104. *Ibid.*, PR, II, ff. 21r–v.
105. I have purposely included the wills of the beneficed in this sample, in part because of the scarcity of wills surviving for the unbeneficed, but primarily because it may be possible to infer religious preferences of more of the unbeneficed named as close friends, executors and supervisors in the wills of the Rectors and Vicars.
106. D.D.R., Orig. Will, George Bayts, Kelloe, Vicar, 1548.
107. *Ibid.*, Orig. Will, Richard Towgall, Gateshead, priest, 1541; Orig. Will, George Read, Parson of Dinsdale.
108. *Ibid.*, PR, II, ff. 299v–301.
109. *Ibid.*, ff. 6v–7.
110. *Ibid.*, Orig. Will, Clement Cockson, clerk, 1598.
111. *TR*, pp. 52, 57, 64, 65, 67.
112. D.D.R., PR, II, f. 225.
113. *Ibid.*, PR, V, f. 104.
114. *TR*, pp. 27, 42, 43, 53. For Adthe, see pp. 27, 45, 52, 58.
115. *Ibid.*, pp. 95, 102; S.S., 22, Appendix, p. 84.
116. D.D.R., Orig. Will, Roland Pratt, Washington, Parson, 1565.
117. S.S., 139, p. 49.
118. B.I., AR, 28, f. 182v.
119. *Ibid.*, ff. 182v–183r.
120 *Ibid.*, ff. 183r–v.
121. Palliser, p. 20.
122. S.S., 112, p. 102; *TR*, p. 59; S.S., 22, Appendix, p. 65; S.S., 21, pp. 143–44.
123. *Ibid.*, p. 113.
124. *Ibid.*, p. 198.
125. S. M. Keeling, 'The Church and Religion in the Anglo-Scottish Border Counties 1534–1572' (Unpub. Ph.D. thesis, University of Durham, 1975), p. 452.
126. D.D.R., Orig. Will, Robert Bedyke, tanner, 1545.
127. *Ibid.*,PR, I, f. 29; *TR*, pp. 53–54.

The Dissolution of the Monasteries in the Border Country

Susan Keeling

The Anglo-Scottish Border counties have generally been regarded as violent, backward and Catholic. Even studies defending the rest of Northern England from such charges tend to conclude that the Borders might be so described[1] and indeed the charges can be substantiated. The barrenness of the country, except in the coastal plain, and the depredations of armies had alike encouraged a society which found the rewards of raiding and rustling greater than those of tilling the soil. The need for some social stability in the midst of this world of reiving and warfare had encouraged a social system which when viewed from outside appeared intensely feudal, but which was in fact based as much on loyalty to a family or 'surname' as on the pattern of landholding. The Borders were above all a self-regarding community. Scottish and English Borderers had far more in common with each other than with their compatriots and their loyalty to a Dacre, a Percy, a Maxwell, or a Scott was greater than that to the sovereign in London or Edinburgh. Whilst the Border remained a national boundary between two frequently warring nations and whilst the two governments were prepared to encourage lawlessness and violence in the opposing realms for their own ends, the basic nature of Border society was unlikely to change. Whilst it remained unchanged both Edinburgh and London found themselves obliged to adapt to the Borderers' ways of behaviour and to govern through local magnates, thus perpetuating the system.

Outsiders appointed to offices in the Borders rarely survived for long. Anthony de la Bastie, appointed Warden of the Scottish East March, was murdered within a year[2] and Hertford, appointed Warden General in the North of England in 1542, feared that

> he that shall serve here had need to be both kin and allied among them of these parts and such are that hath and doth bear rule in the country.[3]

Above all else the Borderers distrusted outsiders, but with their fellow Borderers they shared social and political organization, prejudices and codes of behaviour, everything except nationality. To them the artificial division of the Border was mostly a convenient barrier behind which to withdraw, or across which to escape, when expedient. It is impossible to consider the dissolution of the Northumberland monasteries without putting them into the context of the Border society which they inhabited.

The supposed Catholicism of the North is also an important consideration. The Borderers' distrust of outside influences could be expected to lead them to reject any new ideas and practices introduced from outside and thus appear loyal to the Catholic church, but contemporaries were convinced that in the main the Borderers had 'no knowledge of Christ's gospel'.[4]

> They are more superstitious than virtuous, long accustomed to frantic fantasies and ceremonies, which they regard more than either God or their prince, right far alienate from true religion.[5]

Evidence that this was true of the wilder elements of Border society, the 'delinquent minority',[6] is plentiful.[7] Reivers who according to the Scottish Catholic Bishop Leslie

> never so fervently . . . say their prayers . . ., nor with such solicitude and care, as often as when they have forty or fifty miles to drive a prey,[8]

were almost as far removed from the Catholic as from the reformed church. The majority of the population of the Border counties was less spectacular in its unorthodoxy but suffered, according to contemporary opinion, from lack of instruction and preaching.[9] As a result it was the outward forms of faith which mattered to them; the performance of ritual had a quasi-magical power in this society which clung so much to tradition and in the Border ballads magical rites figure far more frequently than any recognisably Christian motif.[10] The persistence of such attitudes suggests that this lack of teaching, although it hampered the spread of the reformed faith, did nothing to strengthen the old one.

It is against this background that the suppression of the religious houses was enacted in the English Borders.[11] There were in Northumberland before the Dissolution ten monastic houses,[12] three nunneries[13] and seven friaries.[14] They ranged from Hexham, Alnwick, Newminster and Tynemouth, with between fifteen and twenty inmates at their suppression, to the cells of Holy Island, Farne Island and Ovingham with only two or three. According to Bishop Barlow writing in 1535 there were in the Borders 'plenty of priests, sundry sorts of religious, multitudes of monks and flocking companies of friars', but they made little impact on the religious life of the area.[15] In all the Northumberland houses held about one hundred monks and canons, fifty friars and twenty five nuns.[16] Most of the friaries were concentrated in Newcastle, but many of the other communities were situated in the wilder parts of the county. Even Alnwick, Hexham and Newminster (Morpeth), sited like most of their Scottish counterparts in or near towns which were sizeable by Border standards, were still in areas where the Border rather than the national ethos prevailed. Blanchland, Brinkburn and the nunneries of Holystone and Lamley were particularly isolated. That they survived at all was due to their usefulness to Border society and to their absorption, at least partially, into the quarrelsome and violent fabric of that society, from which most of their inmates were drawn.[17]

In 1521 a dispute between Brinkburn and the Lisles over tithes led to the murder of one of the canons.[18] Sir John Delaval had quarrels with both Hexham and Tynemouth in the 1520s. The latter priory was attacked by about two hundred men intending to hold a court there; the Prior prevented their entering, but they threatened him and took the Bursar prisoner.[19] One of the intruders was Sir Thomas Hilton to whom, ironically, the priory was advised to appeal for protection in 1536 when its tenants forcibly withheld rents and again threatened to enter the house.[20]

This involvement in local affairs was partly a reflection of the government's long reliance upon the monastic houses in secular affairs. The Prior of Durham seems regularly to have acted as treasurer of royal money during Border wars and in 1515 the Abbot of Newminster was sent to meet the Queen of Scotland at Morpeth.[21] Tynemouth Priory, sited within the castle, concerned Lord Darcy in 1536 because it was a 'house of very great strength',[22] and the Earl of Northumberland made Alnwick Abbey and Hulne Friary his bases as Warden of the Marches.[23] In 1537 the Abbot of Alnwick was given a store of arms for safekeeping.[24] Evidence from other parts of the Borders reinforces the picture of secular preoccupation. In August 1536 the Convent of Holme Cultram, in Cumberland, asked Cromwell for a commission to elect a new abbot without delay 'as they are continually exposed to danger from the raids of the Scots'.[25] The Abbot of Jedburgh, who harboured the murderers of English officials and himself led plundering expeditions into England,[26] was in a somewhat different position as a lay commendator. The Prioress of St Bothans, however, who gave treasonable assistance to English forces, supplying them with weapons,[27] and the Prioress of Coldstream who acted as an English spy from at least 1523 until her death in 1537,[28] although oustanding examples, were in many ways typical of the heads of Border houses before the Dissolution.

In the 1560s the Earl of Northumberland's surveyor was concerned with local churches still largely from a military viewpoint.[29] In 1566 he suggested that as Long Houghton church, formerly appropriated to Alnwick, was such a great strength to the neighbourhood in times of war, the cost of repairing the chancel should fall on the Crown, as a military expense, thus freeing the Earl from his responsibility as lay rector.[30] Lack of complaints about the monasteries' fulfilment of such obligations would suggest that they kept the churches for which they were responsible in reasonable repair, although the whole of the Border area seems to have been characterised by a reluctance to spend money on repairing buildings so likely to be the target of attacks by either Border thieves or invading armies.[31] In 1556 of twenty-two churches in the Scottish Merse in poor repair nine belonged to Coldingham Abbey, six to Kelso and two to Dryburgh.[32] It is impossible to tell whether the English houses really were more conscientious than their Scottish counterparts.

The general usefulness of monastic houses to Border society is illustrated by Robert Aske's admittedly exaggerated defence of them. As a result of their suppression there was

> no hospitality now kept in those parts . . . and the profits of the abbeys yearly go out of the country to the King . . . Also several of these abbeys were in the mountains and desert places, where the people be rude of conditions and not well taught the law of God and when the abbeys stood the people not only had worldly refreshing in their bodies but spiritual refuge, both by ghostly living of them and by spiritual information and teaching.

Not only was 'the service of God . . . much diminished' but the monks were missed for their provision of education and maintenance of roads, bridges and sea walls.[33] Archbishop Lee's plea that Hexham should not be suppressed was based strongly on such secular considerations:

> if the monastery go down . . . all shall be much waste within the land. And what comfort that monastery is daily to the country there, and specially in time of war, not only the countrymen do know, but also many of the noblemen of this realm that hath done the King's Highness service in Scotland.[34]

The Archbishop, who had visited Hexham in 1534 and had had to issue injunctions about the strict observance of the Augustinian rule and in particular about too free an intercourse with outsiders necessarily encouraged by its secular role, perhaps felt unable to defend the house so firmly on spiritual grounds.[35]

The monastic communities were enmeshed in Border society and their buildings were some of the most obvious reminders of the church in that area, but what of more detailed evidence of their spiritual role? Evidence that the Northumberland houses served in any way as centres of learning is generally lacking, with the exception of Hulne Friary. That Carmelite house was valued at less than £17 in 1539, but it had a library of a hundred and fourteen books, including, as well as missals, service books, the scriptures and several commentaries, works by St Gregory, St Bernard, St Augustine, Odo, Anselm, Bede and Peter Lombard, histories and chronicles, grammar, logic and philosophy books and twenty-two canon law books. The house was also well equipped with vestments and plate, presumably because of the patronage of the Percies, and must have been conspicuous amongst the other Border houses.[36]

The involvement of those houses in Northumberland's parochial organisation was, however, extensive. Eleven Northumberland cures were wholly appropriated to monasteries in the area,[37] and served by a chaplain provided and paid by the monastery, and a further twenty-two vicarages were in the patronage of Northumberland houses. Moreover, those thirty-three parishes had between them twenty-nine dependent chapelries and thus the monasteries were responsible for much of the provision of secular clergy within the Borders. Particularly prominent were Alnwick Abbey, with the patronage of nine cures, and Hexham Priory with eight. Before the Dissolution sixteen of the cures were served by members of the appropriating house and several of the cures for which no evidence survives were probably also so served. The Dissolution did not however remove all these regulars from parochial service. Many continued to serve the same cure for some years after.

From Alnwick Abbey Ralph Galland served as Vicar of Alnham until 1554,[38] Roger Spence as Curate of Alnmouth until 1578,[39] Robert Foster as Curate of Alnwick until 1540,[40] William Marshall as Vicar of Chatton until 1549,[41] Thomas Winfield as Vicar of Lesbury until 1556[42] and Robert Clarke and George Wilkinson successively served Shilbottle until 1554.[43] John Grey, canon of Brinkburn, served as chaplain there until 1546[44] and his fellow canon Edward Hutton was Vicar of Felton until 1547.[45] Henry Spragen, canon of Blanchland, was Vicar of Bywell

St Andrew until 1564[46] and William Thornton, canon of Hexham, served Ovingham until 1567.[47] Also after the Dissolution a number of ex-religious chose to augment their pensions by parochial service and a further fourteen ex-members of Northumberland houses are recorded in Northumberland cures up to 1578. They included the Sub-Prior of Hexham, Vicar of Alnham from 1559,[48] and monks of Tynemouth serving Eglingham from 1559 to 1578[49] and Long Horsley from 1557 to *c.* 1584.[50] At Felton, Hutton was followed by an ex-canon of Alnwick who served until 1554[51] and another ex-canon of Brinkburn served there from 1558.[52]

This continuity of service highlights a major difference between the English and Scottish churches. In the Central and Eastern Scottish Borders fifty-one out of ninety-eight cures were appropriated to local religious houses, especially Kelso and Coldingham,[53] but in only nine cases is there evidence that the religious served the cures themselves[54] and in only four cases, Lessuden, Melrose, Mertoun and Stitchill, is there record of an ex-religious serving in the reformed church.[55] Since the Scottish religious were not turned out of their houses in 1560 and continued to receive adequate portions, there was little incentive for them to take up a parochial cure unless moved by a true devotion to the reformed church. As in England therefore many curses were ill served after the Reformation.

In the 1560s Bishop Pilkington complained that many of the Northumberland cures were of such low value and that the many chapels

> have no livings at all, and many of them never a priest, and those that have any be Scots, vagabonds and wicked men which hide themselves there because they dare not abide in their country and serve for little or nothing . . . Many of the parsonages in these parishes are impropriated to abbeys and while they stood they were better served. Now they be in the Queen's majesty's hand or else sold.[56]

In 1587 Robert Arden made much the same complaint, blaming the low value of so many livings for the dearth of preachers and lack of teaching in the county.[57]

It would seem that the opportunity offered in England by the Dissolution, to take the extensive monastic patronage into the Crown's own hands, or to grant it to sympathetic laity and thus to improve the parochial provision in the Borders, had been entirely neglected. Of those cures whose patronage passed to the Crown, Kirkharle was vacant from 1561 to 1565 and in 1578,[58] Felton was vacant in the 1560s[59] and Bolam in the 1570s.[60] Two chapels of Bywell St Andrews were served by

Scottish curates, as were the chapelries of Corsenside and Holystone.[61] Tynemouth was better provided with vicars, but as the old priory church, within the castle, was used as the parish church, both military and religious interests were seriously inconvenienced.[62] Of the four chapels in Eglingham parish, which had belonged to Tynemouth Priory, only one has left record of any service before 1578, two had no curates even then, when one was served by an unlicensed Englishman and one by a Scot, both of whom absented themselves from visitation.[63] The Rectory of Alwinton, which had belonged to Holystone Nunnery, was leased first to local men and in 1562 to a Londoner, with provision made for the payment of a vicar, but in 1563 and 1578 there was only a Scottish curate there.[64] No chaplains are recorded for its two dependent chapels until 1578.[65] The chapel of Lamley which passed from the priory firstly to the Earl of Northumberland and then to Albany Featherstonhaugh has no recorded chaplain before the Scottish curate there in 1578.[66] Several of the cures belonging to Alnwick Abbey fared particularly badly. Alnmouth had, before the Dissolution, been served by two priests paid by the abbey, but by 1566 there was only one priest who received 53s. 4d. from small tithes and offerings.

> The Prince hath let all the rest by lease and receives the yearly rent thereof so that if it be not by some means foreseen after the death of the vicar that now is who hath also a pension of the Prince (as an ex-canon) there will no priest of any understanding or knowledge take upon him the same and all for lack of living.[67]

At Alnwick, where the canons had served the church, an ex-canon served in 1540, for his pension of £7, but although in 1547 £12 was granted from the abbey lands for a curate no subsequent incumbent is recorded until 1577.[68] Chatton, which had also belonged to Alnwick Abbey, passed into the Crown's hands at the Dissolution and there were three royal presentations between 1550 and 1559, none of which seems to have taken effect.[69] The patronage subsequently passed to the Earl of Northumberland and in 1563 the Vicar, the ex-Abbot of Alnwick, kept a Scottish curate there.[70] The chapel of Braynshaugh in Shilbottle parish, formerly served by canons of Alnwick, fell into complete disuse after the Dissolution. It was in the 1560s leased to Sir John Forster,[71] as were the churches dependent upon Hexham priory, including Allandale, Slaley and St John's Lee, and in 1578 an incumbent was recorded for only one of those, Slaley, where there was an unlicensed Scot.[72] As late as 1587 it was demanded that

> now after he (Forster) has so long time gathered the fleece, he would employ some portion of every of the same livings for finding of preachers.[73]

No more in the distribution of monastic land than of patronage did the English government take the opportunity to encourage new men who might break the hold of entrenched local interests on Border life. Of the three nunneries Newcastle went to James Lawson of Newcastle, the brother of the last Prioress;[74] Lamley was leased to Richard Carnaby, previously its bailiff, and although it was granted to Northumberland in 1553 he immediately conveyed it to another local man, Albany Featherstonhaugh.[75] Holystone went first to Richard Lisle and later to John Heron.[76] The cell of Holy Island was leased to Thomas Sparke, the last Prior, and after his death to the Captain of Berwick[77] and Farne Island went to the Dean and Chapter of Durham. Bamburgh was granted to Sir John Forster.[78] The Crown retained several of the possessions of Alnwick Abbey, but leased others to local families, as it did the site and lands of Brinkburn.[79] Tynemouth was granted firstly to Sir Thomas Hilton, long involved in its affairs, and in 1557 to the Earl of Northumberland.[80] Northumberland also secured a grant of Newminster for one of his officers, William Grene,[81] Receiver for Northumberland, Cumberland and Westmorland and an official of the Court of Augmentations, who also received Blanchland, despite the Earl of Westmorland's attempts to secure it for himself.[82] Hexham was granted to Sir Reynold Carnaby, much to the resentment of certain local interests, but although he was a useful government tool in the North he was also a protégé of the Earl of Northumberland, a member of an old Northumberland family and already the Archbishop of York's officer in Hexhamshire, thus hardly a new man.[83]

Hexham was the only house in Northumberland to offer armed resistance to the Dissolution. In late September 1536 the commissioners for its dissolution were met on their arrival in Hexham with the news that the Master of Ovingham, who had taken charge while the Prior was in London petitioning Cromwell, had armed the house. He appeared in armour and scared the commissioners into retreating to Corbridge, before leading the canons and other armed men to parade outside the priory.[84] By the middle of October the canons were prepared to come to terms with Sir Reynold Carnaby, but the whole incident was prolonged and confused by the intervention of John Heron of Chipchase and the men of Tynedale, ready to take advantage of any unrest.[85] The priory was finally dissolved, without any further resistance, in February 1537 and it seems that the King's order to hang dissident canons was ignored since none had made any resistance since the general pardon to the Pilgrims.[86] The suggestion made in 1537 that the canons of Newminster had been implicated in the revolt is unsubstantiated[87] and nowhere else in Northumberland was there involvement of the regular clergy, who played such a prominent part in the rising in Cumberland[88] and Lancashire.[89]

Most of the other Northumberland houses, all of which except Tynemouth were valued at less than £200, were surrendered in 1537 with no trouble. However, Alnwick, Blanchland, Newcastle and Holystone were all exempted[90] and finally suppressed in December 1539 and January 1540.[91]

The latter month also saw the suppression of the only remaining religious communities, the friaries. Although five of them were in Newcastle their inhabitants may well have travelled considerably in the area. It was Franciscan friars from Jedburgh who were said to have baptised, married and celebrated mass in the wilds of Liddesdale in the earlier sixteenth century[92] and some of their English counterparts may well have done likewise. In 1521 when an English raid had left the Jedburgh friary in ruins, its Warden was given permission to enter the country to preach at Norham[93] and in 1525 at least one Scottish friar was to be found in Tynedale, whose thieves, coming under an interdict imposed simultaneously by Wolsey and the Archbishop of Glasgow in an attempt to curb the lawlessness of the area, ignored the church's displeasure and forced the friar to administer communion to them.[94] Such wandering preachers, whether English or Scots, do not seem to have had any great influence on the wilder Borderers.

Perhaps because they were used to mobility both English and Scottish friars seem to have been more prone than the rest of the clergy to seek refuge in the opposite realm. At least eight English Observants sought refuge in Scotland in 1534,[95] two of whom were amongst a group who re-entered the Franciscan friary in Newcastle during the 1536 Rising. They were expelled and again fled North, but returned to ask for mercy in November 1537.[96] In 1536 Richard Marshal, Prior of the Newcastle Dominicans, who had refused to accept and preach the Royal Supremacy, also fled to Scotland.[97] There was however no trouble when the friaries came to be suppressed.[98] The property of most of the Newcastle houses went directly or eventually to local men, apart from the Austin friary which was reserved for the use of the King's Council in the North. The other two Northumberland houses were also granted to local officials, Bamburgh to Thomas Horsley and Hulne to Sir Robert Ellerker.[99] No friars' names are recorded for the last two houses at their suppression, but of the fifty friars in Newcastle eleven went on to serve in parish churches or chantries.[100]

Most of the inmates of Northumberland's religious houses seem to have been recruited from local families and even those who did not continue to serve in parishes, or find parochial employment after a number of years, are likely to have remained within the area after the Dissolution. The Prioress of Newcastle and her sister the Prioress of Neasham in County Durham ended their days as comfortable small farmers[101] and the Prior of Tynemouth, although originally from Hertfordshire, retired to the former monastic manor of Benwell.[102] William Harrison, Abbot of Alnwick, supplemented his £50 pension with the Rectory of Bothal and perhaps the Vicarage of Lesbury. He was deprived for marriage in 1554, but restored by the 1559 visitors whose deputy he was and he went on to hold the Vicarage of Chatton and to found a prominent county family.[103]

Harrison was obviously a firm adherent of the new faith, but the government was for a long time concerned about the influence of less sympathetic ex-religious in the Borders. In December 1539 it was proposed to send a garrison of a hundred and seventy men to Sir John Heron in Tynedale 'considering that of late there are so many foxes and wolves put at large and let loose out of cloisters.' The force was intended to keep such ex-religious out of the Borders and stop them escaping to Scotland.[104] It probably had little effect however; the escape routes were too well established and too frequently used, by both clergy and laity, to be so easily cut. The English government was happy to encourage the flow of 'gentlemen and clerks who flee out of Scotland, as they say, for reading the scripture in English',[104] whilst King James refused to expel 'friars, priests and other churchmen that are fled into Scotland', but 'leaves the handling of their persons to their ordinaries, Archbishops and other prelates that are their judges by the laws of Holy Church.'[105]

The English religious were of course set free at a time when Scotland was still happy to encourage adherents of the Catholic church. By the time that the Scottish Reformation dislodged a number of Catholic clergy England was a Protestant country intent on keeping out those Scottish priests. And yet many of them found refuge, and sometimes a curacy, in England.[106] As the reformed faith became more firmly established in Scotland those Scottish ex-religious who were truly attached to the Catholic church were moved to leave their livings, which they were assured for life, and to seek more congenial surroundings which they often found in North East England, 'the common refuge of papist offenders that cannot live here and are unworthy to live anywhere.'[107] In 1562 the English ambassador in Scotland was warning of certain 'wicked friars' who, leaving Scotland for fear of punishment, were being employed as ministers in England.[108] As we have seen many of them found employment in cures once served by the English monasteries. 'The country is willing to take them that will serve best cheap'.[109] Bishop Pilkington was naturally concerned that the vacuum created to some extent by the Dissolution should be filled by those regarded as too Catholic or too unlearned to serve in the Scottish church. The government was concerned for the security of the Borders when these Scots could 'conduct all Scotland into the realm.'[110] Once again secular and spiritual problems were intermingled and stamped by the peculiar considerations of the Borders.

One commentator on the Scottish Border abbeys concluded in the nineteenth century that the great Mediaeval houses had sadly degenerated by the sixteenth century and as a result 'whole districts had lapsed practically into barbarism'.[111] The true picture on both sides of the Border seems to have been less spectacular. The Border houses did however adopt to a large extent the protective colouring of their surroundings. Much of the evidence relating to them in the sixteenth century displays them in a political, economic or even military context, rather than a spiritual one. To some extent they chose to adopt the values of the society in which they lived, rather than to uphold the still sometimes alien values of the church. The picture is not one of gross corruption, but of neglected opportunity. The large number of religious in the pre-Reformation church did indeed help to serve the Border parishes, but did little to dispel the general ignorance and superstition of the area.

Despite the 1536 Rising's championship of the monasteries the Border houses seem to have attracted little popular support. The tenants of Tynemouth seized the opportunity of the rebellion to act against the priory as a landlord. The Percies' devotion to the Rising was entirely political, as was the involvement of the thieves of Tynedale and Redesdale, who saw a golden opportunity to run riot unchecked by any authority. The Charltons alone refused to accept a pardon and take the King's oath unless they could make a reservation in favour of Hexham Priory and their loyalty to the priory was due not so much to their previous oath to uphold it, as to a retainer of twenty nobles a year paid to each of their leaders.[112] Perhaps the monasteries had blended too well with their surroundings, since there were few who seemed to miss them, except as providers of parish clergy or of hospitality.

With their passing the government also missed an opportunity. Their extensive patronage and their possessions might have gone to secure the government's influence on the churches and the political organisation of the area, but instead the lands went largely to long-established Border families and the patronage was abused or misused. It might have given the reformed church an effective tool in the evangelisation of this 'dark corner of the land' but instead the church found itself more poorly equipped than before to deal with the large parishes, the unsettled conditions and the entrenched conservatism of the Borders.

NOTES

1. e.g. B. W. Beckingsale, 'The Characteristics of the Tudor North', *N.H.,* 4 (1969), pp. 79–80.
2. T. I. Rae, *The Administration of the Scottish Frontier* (1966), pp. 104, 237; G. M. Fraser, *The Steel Bonnets* (1971), p. 132.
3. *Hamilton Papers*, ed. J. Bain (1890), I, Appendix 1.
4. *C. S. P. Scot.*, I, no. 33.
5. *L.P.*, VIII, no. 955.
6. *N.H.*, 4, p. 79.
7. See S. M. Keeling, 'The Church and Religion in the Anglo-Scottish Border Counties, 1534 to 1572' (unpub. Ph.D. thesis, Durham Univ. 1975), pp. 288–91.
8. John Leslie, *History of Scotland*, ed. E. G. Cody, I (Scottish Text Society, 1888), pp. 101–2.
9. L.P., XI, no. 1410.
10. See J. Reed, *The Border Ballads* (1973), pp. 179–200; M. E. James, *Family, Lineage and Civil Society* (1974), pp. 52–3.
11. The Scottish houses were never suppressed in the same way. Their religious life came to an end but they survived as economic entities for some time. See D. E. Easson, 'The Reformation and the Monasteries in Scotland and England, Some Comparisons', *Transactions of the Scottish Ecclesiological Society*, 15 (1), (1957), pp. 7–23.
12. Alnwick, Bamburgh, Blanchland, Brinkburn, Farne Island, Hexham, Holy Island, Newminster, Ovingham, Tynemouth.
13. Holystone, Lamley, Newcastle.
14. Bamburgh, Hulne, Newcastle: Austin, Carmelite, Dominican, Franciscan, Trinitarian.
15. *C. S. P Scot.*, I, no. 33.
16. Keeling, thesis, p. 588.
17. The little surviving evidence for recruitment to the Northumberland monasteries suggests that like Durham in the fifteenth century and the Lancashire houses in the sixteenth they were filled mostly by local men. See Keeling, thesis, p. 182; R. B. Dobson, *Durham Priory 1400–50* (1973), p. 58; C. Haigh, *Reformation and Resistance in Tudor Lancashire* (1975)p. 126.
18. *L.P.*, III (2), no. 1920.
19. *Ibid.*, IV (2), no. 145; W. S. Gibson, *The Monastery of Tynemouth*, II (1847), p. 108.
20. *L.P.*, XI, no. 1293.
21. D. Hay, 'The Dissolution of the Monasteries in the Diocese of Durham', *A.A.*, 4th series, 15 (1938) pp. 75–6.
22. *L.P.*, XI, no. 1293.
23. *A.A..*, 4th ser. 15, p. 78.
24. *L.P.*, XII (2), no. 548.
25. *Ibid.*, XI, no. 276.
26. *Ibid.*, XII (1), no. 859; National Library of Scotland, Armstrong MS 6115, f. 200.

27. *R(egistrum) S(ecreti) S(igilli Regum Scotorum)*, III, no. 1732.
28. B.L., Cotton MS, Caligula B III, f. 255; *L.P.*, XII (1), no. 422.
29. A.C., MS A1, parts 1–16, *passim*.
30. *Ibid.*, part 5, f. 15v.
31. See Keeling, thesis, pp. 64–75.
32. Scottish Record Office, Ecclesiastical Documents, Ch 8/16.
33. *L.P.*, XII (2), no. 901.
34. B.L., Cotton Ms, Cleopatra E V, f. 286.
35. *The Priory of Hexham*, ed. J. Raine, S.S., 40 (1864), doc. xciv.
36. G. Tate, *History of the Borough, Castle and Barony of Alnwick* (1866), II, p. 51.
37. For details see Keeling, thesis, pp. 442–91.
38. *Registers of Cuthbert Tunstall, Bishop of Durham 1530–59, and of James Pilkington, Bishop of Durham 1561–76*, ed. G. Hinde, S.S., 161 (1946), nos. 146, 301.
39. *N.C.H.*, II, p. 490; *Injunctions and other Ecclesiastical Proceedings of Richard Barnes, Bishop of Durham, 1577–87*, ed. J. Raine, S.S., 22, (1850), p. 38.
40. Ann Forster, 'Bishop Tunstall's Priests', *Recusant History*, 9, p. 184.
41. *N.C.H.*, XIV, pp. 198–9; Hinde, *Registers of Tunstall and Pilkington*, no. 273.
42. *Ibid.*, nos. 48, 317.
43. *Ibid.*, no. 145; *C.P.R.*, *Mary*, II, p. 214; *Fasti Dunelmensis*, ed. D. F. Boutflower, S.S., 134, (1927), p. 26.
44. C. H. Cadogan, 'Brinkburn Priory Minister's Account of 1535–6', *Berwickshire Naturalists Club*, 12 (1887), p. 124; Forster, *Recusant Hist.* 9, p. 185.
45. Boutflower, *Fasti Dunelmensis*, p. 194; Hinde, *Registers of Tunstall and Pilkington*, no. 260.
46. *Ibid.*, nos. 111, 430.
47. *Ibid.*, nos. 60, 460.
48. *The Royal Visitation of 1559*, ed. C. J. Kitching, S.S., 187, (1975), p. 103; Forster, *Recusant Hist*, 9, p. 185.
49. Hinde, *Registers of Tunstall and Pilkington*, nos. 358–9; Raine, *Proceedings of Richard Barnes*, p. 37; Forster, *Recusant Hist*, 9, p. 181.
50. Hinde, *Registers of Tunstall and Pilkington*, no. 331; Raine, *Proceedings of Richard Barnes*, pp. 35, 76, 134–5.
51. Hinde, *Registers of Tunstall and Pilkington*, no. 260; Forster, *Recusant Hist*, 9, p. 184; *C.P.R.*, *Mary*, II, p. 252.
52. *Ibid.*, IV, p. 246; Hinde, *Registers of Tunstall and Pilkington*, no. 343; Forster, *Recusant Hist.* 9, p. 184.
53. See Keeling, thesis, pp. 522–72.
54. Eckford, Hownam, Jedburgh, Lamberton, Lessuden, Melrose, Mertoun, Oxnam, Stitchill.
55. Keeling, thesis, pp. 531, 533, 566, 569.
56. P.R.O., SP 15/12/108.
57. M. C. Cross, 'Berwick-on-Tweed and the Neighbouring Parts of Northumberland on the Eve of the Armada', *A.A.*, 4th ser., 41 (1963), p. 133.

58. P.R.O., SP 15/12/272; Raine, *Proceedings of Richard Barnes*, p. 35.
59. P.R.O., SP 15/12/272; B.L., Harleian MS 594, f. 192.
60. D.C.L., Hunter Ms 37, f. 89v; Raine, *Proceedings of Richard Barnes*, p. 34.
61. B.L., Harl. MS 594, ff. 192, 194; Raine, *Proceedings of Richard Barnes*, p. 31.
62. *A.P.C.*, I, p. 316; VI. p. 382; *C.S.P.*, *Addenda, 1566–79*, p. 18; *N.C.H.*, VIII, pp. 127–8.
63. Raine, *Proceedings of Richard Barnes*, pp. 37, 41, 77; *N.C.H.*, XIV, p. 365; Keeling, thesis, p. 457.
64. *L.P.*, XXI (1), no. 650; *C.P.R.*, *Elizabeth*, II, pp. 243–4; B.L., Harl. MS 594, f. 194; Raine, *Proceedings of Richard Barnes*, p. 38.
65. Keeling, thesis, p. 445.
66. J. Hodgson, *History of Northumberland*, III (3), p. 96; C.P.R., *Edward VI*, V, pp. 180–1; Raine, *Proceedings of Richard Barnes*, p. 31.
67. A.C., MS A1, part 12, f. 5.
68. Tate, *Hist. Alnwick*, II, pp. 21, 114.
69. *C.P.R.*, *Edward VI*, III, p. 325; *Mary*, I, p. 359; *Elizabeth*, I, p. 268.
70. Hinde, *Registers of Tunstall and Pilkington*, nos. 395, 429; B.L., Harl. MS 594, f. 194.
71. A.C., MS A1, Part II, f. 30v.
72. Keeling, thesis, pp. 442, 464, 484–6; *C.P.R.*, *Elizabeth*, IV no. 1500.
73. *A.A.*, 4th ser., 41, p. 134.
74. *L.P.*, XVI, no. 1500 (188*b*).
75. P.R.O., Exchequer, Augmentation Office, Miscellaneous Books, E 315/281/12; *C.P.R.*, *Edward VI*, VI, p. 180; J. Brand, *History and Antiquities of Newcastle-upon-Tyne* (1789), I, p. 334.
76. W. Dugdale, *Monasticon Anglicanum*, IV, p. 197.
77. *C.P.R.*, *Elizabeth*, III, no. 1041.
78. Dugdale, VI, p. 103; *N.C.H.*, I, p. 94.
79. Tate, *Hist. Alnwick*, II, pp. 25–9; *N.C.H.*, VII, p. 469; *L.P.*, XXI (1), no. 814.
80. *C.P.R.*, *Edward VI*, V, p. 244; Gibson, *Monastery of Tynemouth*, II, p. 216.
81. *L.P.*, XI, no. 529.
82. *Ibid.*, XIV (1), no. 344; XIV (2), no. 482; XVI, no. 1500 (140*b*).
83. *Ibid.*, XI, no. 529; XII (1), nos. 546, 1090; M.H. and R. Dodds, *The Pilgrimage of Grace and the Exeter Conspiracy* (1915), I, pp. 31–3.
84. *L.P.*, XI, no. 504.
85. *Ibid.*, no. 1090 (iii).
86. *Ibid.*, nos. 479, 546.
87. *Ibid.*, no. 479.
88. Dodds, I, pp. 220–5; *L.P.*, XII (1), nos. 687, 1259. S. M. Harrison, *The Pilgrimage of Grace in the Lace Counties, 1536–37*, Royal Historical Society Studies in History, 27, 1981, pp. 104–6.
89. Haigh, pp. 118–38.
90. *L.P.*, XII (1), no. 311 (36–7); R. Welford, *History of Newcastle and Gateshead*, II (1885), p. 160.

91. *L.P.*, XIV (2), nos. 701, 715, 722; Welford, II, p. 198.
92. R. B. Armstrong, *History of Liddesdale, Eskdale, Wauchopdale, and the Debateable Land* (1883), p. 105.
93. W. M. Bryce, *The Scottish Greyfriars* (1909), I, p. 76.
94. B.L., Cotton MS, Calig, B I, f. 42.
95. *L.P.*, XV, no. 1607; Moir Bryce, I, p. 79 gives the number as 18.
96. *L.P.*, XI, no. 1372; XII (2), nos. 1045, 1076; Welford, p. 161.
97. *L.P.*, X, no. 1536; *Essays on the Scottish Reformation*, ed. D. McRoberts (1962), pp. 326–9.
98. *L.P.*, XIV (1), nos. 39–40, 43–5.
99. *A.A.*, 4th ser., 15, pp. 99–100; Welford, pp. 167–72; Tate, *Hist. Alnwick*, II, pp. 55–6.
100. *A.A.*, 4th ser., 15, pp. 105–6; Forster, *Recusant Hist*, 9, pp. 185–7.
101. *Wills and Inventories*, ed. J. Raine, S.S., 2 (1835) pp. cxx, clxxii; Dugdale, IV, p. 487.
102. Welford, p. 173; Gibson, *Monastery of Tynemouth*, II, pp. 91–4.
103. *N.C.H.*, II, p. 436; Forster, *Recusant Hist*, 9, p. 184.
104. *L.P.*, XIV (1), no. 625.
105. *Ibid.*, (2), no. 612.
106. Keeling, thesis, pp. 347–9.
107. *C.S.P. Scot.*, II, no. 8–9.
108. *Ibid.*, I, no. 1155.
109. P.R.O., SP 15/12/108.
110. *Ibid.*,
111. R. Borland, *Border Raids and Reivers* (1895), p. 52.
112. *L.P.*, XII (1), no. 421.

The Durham Palatinate and the Courts of Westminster under the Tudors

Christopher Kitching

Surtees remarked with a sigh that 'Bishop Tunstall bowed to the storm in silence'.[1] He was lamenting, like some of the Pilgrims of Grace before him and countless historians afterwards, the beginning of the end of Durham's distinctive Palatine jurisdiction as signalled in the Franchises Act of 1535.[2]

Until July 1 1536 when that Act was due to come into effect, the Palatinate of Durham had a judicial system virtually sealed off from the rest of the kingdom. Civil litigation there was properly a matter for the Court of Pleas at Durham. Criminal offences committed within the Bishopric were triable only before the Durham Justices of the Peace, of Assize or of Gaol Delivery – all of whom were commissioned by the Bishop, not by the King, though in practice the Bishop's Assize Commission included the Justices of the King's Northern Circuit. The common law courts at Westminster had no machinery for initiating actions concerning the inhabitants of the Bishopric, save in the rare circumstances of appeals on a writ of error to King's Bench from one of the Palatine courts.[3] For equity matters too the Bishop had his own Chancery court and as yet even the outpost of royal conciliar justice at York had had little impact in the Bishopric, even though the Bishop and several Palatine officials were of the Council.[4] In Durham writs ran in the Bishop's name. It was *his* peace, not the King's, which might be broken. And when traitors or felons were condemned there it was to the Bishop that their forfeited lands and goods reverted. Occasionally, Durham residents might appear before a Westminster court: notably Chancery, Star Chamber or Requests. The number of such cases, however, was small and in most of these the other party concerned lived outside the Palatinate. Even while Wolsey was simultaneously Lord Chancellor of England and Bishop of Durham there was no upsurge of Durham cases at Westminster.[5]

There is no doubt that the Franchises Act was designed to make the Durham jurisdiction (among others) more consonant with the Royal Supremacy in church and state. Henceforth, Justices were to be appointed and writs were to run exclusively in the King's name, whilst nobody save the King would pardon traitors and felons. But – very significantly – no attempt was made to suppress the existing Palatine courts or, as was subsequently proposed, to annexe the jurisdiction to the Crown. Moreover, by a specific proviso, the Bishop and his Chancellor were to remain *ex officio* members of the Durham Commission of the Peace. So, although the fact was not made sufficiently clear (as perhaps it might have been had Durham been represented in Parliament) residents of the Bishopric would still have privileged access to justice near home. The most important change was that it would be justice in the King's name. It was not a 'storm' and Tunstall probably nodded rather than bowed to it.

The Pilgrims rose before the Act could be seen at work. And the fact that such a momentous insurrection brought forth military and judicial aid from beyond the Palatinate has tended to confirm historians in the belief that the Act had indeed signalled the end, even though subsequent evidence shows the Palatinate and its courts flourishing. This external aid deserves a closer look. Rather than leave the residual rebels to the normal course of justice at the Durham Assizes, the King issued a special commission to the Duke of Norfolk as Lieutenant in the North (thus superimposing him, like Northumberland before him, on the Council of the North and openly proclaiming that Tunstall as President of that body lacked the strength to enforce its authority, especially in these particularly difficult circumstances).[6] Had there been any brooding long-term intention on the Crown's part to annexe or dissolve the Palatinate, here was the very occasion; but no such move was made.

The provision for the King rather than the Bishop to pardon traitors and felons now, unexpectedly soon after the Act, had to be widely implemented. A general pardon for rebels not already apprehended was published on December 9 1536 and at the end of that month Lancaster Herald arrived in Durham to proclaim it, triggering off fresh local exhortations to insurrection and even an attempt to murder the Herald himself in Durham market place.[7] On March 9 1537 Norfolk and the greater number of his fellow commissioners including Tunstall arrived in Durham to try those charged with these most recent disturbances. Norfolk wrote to the King that the commissioners realised shortly before the trial that their authority did not, in so many words, extend to

Durham, but they decided nevertheless to proceed to justice. In some embarrassment, however, they then discovered another irregularity: the prisoners had been captured after the date on which the royal commission to Norfolk had been issued. So the trial was adjourned for a month, pending the King's authorisation to proceed.[8]

Meanwhile, we must note something that could be easily overlooked, namely that the Durham Lent Assizes sat as usual and with the old balance of Northern Circuit Justices and Palatine officials. What is more, the commission was entered on the rolls as before (perhaps by some oversight) in the Bishop's name not the King's![9] Norfolk returned with a somewhat smaller contingent of commissioners in April and sentenced all the prisoners from his adjourned hearings to death. This time, in contrast to the preliminary hearing, a formal record was kept, entered up in the same manner as the Durham Judgement Rolls: it has survived among them in the Public Record Office.[10] At its head is enrolled a commission dated January 17 to Norfolk and his colleagues to try all cases concerning treason, rebellion and related offences throughout the North, *including the Bishopric of Durham*. This was surely a judicial fiction, ante-dated to put the record straight. For if Norfolk had had this instrument in March there would have been no objection to the preliminary hearings. Whatever its basis in law, it was important in signalling the incorporation of the Palatinate within the conciliar authority of York – a fact which, far more than the impact of the Franchises Act, was to have important repercussions on the relative prestige of the Palatinate.

Even so, the Palatinate survived Henry VIII and its records thereafter amply testify that it was not a corpse. Those for the Durham Chancery Court have, alas, suffered sundry mishaps – some reputedly at the hands of the Pilgrims of Grace and some by administrative laxity.[11] But the Judgement Rolls (recording proceedings before the Justices of Assize and of Gaol Delivery) are well represented. A detailed survey of their contents must one day be undertaken, but it can be seen at a glance that Durham residents of every walk of life pleaded and were impleaded there at common law and that all manner of criminal charges continued to be heard.

If we look forward a few years, to the rather unlikely context of the abolition of the Bishopric under Edward VI, we find further confirmation of the Crown's high regard for the Palatinate and its liberties. In May 1553 Edward prepared, by Letters Patent,[12] to annexe the Palatinate to the Crown under the new title of 'King's County Palatine'.

Had this instrument come into effect, Durham would have secured its Parliamentary representation but for our present purposes we need only hear what it said of the Palatine courts. They were

> very commodious, easy and profitable to the inhabiters and dwellers within the jurisdiction, limits and bounds, of the said County Palatine, forasmuch as their causes, matters and titles were ordered, judged and discussed by such ordinary judges, officers and ministers as were appointed within the said County Palatine, being nigh to their habitations and dwelling places for the hearing and determination of the same.

This was anything but a death threat, but it is of no more than passing interest since Mary's restitution of the Bishopric very soon restored the *status quo ante*. Elizabeth's reign was not far advanced before another statute[13] reaffirmed (in passing) that the Queen's writ did not run in Durham. The 1569 Rising, however, again placed a great strain on the relationship between Crown and Palatinate and, as in 1536, exposed the Bishop and Palatine authorities not only as incapable of maintaining law and order unassisted, but even as too prudent to stay behind to face the consequences, in stark contrast with the warrior Bishops of earlier generations who had led their troops in battle against the Scots. The rebels were accordingly dealt with not by the regular Palatine courts but by a special commission of oyer and terminer in the absence of both the Bishop and the Dean.[14] The Earl of Sussex acknowledged to Cecil what many of his troops and others at Westminster were feeling, that whilst by the law of the realm the Bishop should have all forfeits within the diocese, a windfall on this scale would be 'too great for any subject to receive'.[15] Pilkington, of course, tried to press his privileges, by *quo warranto* proceedings in King's Bench,[16] though he died before judgement was reached and in any case the matter was overtaken by an Act of Parliament which, while granting the rebel lands to the Crown on this occasion, nevertheless safeguarded the Bishop's theoretical rights.[17] It is not surprising that a paper was circulated in the 1570s arguing again the case for abolishing the Palatinate or annexing it to the Crown.[18]

The growing storm over tenant right in the Northern counties also helped to keep the issue very much alive. But the lobbyists for abolition were to make no solid progress for the remainder of the reign. A judgement much to Toby Matthew's satisfaction towards the end of the century showed that the courts really did accept the theory: the Exchequer proclaimed that '*iura regalia* and forfeitures at the common law between the rivers Tyne and Tees' appertained to the Bishop, 'notwithstanding that the freehold and inheritance of the soil of the premises be in her majesty.'[19]

I have suggested, then, that the Franchises Act was not, and was not intended to be, quite the watershed in Durham affairs that many have supposed. But it would be wrong to dismiss it altogether as a factor in the Palatinate's relative decline in the Tudor period. It certainly brought about a change of ethos, with every judicial instrument and commission now issuing in the Crown's name, putting the Bishop rather in the background. On the other hand, few were lured by this into thinking that any real change had come about in the Palatinate's powerbase or the impartiality of its courts. And when they truly wanted the King's justice, Durham men turned elsewhere.

Indeed, they were given every opportunity to do so. In revising and strengthening the Council of the North at York in 1537 and finally extending its authority to Durham, using initially the opportunity of Tunstall's own short-lived Lord Presidency, the Crown provided a ready outlet for Durham residents frustrated by, or apprehensive of, Durham courts. The sad loss of that Council's records prevents us making a full assessment of its impact in Durham, but incidental evidence, particularly from Westminster cases cited below, proves that Durham men did take many of their grievances to York, which must clearly have deprived the Durham courts of potential business.

The Council's historian has shown that it occasionally intervened to stay proceedings in the Durham courts and that in the 1580s and 1590s unsuccessful attempts were made by the Bishop and others to have Durham removed from the Council's sphere of authority.[20] Meanwhile, some cases are known to have been turned away by Chancery at Westminster when both parties were found to live within the Council of the North's jurisdiction, although this was not always done.[21]

There were frequent tactical and logistical arguments over the most sensible venue for a court hearing, largely betraying the conflicting interests of the parties. And judging by the large number of cases concerning Durham finally brought to the royal courts at Westminster in the second half of our period the appeal of justice near at hand was strictly limited, however fiercely Durham men could fight for the privilege when it was under threat. When in 1593 the Mayor of Hartlepool, William Porrett, was impleaded in Chancery at Westminster by a Hartlepool fisherman, Christopher Chester, he pointed out that Chester, 'if he had any just cause of complaint either in law or conscience, might have had remedy in divers places within forty miles – yea, a dozen miles – of his dwelling' rather than some two hundred miles away.[22] But it is clear from further evidence that the Council at York had already heard the case, or a related issue, and that the plaintiff doubted the impartiality of Durham in defending his interest: it was not difficult to find an excuse.

Chancery was just one of the Westminster courts to which Durham men might turn, but it provides us with a good starting point. The available lists of Chancery Proceedings contain mention of up to two hundred Durham cases in the sixteenth century.[23] This may not seem an impressive total compared with those for other English counties, but given the existence of the courts at Durham and York it is surprisingly large. Many more of the cases fall within the second half of our period than the first. This may be partly attributable to better survival of records; another important factor was undoubtedly the general increase in litigiousness as the century progressed. Since it is usually difficult and often impossible to date the case papers, no precise graph of the trend towards pleading at Westminster can be drawn. Large issues such as the tenant right disputes of the 1560s to 1580s undoubtedly boosted the flow South,[24] as did the massive forfeiture of lands after the 1569 Rising (though this was felt more in the Exchequer). But on the whole the move towards litigation at Westminster in preference to Durham was probably a gradual process: a matter of Durham men getting used to litigation at a distance.

Some of the cases from the 1540s onwards fall into the old familiar pattern, involving at least one non-Durham resident or title to lands in an additional county; cases involving Crown servants, peers of the realm, merchants and others whose business made it even more convenient to proceed at Westminster. But to a greater extent there now appear to be also cases which look ready-made for the Durham courts. And even though it was still an essential part of the courtly ritual to argue over the jurisdiction, Chancery (and for that matter the other equity and prerogative courts at Westminster also) seems almost always to have proceeded with matters presented there, turning a blind eye to the Palatinate's theoretical privileges.

Nobody was better placed to defend the Durham jurisdiction than the Bishop himself. In Mary's reign, Tunstall, finding himself impleaded along with the Earl of Westmorland by Edward and Joan Waldegrave over a mine at Eggleston, produced a solemn statement of Palatine rights:

> All suits and titles for and concerning any title of freehold or inheritance pretended by any person or persons to any lands, tenements or hereditaments lying or being within the said County Palatine hath always been, time whereof the memory of man is not contrary, determined and yet are determined according to the laws of the realm within the said County Palatine and not elsewhere.[25]

Nevertheless (of course) he went on to defend himself, thereby implicitly acknowledging Westminster's jurisdiction. His co-defendant the Earl, by contrast, took a stand on this principle, claiming that it was in the Palatine courts that he and his ancestors had always pleaded and been impleaded.[26] Chancery certainly continued the hearing, though the later papers in the case are lost (or quite probably the case lapsed before it came to a final decree). The problems of enforcing Westminster's will at such a distance are illustrated by the fact that the first commission of enquiry arising in this case was issued in October 1557, with orders to report by Lent following, but failed to do so; and the problem of communications between parties (a phenomenon by no means confined to Durham cases) is underlined by the defendants' being instructed to give the plaintiffs three weeks' notice of the eventual execution of the commission by leaving a message at a house in Watling Street.[27]

Quite commonly, one party had a distinct advantage if his case were heard at Westminster and the other if it were heard at Durham. Sir Richard Rede, Master of Sherburn Hospital under Edward VI, was ousted by Mary on the reinstatement of Tunstall as Bishop, with an annuity in compensation. As Master in Chancery he naturally pursued there his grievance when a subsequent Master of Sherburn (and Dean of Durham), Ralph Skinner, suspended his annuity. Skinner, equally naturally, argued that the case was triable in Durham, though his choice of words – 'in the court of the Lord Bishop of Durham for the time being' – serves to underline how establishment figures continued to regard the Palatine authority even after the Franchises Act.[28]

The rhetoric is exposed whenever we find a prime advocate of the Palatine courts actually choosing to take a case to Westminster. Again, Tunstall can stand as an example, although he was doubly fortunate in that as a former Lord Keeper of the Privy Seal he knew the Westminster machinery exceptionally well. His willingness as Bishop of Durham to initiate actions at Westminster – we shall see that this extended also to the Court of Augmentations – may have been a factor encouraging other Durham residents to do the same. Tunstall had had a long-standing dispute with Sir Robert Constable over the Stewardship of Howden and having failed to gain satisfaction before the Council of the North, he brought the issue to Chancery.[29] Again, during Wriothesley's Chancellorship (1544-47), he brought an action against Ralph Neville, Earl of Westmorland, concerning the wardship of one William Claxton. After making the precautionary remark that within the Palatinate the Bishops had 'all such right and prerogative royal concerning ward and marriage' as the King had elsewhere, he added that settlement at the common law would take too long for his purposes, since the heir would be over his majority before judgement could be reached. He had offered to allow the matter to be determined by the Assize Justices in Durham, but Westmorland – true to form – had insisted on a hearing at common law in Durham.[30] Thus, in effect, the Bishop was here using the royal Chancery as the only way out of an *impasse*.

In contrast, anyone resident outside the Palatinate, or anyone pitted against a weightier opponent there, had strong grounds for resisting litigation in Durham. During Gardiner's Chancellorship (1553-55), Sir John Legh who was in dispute with Henry Neville, Earl of Westmorland, over tithes, came to Westminster because his adversary was 'of great power and authority in the said Bishopric of Durham and greatly landed, friended and allied there': redress in the local courts of common law was impossible.[31] The sentiment is echoed by Robert Waldoo of London, who claimed that although he had a lease from Tunstall of certain windmills in the Bishopric, local men who had detained his deeds were:

> men of very great riches and ability and greatly friended and allied in the said County of Durham . . . and your said orator a mere stranger there, unfriended, unacquainted.[32]

Similarly, when John Pette 'dwelling in Kent', laid claim to books left at his death by Ralph Skinner, late Dean of Durham, his antagonists were none other than Robert Swift, Chancellor of Durham, and Prebendary Pilkington, men:

> in great authority within the said county and by reason thereof . . . greatly maintained, favoured and borne by the most part of the men of worship and others within the said county, by means whereof your said orator standeth greatly in doubt of remedy herein by the due order and course of the common law.[33]

Supremely, anyone with a grievance touching the Bishop himself – and there were few Durham cases that could not arguably be interpreted in this light – might feel he had a better chance of gaining ground at York or Westminster. It was an old lament that the Bishop was both judge and jury in his own courts.[34] In the time of Bishop Barnes, Lord Eure laid claim to certain commons and estovers in Weardale Forest and was fined at Quarter Sessions, in the presence of the Bishop, for grazing his cattle there. The dispute ricocheted off the Council of the North and the Durham Assizes and into Chancery at Westminster, where Eure took the now familiar line that he could not effectively plead his cause in any court in the Palatinate.[35] Or – to take a humbler plaint – in 1582 copyhold tenants at East and West Boldon complained that Henry Bisham, a servant of the Bishop, had launched ejection proceedings against them at the Durham Assizes and that since the Sheriff whose job it was to return the jurors was appointed by the Bishop, justice could not be expected.[36]

This alleged partiality of justice at Durham[37] led to several instances of Chancery, like the Council of the North, being used more or less as a court of appeal. In the Michaelmas Term, 30 Henry VIII, Robert Johnson, a former Durham yeoman entangled in an action for debt in the Palatinate (adjourned because of an outbreak of plague) migrated, apparently with no malice aforethought, to London, acting on the advice of a Durham lawyer that he might just as well go about his business unless he were called on again. No sooner was he settled in London than the action was re-started in Durham, even though he himself claimed to have settled the debt long since. He came to Chancery in an attempt to get the action quashed.[38] Similarly in the latter part of Mary's reign, under Chancellor Heath, Richard Robinson came to complain of harassment in the Durham courts by John Layton and Nicholas Younge, the former a friend and the latter a servant of Robert Meynell (serjeant-at-law in the Palatinate). Robinson had successfully escaped one charge of trespass in the Court of Pleas at Durham on a non-suit, but had been hooked on another charge by his opponents.[39]

It is not always easy to see whether grievances brought to Westminster were genuine or whether, as so often in the Tudor courts, actions were simply opened on as many fronts as possible to put opponents to the maximum trouble and expense. In Mary's reign, Lord Lumley – noticeably less keen than the Nevilles to have his hearings in Durham – was having trouble with his kinsmen Richard and Percival Lumley and their henchmen over his estates at Butterby, Bradbury and Great Lumley. Having taken Richard with others before Durham J.P.s whose censure was to his mind less than adequate, he pressed charges of riot against them in Star Chamber, seeking 'more condign' punishment and launched a concurrent bill against them in Chancery for good measure.[40] He took Percival to Star Chamber separately on another charge,[41] nobody seemingly having challenged *that* court's right to hear the case, and laid bills in Chancery against John Sanders for detinue of deeds concerning fishing in the Wear at Lumley,[42] against Lionel Smith for riot at Great Lumley[43] and against Henry Gascoyn for refusing suit of court[44] – a lawyer's friend indeed!

In these examples, drawn primarily from Chancery, we have seen some reasons why Durham litigants chose to come South, or resisted doing so. (In many instances the matters in dispute could actually be settled by commissioners of enquiry deputed by Chancery to sit locally and examine witnesses or take answers from defendants, so that a Durham party, provided he had a good attorney, might not need to appear in person at Westminster.) Similar arguments for and against the Durham jurisdiction were, of course, heard by Requests, Star Chamber and the Exchequer. The records of the Courts of Requests and Star Chamber are much less complete than those of Chancery, but the lists[45] show only a handful of Durham cases in Requests before Elizabeth's reign and only a score or so during that reign. For Star Chamber up to the end of Mary's reign there are very few Durham cases and thereafter there is no topographical finding aid, so the position under Elizabeth is impossible to assess. In both courts the tendency among the known cases is for the issues or parties to have some non-Durham connection. In one case[46] between John Browne of Hartlepool and some local men whom he accused of wrecking his rabbit warren at Stranton, the defendants were adamant that the matter hinged on rival titles to the warren, and so should be settled at common law by the Durham Justices of Assize; if not, and if it were an equity matter, then it could be heard before the Bishop and his Temporal Chancellor in Chancery at Durham. If even *that* were not satisfactory, there was the Council of the North, but 'no writ of this Her Highness's Court of Requests nor any other Her Highness's courts at Westminster are current within the said County Palatine'. It is virtually certain that the sort of cases which Durham men might have brought before these conciliar courts were in fact normally heard by the Council of the North, but in this case Requests certainly did proceed – there are extant interrogatories and depositions – and it is clear that the judges agreed with the plaintiff that the Queen's jurisdiction 'extendeth generally over all her subjects'.

If we turn now to the Court of Augmentations and to the Exchequer, we are in a different world, for here there were few doubts about the

Crown's jurisdiction. The confiscations of land and revenues following the Dissolutions and the 1569 Rebellion – not to mention the manipulation of episcopal estates *sede vacante*[47] – could scarcely have done more to further the habit of litigation at Westminster had this been their prime purpose! For bailiffs and receivers of Crown revenues in County Durham as elsewhere were accountable at Westminster and disputes (other than essentially common law matters) arising from Crown ownership had to be resolved there, completely by-passing the Palatine courts. Some forty cases concerning Durham are represented in the Augmentations records,[48] nor was this the end of the story, for with the absorption of Augmentations into the Exchequer in 1554 similar cases continued to be heard in the latter court: well over a hundred in Elizabeth's reign.

Tunstall again showed himself willing to accept the jurisdiction, exhibiting a bill of complaint over lands and rents in Stanhope and Wolsingham which the King claimed as part of the dissolved monastery of Blanchland.[49] This also highlights the fact that several religious houses situated outside the Bishopric had held lands within it. Three or four distinct cases arose, for example from the pre-Dissolution leases made of Durham lands by the Nunnery of St Bartholomew, Newcastle.[50] In Gateshead in particular the Crown now rubbed shoulders with the Bishop and his tenants, with rival claims to coalpits and several boundary disputes.

Bringing in the royal land-revenues was not always an easy task, as is demonstrated by a letter in August 1556 from Lord Treasurer Winchester to Shrewsbury as Lord President of the Council of the North and to Wharton as Lord Warden of the Eastern and Middle Marches, asking them to assist the Receiver of Northumberland and Durham in his duties.[51]

The tremendous upsurge in Exchequer business (administrative as well as judicial) after the 1569 Rising is evident from the bulk of the resulting records. The rebels' lands, and notably those of the Earl of Westmorland, were sufficiently large to require a distinct series of Ministers' Accounts rather than be integrated into the general accounts for County Durham.[52] Over sixty bailiffs, collectors and farmers had to be employed to account for these extra lands. Most of the property was subsequently leased out by the Crown – in virtually every case to the sitting tenants (provided they were not themselves rebels) – as old leases and tenancies fell in.[53] They were treated on exactly the same terms as Crown lands elsewhere, the entry fines averaging two to four years' rent, although incentives were given to those undertaking to prospect for coal or occupy 'decayed' properties. In the 1580s and 1590s, in an unsuccessful attempt to prevent further disputes over tenant right, the Crown sought to define more clearly the obligation of border service in the terms of the leases. But the difficulties were considerable, as is demonstrated by an extant warrant from Burghley in 1594 staying further leases in Durham and Northumberland 'until order were taken how to bind the tenants to service in the Borders in better sort than heretofore they have been'.[54]

This major transfer of land could not fail to have its impact on the litigation coming before the Exchequer, where the file of Bills and Answers for Elizabeth's reign provides a convenient window into court business.[55] Virtually every case hinged (or was said to hinge) on rights or titles conveyed by the Crown in Letters Patent, leases and so on; rival claims to the rents and profits of ex-church or rebel lands are strongly represented, together with at least one case concerning concealed lands[56] and one breach of the playing cards monopoly.[57] The two-year vacancy following the death of Barnes (1587-89) occasioned at least eight actions which could have been heard in Durham but for the fact that the Crown was temporarily administering the Bishopric lands.[58] I have noted only one case where the Exchequer actually overruled a Durham court[59] and that was a prohibition in a tithe cause before the Durham Consistory, a church court not a Palatine one, when the point mainly at issue was the interpretation of royal Letters Patent, which it fell outside the church courts' power to settle. Another case, unfortunately incompletely documented, shows how parties might use other courts in an attempt to subvert or circumvent judgements already made against them. In the wave of concealment-hunting in the mid 1580s, a Surrey man, John Awbrey, told the inhabitants of Wolviston chapelry (in Billingham) that their chapel had been concealed from the Crown and that unless they compounded with him for forty marks he would have it pulled down. With a gang, he stripped lead off the roof and cut the bell ropes before George and William Thorpe entered into bonds with him to raise the forty marks. They then, however, complained to the Council of the North at York; Awbrey was arrested and ordered to discharge them of the bond, as he had no local sureties himself. Thereupon, he returned to London and began a case at common law to 'recover' his debt, but was thwarted when the Thorpes, with the support of the Dean and Chapter of Durham, reported all the earlier proceedings to the Exchequer.[60]

A small group of Exchequer cases directly concerned the Bishop himself and the extent of the Palatine jurisdiction, so they deserve rather more detailed consideration. Anyone familiar with the earlier history of the Palatinate will smile as he savours the *déjà vu*.[61] In the early 1580s the aspiring lawyer, John Barnes, aged 22, defined the boundaries of the Palatinate thus:

> The Bishopric and County Palatine aforesaid is in form triangular and is divided from Yorkshire by the river of Tees Southward; and in the West part thereof hath the two heads of the rivers Tees and Wear, commonly called Teesdale and Weardale. And from the said West point runneth the water of Derwent into the river of Tyne which parteth this county from Northumberland Northward. And that the East side or basis of the said triangle is beaten upon with the German sea, in the very point whereof Southward lie the . . . manor of Hart and Hartness and the . . . town of Hartlepool, being divided from Yorkshire by the Tees and being twenty miles distant from any part of Northumberland.[62]

But natural boundaries and distances as the crow flies are deceptive measures of effective jurisdiction and the Palatinate was distinctly vulnerable at its 'corners'. It had to fight off repeated challenges to its power over Gateshead, Hartlepool and, to a lesser extent, Barnard Castle. Moreover, some of the resulting case-papers contain a wealth of incidental detail for the history of industry and commerce in the North East – a source which has hardly yet been tapped.

Gateshead in particular provides us with cases rich in detail. The principal cause of friction here was that the citizens of Newcastle, across the Tyne, wanted to control their Southern neighbour (in rather the manner that London absorbed Southwark). For a while in the middle of the sixteenth century they did, of course, annexe it by Act of Parliament,[63] but this was a short-lived triumph, for the town was fully restored to the Bishopric under Mary, although not without prolonged discussion.[64] Tunstall went some way to appeasing the Newcastle corporation by granting them a four hundred and fifty year lease of the Gateshead salt-meadows and the borough tolls and in 1578 and 1582 Bishop Barnes leased the manor, along with that of Whickham, to the Crown, which quickly assigned its interest to two aldermen of Newcastle who in turn assigned to the corporation.[65]

The burgesses of Gateshead were fiercely proud of their independence. When the mayor of Newcastle used the episcopal vacancy after Pilkington's death to re-introduce a Bill in Parliament to annexe the town, the population of some three thousand feared for their livelihood and submitted a spirited defence. There were, they said, 'a great number of substantial honest men, faithful and good subjects, some merchants, some drapers and other honest artificers, whom the town of Newcastle doth envy because they do well and thrive so much there'. Their resources – especially grazing land and coal mines – would be exploited, whilst the town itself would be neglected as being outside the walls. Gateshead men had already occasionally found themselves debarred from trading in Newcastle or taking apprenticeships there. They resented Newcastle's insinuations that they bred nothing but hooligans, and polluted the Tyne with their rubbish for, they said, the bailiff (appointed by the Bishop) kept regular courts and the river (considerably deeper on the Gateshead side) was well tended.[66] Life under the Bishop, we must conclude, was easier than that proposed by the enemy across the water. They successfully fought off annexation, affirming the town to be 'the key of the Palatinate, the people religious, godly and good Protestants and besides, men of good wealth and very civil behaviour'.

When they were not actively pursuing their claim to overall control, the men of Newcastle contented themselves with taunts and threats. It can scarcely be coincidental that tension came to a head during vacancies in the Durham see. A common pattern of events evolved: someone from Newcastle would attempt heavy-handed action, hoping that Durham would be at best half awake, the aggrieved Gateshead party then turning directly to Chancery at Westminster rather than wasting time in the Durham courts.

To take just one example, Wolsey while Bishop of Durham leased his Gateshead coalmine for one year to John Broke, a London mercer, for two hundred marks. The mine was adjacent to another owned by James Lawson, Mayor of Newcastle, who had to cross the land of the Gateshead mine to get his own coal to the river. Broke and Lawson agreed that Broke should have the right of carriage three days out of four and Lawson on the fourth, Lawson paying £4 for the concession and also lending Broke £26 13s. 4d. as part of the deal. During the year Broke gave Lawson £20 in coal to clear some of his debt, but when he sent his kinsman Thomas Broke to oversee the mine Thomas found himself arrested and gaoled by Lawson 'among felons' for the outstanding £6 13s. 4d. which was properly John's affair. From his prison where he found himself at a distinct disadvantage being an isolated Londoner and with Lawson in a comfortable position as Mayor, he appealed for a *corpus cum causa* to refer all the proceedings to Chancery (Wolsey having meanwhile been translated to Winchester).[67]

Another regular source of friction in Gateshead was the Tyne Bridge: vital strategically for the passage of men and munitations to the Borders and commercially, for access by Durham merchants and shoppers to the port and market of Newcastle. On the one hand, boundary and maintenance disputes arose between Newcastle and the Bishopric and on the other hand there was internal dissension South of the river over who should pay to maintain the Durham portion of the bridge. The Palatine courts were quite the wrong place to attempt to resolve these differences, but experience was to show that even the outside help of the Council of the North might prove insufficient. The bridge was stone-built, with shops and houses on top; tolls were charged at each end, twice as heavy at the Newcastle end, reflecting both the relative scope of jurisdiction and the relative cost of upkeep. The boundary was marked by two blue marble stones (the 'Cuthbert Stones') where the respective Sheriffs would meet as occasion demanded to exchange prisoners. The stones had more than once been dug up by Newcastle men asserting control over the whole bridge. In the aftermath of one such attack in 1383, Bishop Langley had had to reassert his claim to one third of the bridge through Parliament, Chancery and King's Bench, beginning in 1410 and emerging victorious only in 1417.[68] This precedent was recalled in the sixteenth century proceedings. Indeed, the Palatine courts never seem to have been at a loss for documentary precedents.

These earlier disputes had also effectively established that the Northern two-thirds had to be maintained by Newcastle and the Southern third by Durham. In practice it had been the Bishop himself who paid: Ruthall, Wolsey and Tunstall all certainly continuing the tradition. But under Pilkington an inquiry by J.P.s reported that responsibility for the Southern third, despite past practice, was not certain at law. The Council of the North intervened in April 1565 by signet letter, instructing the J.P.s to levy the inhabitants of County Durham to maintain the bridge. Charges were brought before the Council of the North against some defaulters, and an abortive suggestion was made to have the matter referred to Chancery. In April 1568 a further levy was raised; 'and then the time of Rebellion troubled the country so that no more was done for Tyne Bridge till the Assizes'. In August 1576 the Assize Judges suggested a special commission of enquiry to assign everyone's share of responsibility, but Newcastle protested loudly that it had been paying five hundred marks a year for the past seven years and (in effect) would not lift a finger to help Gateshead and Durham residents off the hook. A further shilling levy was accordingly made throughout Durham, but in the early 1580s the Crown tenants in Gateshead secured an Exchequer order shifting liability back on to the Bishop.[69] Here then, the Exchequer at Westminster was used as a last resort when neither J.P.s nor Assize Justices, nor even the Council of the North, had been able to arrive at a long-term solution to a pressing problem.

Hartlepool, like Gateshead, was a source of both internal and external conflict for the Palatinate. Well past its heyday by the early sixteenth century and of little commercial importance compared with Newcastle, which nevertheless feared its rivalry, it had some strategic significance at the South Eastern tip of the Palatinate. It had no fully-fledged customs service of its own, but (like Sunderland and Stockton) came under the port of Newcastle[70] which in 1560 alleged that its 'uncertain jurisdiction' – of which we shall hear more in a moment – had turned Hartlepool into a haven for London debtors. This 'hazard-to-law-and-order' charge seems to have been a regular tactical weapon of the men of Newcastle.

Newcastle's merchants had been quite content to see Hartlepool remain a 'fisher town', but they alleged that these unsavoury Londoners had settled in and dabbled in wool-fells, lead and other commodities, evading duty 'for that there is neither searcher, customer, controller or weighmaster there save only one of themselves as deputy to the customer of the port of Newcastle'.[71] They feared that Newcastle's rising generation would be beguiled by the easy life, to the city's detriment. Very sensibly, however, Cecil turned a deaf ear to these entreaties, though it is strange that he did not think it necessary to sort out the alleged 'uncertainty' of the jurisdiction over Hartlepool, for here lay both past and future trouble.

When Sir Robert Chamberlayne and a band of rebels had been besieged and held in Hartlepool in 1492, the Bishop had claimed their goods as within 'the franchise of St Cuthbert' and Henry VII chose to allow it 'for the honour of God and of that glorious confessor St Cuthbert'.[72] But in later encounters on this, as on so many other issues, Cuthbert's power proved less enchanting.

In Wolsey's time, Chancellor Frankelyn had urged the improvement of the haven,[73] showing that he, at least, believed it to be in the Bishopric, but at some time in the 1530s Parliament discussed a Bill to declare Hartlepool, along with Barnard Castle, to be actually in North Yorkshire.[74] Residents of the town continued styling themselves 'of Northumberland', in an attempt to escape the Palatine jurisdiction, following an old claim[75] of the Clifford Earls of Cumberland, lords of the town and of Hartness, who refused to recognise the Bishop's jurisdiction.

For our present purposes the failure to resolve this dispute had the happy consequence that a further test case was brought in the Exchequer in the 1580s, in which the depositions[76] add further significant pieces to the jig-saw of jurisdictional relationships at this time. On June 17 1581 a pirate ship with a crew of thirty, commanded by Thomas Browne, had been blown into Hartlepool in a storm. The townsmen informed not the Bishop (whose jurisdiction they still claimed not to recognise) but Lord Eure, Vice President of the Council of the North, asking for the pirates' removal, or for financial help in maintaining them in gaol. Very properly, Eure ordered the pirates to be sent to Durham gaol and informed the Bishop, who sent his sheriff (Sir William Hilton) to Hartlepool to collect them. The Bailiff refused to hand them over and on receiving a further order from the Council, the townsmen took the law into their own hands by setting off with the pirates to Newcastle, to the county gaol for Northumberland, ignoring a deputation that intercepted them and urged them to go instead to Durham. The matter was again referred by the Durham justices – including the Earl of Cumberland – to the Council of the North, but also raised in the Exchequer at Westminster. J.P.s and Palatine officials produced documents as precedents, showing that Hartlepool men had pleaded and been impleaded in the Durham courts and that some fifteen years previously the then Mayor, William Tarlton, had sent two suspected felons to Durham gaol. The port was regularly described as 'in the County of Durham' and it had even been assessed with the Stockton Ward during Pilkington's episcopate. The Bishop had granted charters and even though he was not the immediate lord he held the higher jurisdiction there. The dispute simmered on for several years, the Earl of Cumberland himself intervening to support his claim to an independent jurisdiction,[77] but just as it seemed the Exchequer was likely to rule in favour of the Bishop, Cumberland threw in the sponge by selling the manor of Hart with Hartlepool and Hartness to Robert Peter and John Morley, agents of Lord Lumley in 1586, forestalling a ruling.[78] In 1593 Lumley obtained for Hartlepool a Royal Charter[79] – significantly not an episcopal one – which defined the town as within the Bishopric of Durham (though not specifying the *County* of Durham). Only after a further legal battle and arbitration was the Bishop's case finally vindicated.

This introductory review of the records of Durham litigation at Westminster begs a number of important questions which with more extended research (even allowing for lacunae in the records) might be answerable. For example, how many of the cases continued through to a final decree or order? Did the Westminster courts return many cases to the courts at Durham and York for trial? Just how buoyant, meanwhile, was the business in the Durham courts themselves? We have seen enough to conclude that for many parties there were serious inconveniences associated with pleadings at Westminster and yet the cases continued to come forward. We have seen, too, that some of the old privileges of the Palatinate were protected in theory and respected by the courts in practice, though the Crown was easily able to manipulate and override the theory to serve its own ends and certainly had little to fear from what remained of Palatine independence. That independence, however, survived to be challenged in future centuries. We can perhaps use as a measure of its resilience the virulent condemnation of 'St Cuthbert's patrimony' as on a par with that of St. Peter in Rome – not in the fourteenth or fifteenth centuries but as late as the eighteenth – by the editor of the 1729 edition of Spearman's *Enquiry into the Ancient and Present State of the County Palatine of Durham*,[80] who added to the main work his own charges of oppression of tenants, nepotism in offices and the insulation of the jurisdiction from other English courts, noting that 'even those privileges now remaining in the County Palatine are too great for a subject and as little become a clergyman as a suit of armour would when he officiates at the altar'.

APPENDIX

Published finding-aids to the records of the Westminster courts:

(a) P.R.O *Lists and Indexes*:
Early Chancery Proceedings: lists covering the years 1467 to 1558 are printed in nine distinct volumes of this series: XVI, XX, XXIX, XXXVIII, XLVIII, L, LI, LIV, LV.
Chancery Proceedings, Series II are listed in vols VII, XXIV (period 1558–1621).
Star Chamber Proceedings: vol. XIII and Supplementary Series IV (i).
Court of Requests Proceedings: vol. XXI and Supplementary Series VII (i).

(b) Record Commission Publication:
Proceedings in Chancery in the Reign of Queen Elizabeth . . ., ed. J. Cayley and J. Bayley, 3 vols (1827–32): a selective calendar of Series I; a typescript supplement covering the omissions is available in the P.R.O.

(c) *Deputy Keeper's Report* XXXVII (1877)
Appendix II contains a calendar of the Exchequer Depositions by Commission.

NOTES

1. R. Surtees, *The History and Antiquities of the County Palatine of Durham*, 4 vols (1816–40), I, p. lxix.
2. 27 Hen. VIII c. 24.
3. R. L. Storey, *Thomas Langley and the Bishopric of Durham, 1406–1437*, (1961) p. 52.
4. R. R. Reid, *The King's Council in the North* (1921), p. 108.
5. For a list of the published finding-aids consulted in the preparation of this paper, see Appendix.
6. Reid, pp. 115–6. The exact date of Norfolk's appointment is uncertain, but see *L.P.*, XI no. 1410, and XII (i), nos. 97–8.
7. M. H. and R. Dodds, *The Pilgrimage of Grace*, 2 vols (1915), II, pp. 28, 30.
8. *Ibid.*, II, pp. 125, 133; *L.P.*, XII (i), nos 478 pt 2, 609, 615, 918.
9. P.R.O., Palatinate of Durham, Judgement Rolls, DURH 13/257 (first roll). Unless otherwise stated, all original manuscript sources cited in this paper are in the Public Record Office.
10. *Ibid.*, (second roll).
11. G. T. Lapsley, *The County Palatine of Durham* (1900), p. 189. Dodds, I, p. 205.
12. Chancery, Patent Rolls, C 66/858 m. 20. Cf. D. M. Loades, 'The Last Years of Cuthbert Tunstall', *Durham University Journal*, 66, (1973–74), p. 10.
13. 5 Eliz. c. 23, s. 6.
14. C. Sharp, *Memorials of the Rebellion of 1569*, p. 226, *Depositions and Ecclesiastical Proceedings*, ed. Raine, S.S., 21 (1840), p. 135.
15. *Ibid.*, p. 119; cf. Storey, p. 53 for precedents.
16. E. Coke, *The Fourth Part of the Institutes* (1648), p. 218. Sir James Dyer, *Reports of Cases*, ed. J. Vaillant, 3 vols (1794), III, p. 288b.
17. 13 Eliz. c. 16, s. 6.
18. SP 12/103, no. 42.
19. Exchequer KR, Entry Books of Decrees and Orders, Series I, E 123/26 f. 256v.
20. Reid, pp. 319, 321.
21. *Ibid.*, pp. 342, 349.
22. Chancery Proceedings, Series I, C 2/Eliz. I/C4/32.
23. See Appendix: analysis has been taken down only to the year 1596.
24. For the celebrated cases concerning the tenants of the Dean and Chapter of Durham, see Claire Cross, *The Puritan Earl* (1966), pp. 187–8. The dispute involved the Privy Council itself, in its famous arbitration of 1577, which was enrolled to be 'of record' in King's Bench and also at Durham and York. See also Linda Drury, Sir Arthur Hesilrige and the Weardale Chest', *Trans. Archit. and Antiq. Soc. of Durham and Newcastle*, n.s. 5 (1980), p. 129.
25. Early Chancery Proceedings, C 1/1485 no. 3.
26. *Ibid.*, no. 6.
27. Chancery, Entry Books of Decrees and Orders, C 33/18, ff. 39, 182v.
28. Chancery Proceedings, Series II, C 3/154/12. Arguably, he could have been referring to the Bishop's *ecclesiastical* court.

29. C 1/683, no. 42.
30. C 1/1164, nos. 38–43.
31. Star Chamber Proceedings, Edw. VI, STAC 3/6/83; C 1/1365, nos 41–4.
32. C 3/195/68.
33. C 3/136/82–3.
34. Storey, pp. 126–7.
35. C 2/Eliz. I/E4/71.
36. C 2/Eliz. I/B12/25.
37. On the ill reputation of John Barnes in the ecclesiastical courts at Durham, see W. Hutchinson, *The History and Antiquities of the County Palatine of Durham*, 3 vols (1823), I, p. 572.
38. C 1/831, nos 67 and 69; the case is incomplete.
39. C 1/1464, no. 30.
40. Star Chamber Proceedings, Philip and Mary, STAC 4/1/14; C 1/1446, no. 96.
41. STAC 4/6/63.
42. C 1/1307 nos. 56–7.
43. C 1/1446 nos 94–5.
44. C 1/1024 no. 67.
45. See appendix.
46. Court of Requests, Proceedings, REQ 2/106/55 (24 Eliz. I).
47. For the prime instance, preceding the restitution of temporalities to Pilkington, see *VCH Durham* II (1907), p. 165; F. Heal, *Of Prelates and Princes* (1980), p. 270; and the original receiver's account: SC 6/Eliz. I/596.
48. Proceedings of the Court of Augmentations, in classes E 321 and E 315, are described in manuscript lists in the P.R.O.
49. E 321/24/71.
50. E 315/109 ff. 13–4; E 315/111 ff. 16–9; E 315/112 ff. 17–20. Note that cases in some measure arising from the dissolutions also came before other courts: see, for example, the following instances from Chancery Proceedings (all in class C 1): 1204 nos 110–34; 1216 nos. 36–7, 1243 no. 19; 1281 no. 53; 1319 no. 30.
51. Exchequer, Auditors of Land Revenue, Enrolment Books, LR 1/179 f. 103r.-v.
52. SC 6/Eliz. I/628 is the first roll in the series.
53. Exchequer, Augmentation Office, Particulars for Leases, E 310/12, portfolios 34–39. When the lessee was not the sitting tenant the surveyor was careful to explain why not, e.g. portfolio 34 no. 16, ptfo. 37 no. 40.
54. *Ibid.*, ptfo. 34 no. 45.
55. Exchequer, KR, Bills and Answers, E 112/13, for which a manuscript list is available in the P.R.O.
56. *Ibid.*, no. 57.
57. *Ibid.*, nos 52–3.
58. *Ibid.*, nos 48–50, 54–6, 58, 60.
59. *Ibid.*, nos 71, 78.
60. *Ibid.*, no. 38, and (*ex inf.* Mr Ted Prince), Durham Cathedral Dean and Chapter Misc. Cart. 2592.
61. Cf. Storey, pp. 54, 120.

62. Exchequer KR, Depositions Taken by Commission, E 134/28–29 Eliz./ Mich. 13.
63. 7 Edw. VI c 10; repealed 1 Mary st. 3, c. 3.
64. *C.J.*, I, 34 (16–7 Apr., 1554).
65. Surtees, II, pp. 111–2. Even at Whickham they ran into some difficulties, e.g. E 112/13 no. 39A.
66. SP 12/107 nos 54, 57.
67. C 1/608 no. 30.
68. Storey, p. 54; Lapsley, p. 276.
69. For proceedings concerning the Tyne Bridge, see particularly E 134/23–24 Eliz./Mich. 17; E 112/13 nos 2 and 5; E 123/8 f. 106; Surtees, II, p. 113.
70. For examples of Port Books concerning Hartlepool see E 190/185–6.
71. SP 12/13 no. 13.
72. *Letters and Papers illustrative of the Reigns of Richard III and Henry VII*, ed. J. Gairdner, Rolls Series (1861), I, p. 99.
73. Surtees, III, p. 101.
74. B.L., Harley Charters 58E5. For more on the status of Barnard Castle see Surtees, IV, pp. 64–7.
75. Surtees, I, p. lxiii.
76. E 134/28–29 Eliz./Mich. 13.
77. E 112/13 no. 1; E 123/13 ff. 42–3.
78. E 123/12 f. 159.
79. C 66/1403 m. 17; Surtees, III, p. 102.
80. B.L., (Printed Books), shelf-mark 578 g.5, especially pp. 41 and 52.

More stout than wise: tenant right in Weardale in the Tudor period

J. Linda Drury

Tenant right, an issue in the North of England in the sixteenth and seventeenth centuries, meant different things in different manors.[1] Basically the term meant the right of a tenant to pass his holding on to his heir with little or no landlordly interference, or to sell it, but who his heir was, the circumstances surrounding the inheriting or sale and the payments and services due to whom for such holdings, varied in their type, presence or absence, according to local custom which could alter in the same place over time. What the situation was about 1500, how that custom developed into tenant right in the High Forest of Weardale and Stanhope Park and how landlordly policy attempted belatedly to modify this evolution of land tenure in the Tudor period, are the subjects which this paper will treat in turn.

Where, then, is Weardale, who were the landlords there and of what nature were the tenures in about 1500? Weardale, where the many small streams forming the headwaters of the river Wear rise and join in the Pennine moors, is the Northwesternmost corner of County Durham, marching with Northumberland and Cumberland. The area was the remotest part of the estates of the Bishops of Durham and as in inhospitable hill country anywhere, weather and remoteness from administrative centres developed toughness and independence in the inhabitants. Upper Weardale was the Bishop's multiple manor of Wolsingham, divided into townships (containing mainly copyhold tenure) and two other divisions farther West, the High Forest of Weardale, lying in the Tudor period West of Eastgate, between about seven hundred and two thousand two hundred feet above sea level and within it, Stanhope Park, lying against the Forest's eastern edge, its two main gates now the villages of Eastgate and Westgate. Within the Park and Forest lay the customary holdings which exercised the Bishops throughout the century following 1500. Weardale customary tenure was by payment of rent (or animals), services, including border service and suit of the Forest Court. It was not a copyhold tenure, of which there never was any in the Park and Forest.

The over thirty thousand acres of Park and Forest contained some unfenced red deer and in 1458 there were two hundred fallow deer in the Park, but only forty in 1595. Episcopal hunting had long ceased. The Forest was rich in minerals, pasture and meadow, not timber trees. For centuries the Bishop's stockmen had worked in the Forest, which was only one of the episcopal stock-breeding or fattening areas. By 1500 this demesne stock-raising had declined considerably.[2] As the Bishop's stockmen moved beasts about, bought and sold at fairs and took animals in lieu of cash, the amount of grazing needed for them in the Forest fluctuated. Having allowed also for the needs of the deer, the custom was that surplus grazing was let out from year to year by the Master Forester. Except for a few charter holders, the tenure of land was therefore somewhat precarious. Other moors in Wolsingham Manor, such as Bolihope and Stanhope Common were left unstinted, so they could absorb stock owned by Stanhope and Wolsingham tenants, at times when the Forester had not admitted it to seasonal shielings in the Forest.

The last Forest Justices had been appointed by Bishop Fordham in the 1380s. In 1436 had begun the hereditary succession in the Lumley family of the Master Forestership to the Bishops of Durham. Their patents of office empowered them to hear and determine all forest causes and to demise grazing, affording the family opportunity for patronage, profit and military leadership.[3] In the 1490s they occasionally failed to submit for inspection the rolls of their Forest Courts.[4] Such action called attention to such entrenched advantage and self-aggrandizement in a family containing Plantagenet blood as would not much longer be tolerated by Tudor-appointed Bishops unused to Northern manners.[5]

Tenant right, rather than privilege, could not have become established in the High Forest of Weardale in the period when the Master Forester possessed the right to regulate the grazing and exercised it. Lists in transumpt books of tenants and payments for the customary grazing of the High Forest in the closing years of the fifteenth century showed that with the shrinkage of episcopal stock-keeping, holding by tenants for a whole year round had become more common than summer-only tenure. The rent arrears lists for some tenancies such as

Blackclough and Daddryshield still contained various former tenants, whereas for others such as Burtreeford and Middleblackdean, the arrears contained the names only of the men who were also the current tenants, showing that tenure by the same family of the same holding for years on end was being established. As almost all of these family names occurred as copyholders in the more sheltered townships of the manor down-dale, it was unlikely that many of the Forest holdings were lived in throughout the year. In the North of England, political reasons, as well as altitude and weather, prolonged the use of grazing grounds in summer only. It was not wise to remain in dispersed shielings in the raiding season, October to February, hence the persistence of half-year lets.[6] Geographically the Forest was prey to raiders from other lordships, Cumberland, Tynedale and Scotland and also, as the locations for the autumn and winter night watches show, even from Teesdale to the South. In the winter of 1491/92, a Scottish raid burned a building at Ireshopeburnmouth on the valley floor, not an outlying part of the Forest, and even in the 1530s raiding caused some customary holdings to be forsaken.[7] It was an area where men chose to settle their differences in their own ways, which made it lawless from the Bishop's point of view. The Bishop's stock apart, the area returned little in cash, timber or venison. The rents of the Forest and the richer Park in 1500 amounted to only about £42 and £67 respectively. What political and military value it had lay with the Lumleys. Episcopal interest awoke with the advent of the Tudors.

In 1479 Duke Richard of Gloucester had obtained a grant of the Park and Forest from Bishop Dudley, which as King he retained till his death.[8] Bishop Sherwood (1485-1493) was the first Bishop for decades to visit the Forest,[9] which he did in August 1490 and ordered repairs to Westgate Castle. The decision was made to form a small new park within Stanhope Park and to divide up the rest of the land into farmholds to be let out permanently in those parts of the Park where customary holdings had not become entrenched nor where the grazing was needed for episcopal stock. First mention of the New Park found so far was in 1495/96 when a new payment for a strip of grazing between the Wear and the wall of the New Park was recorded.[10] Bishop Fox, Sherwood's successor (and a close associate of Henry VII), continued the building of the New Park. He appointed in 1499 a surveyor of all the episcopal estates, specifying forests, chases, woods and herbage, possibly in preparation for altering tenures in Weardale, which contained land recently in hand and therefore able to be leased.[11] However, his

Halmote Court Books show that Fox was still making small new grants of land elsewhere, as traditional, life-long copyhold tenures.[12] Fox departed for Winchester in 1501, leaving a vacancy for a year during which evidence of Sherwood's and his Weardale policy can be seen.

Henry VII knew something of the Bishopric and its tenures from his visit after the Simnel Rising in 1487. His commission of May 2 1502 regarding the temporalities, to William Senhouse Bishop of Carlisle, (Keeper of the Temporalities and soon Bishop of Durham) and others, was to survey all the episcopal estates and assets and to investigate means for their improved profit, exploitation and the King's advantage. They were to make grants for a year and report back.[13] They had power to summon, compel and chastise all tenants and officers. Parks, chases, wild beasts, and woods were specifically included. The Crown, perhaps on information from Fox, was taking the initiative in bringing certain Durham tenures into line with other parts of the country.

The survey does not survive, but the terms of some of the one-year demises in Chancery do.[14] These included mills at Auckland and Sedgefield, which had earlier been copyhold, Wolsingham Park, some twenty nine holdings in the High Forest, Stanhope Park demised in four quarters and the New Park. Stanhope Park and the Forest were being singled out of the Bishopric estates for an attempted severe re-ordering of tenants who had long enjoyed the area on casual terms advantageous and convenient to themselves. There had been as much grazing as local people had wanted, as empty holdings showed. Grazing had been let for a year or a half at a time and arrears often written off or compounded, so tenants had not been over-burdened with financial responsibility. In this vacancy rents were not altered, but tenants' conditions were. These new conditions of tenure for Park and Forest were draconian and impolitic. To impose such written conditions for a mere one-year let must be viewed as an experiment for longer engagements. Being in Latin, it was unlikely that the tenants could have any copies read out easily, locally. The conditions regarding maintenance of buildings, prohibition on wasting wood or undergrowth, disturbing, hunting or killing game were unexceptionable, but what followed was more stringent. Tenants might not participate in nor knowingly permit fornication nor adultery on the premises. None might enter the holding who were of bad reputation or suspected or indicted of felony or murder. No inhabitants of Tynedale, Redesdale or Gilsland were to be given any hospitality or comfort. Tenants were not to have secret meetings but hold discussions at church or market. Card playing was limited as to places and season. Goats, greyhounds, bloodhounds or other hunting dogs were forbidden except by licence. The size of stocks of farm animals was to be set by the lord's servant. (Goats, dogs and stock had already been regulated in the Forest). No part of any tenure could be sublet without licence on pain of forfeiture. £10 in cash or kind was the penalty for breaking any condition during this one year. The Park and Forest tenants came to Durham on May 6 1502 and in person took their holdings from May 3, the usual spring entry day, showing that the tenants had continued to occupy these holdings since they were last granted them by the Master Forester. These lands, being treated as demesne, comprised the holdings some of which became leasehold, but most of which developed through tenant right into customary freeholds.

Bishop William Sever or Senhouse received the Durham temporalities in October 1502. Probably born at Shincliffe near Durham, a connection of the Cumberland Senhouses and therefore familiar with Northern tenures and tenacity, it might have been deliberate policy on his part, rather than lack of time, which explains why no evidence survives in the appropriate sources to suggest that he pursued the 1502 initiative. From Michaelmas 1502 till the end of his episcopate in May 1505 the Forest Courts were held regularly (usually May and Michaelmas) and presumably the customary forest tenure continued as before.[15] Senhouse, another conservative, also permitted many new copyholdings to be created throughout his Durham estates.

After his death Henry VII kept the see vacant two years, Bishop(later Cardinal) Christopher Bainbridge, a Westmorland man, not receiving the temporalities until November 1507. Policy in this vacancy, when Prior Castell and William Bulmer, Senhouse's Sheriff, were guardians, was a development of that in the previous one, in demising for longer terms, already the practice on Priory copyhold lands.[16] Over Horsley, alias Horsley Head, in the Billingside quarter of Stanhope Park was let for eighteen years in February 1507 to John Rakett, an episcopal clerk and on January 20 1507 came the first long let of Eastgate which soon developed into an undisputed leasehold. George, son of Geoffrey Emerson was, by special grace, granted a twenty-one-year lease of the messuage called Eastgate in Stanhope Park with specified appurtenances. In 1527 Wolsey let it to him for another sixty years.[17] A few new copyholdings were created also in this vacancy and in Bainbridge's brief tenure, but not in the Park and Forest which were almost ignored.[18] In September 1508 Bainbridge was translated to York, after granting by charter a weekly market and fair at Wolsingham, under supervision of the Master Forester and a bailiff and he leased for twenty years to Roland Tempest all of nearby Wolsingham Park (for which Forest Courts were being held) with elaborate safeguards for the preservation of deer. The habitable buildings in the Park were not to be occupied except for specified purposes.[19] Like Stanhope Park, this one had earlier been treated in quarters (or less), according to the needs for episcopal stock. Henry VII died in April 1509 without appointing Guardians of the Temporalities and no particular initiative was apparent in this vacancy.

Land, the occupation of which had been arranged in Forest or Halmote Courts, was gradually and inconspicuously becoming subject to stricter lettings for definite periods, but as new copyholdings were still being made, no wholesale threat to old tenures seemed imminent. The question of 'tenant right' had not been raised.

On July 3 1509 Bishop Thomas Ruthall received the Durham temporalities. Born in Gloucestershire and later a Prebendary of Wells and Dean of Lincoln, he had knowledge of estate management, but not in the North of England. Being Secretary to Henry VIII, he was much employed in Scottish and other public affairs. Forest Courts were held for Ruthall's first year, John Rakett assisting, but on March 1 of the second year, 1511, the Bishop issued a patent[20] to Thomas Kaye (Bachelor of Law and Keeper of the Seal), Sir William Bulmer, William Hilton, Baron of Hilton (made Chief Forester the previous June), Thomas Tempest (Steward), John Rackett and John Bentley (later Escheator, both with experience in Weardale and who must have guessed the outcome) to survey and let to farm the lands and tenements of the Forest of Weardale and the two Stanhope Parks, for the Bishop's profit, for terms of thirteen years or less, thus converting the tenure to the leasehold so common outside Durham Bishopric estates.[21] One part of the indenture, with whomsoever made, was to be lodged in Durham Chancery within a month of its making and to be kept safe. The commissioners were to certify whatever they signed, for the security of the Bishop and his successors.

This stress on the written evidence was unusual. The results were enrolled on Ruthall's Chancery Roll. Fifty-six holdings and shares of holdings (which in some cases exceeded the whole) were supposedly let, most for five years, but large areas were kept in hand including Kilhope, Welhope, Burnhopeshield and pasture. As it was intended that the terms be written in indentures, part to be kept by the tenant, the language used was English, which over a century later was still not widely written or read in Weardale. The demises of Dirtpot in Forest and the herbage of New Park were dated March 4, so soon after the commission that these initiatives must have been begun beforehand. Letting to farm the Forest herbage etc., under the supervision of the Steward had been a privilege already granted to Lord Richard Lumley and his son John in their patent of August 31 1508 from Bainbridge.[22] Possibly the new Steward and Bishop now realised that this was potentially too valuable to be left to a new inexperienced Master Forester. John Lumley, born about 1492, had lost his father and grandfather in 1508 and 1510. The Master Forestership was in less strong hands than formerly and a policy of resumption might now have success. Despite young John's patent, Hilton was made Chief Forester and new terms were devised for the Forest holdings.

The terms for all the so-called demises of 1511 included some of those of 1502, regarding upkeep of buildings, waste, interference with game, aid to suspicious people, secret meetings, goats and hounds. What was added was that no tenant should be retained by word, badge, livery, promise or any other way, by anyone but the King or the Bishop, their successors or assigns. Tenants would take this as a reference to the Lumleys on whose favour grants of Forest grazing had hitherto depended and who led them to service on the Scottish border.[23] The tenants were to be ready with sufficient defensible array and harness, with bow, spear, bill or other weapon, to attend upon only the King, Bishop or assigns and must be ready to follow the hue and cry within the 'Country of Weardale'. If the rent were forty days late or the tenant died, the grant was void. These leases could not be inherited. Ruthall tried to prevent what Wolsey and Tunstall let escape, he forbade the assignment of holdings without licence. Rents were to be paid at the Exchequer in Durham, bypassing the Master Forester. All but a handful of these so-called lessees had the same surnames as families already resident in the various other townships comprising Wolsingham manor, i.e. Stanhope, Bishopley, Wolsingham, Wigside, Greenwellside, Lynesack and Bedburn.[24] The only obvious incomer was John Lowther, gentleman, possibly from Cumbria. Some men were to hold more than one holding in the Park and Forest and some families, several, the Emersons outstripping the rest with fifteen.

Ruthall's reason for trying to increase his control over the inhabitants of Upper Weardale was political as well as economic. In August 1509 at Durham Court of Pleas the Sheriff was instructed to distrain the 'villat de Stanhop' to come and answer for divers transgressions and contempts. In all the Durham Plea Rolls for the sixteenth century there is no other such sweeping condemnation of any one whole township. By clamping down on the Park and Forest, Ruthall hoped perhaps to prevent the long lists of malefactors summoned by name from the Stanhope area in 1509-12 from taking refuge in the Forest where, in practice, the Bishop had little control.[25]

Very few of those summoned to Durham, who included few, if any, of the 'lessees', heeded the summons and this mass contempt for law and order would encourage the feeling among the episcopal administrators that Weardale was more trouble than it was worth. The commissioners in spring 1511 had also held Sessions of the Peace in Weardale.[26] Obviously trouble was expected, but the record itself does not survive. It was rare for such sessions to be held in County Durham outside Durham City. What actually occurred in Weardale in 1511 is not known exactly. The tenants were on home ground, not in Durham as in 1502, and it is unlikely that they signed or sealed anything, except perhaps for Sunderland (Sir Ralph Bowes) or Horsley Head (Edward Sanderson), both in the Park.

The authorities were trying to do far too much too suddenly for acceptability to tenants who were used to pleasing themselves. Later evidence shows that they just stayed where they were, paying what had been paid and undertaking no extra obligations. Ruthall knew the value of signed, sealed or marked counterparts, which would have been trump cards in later court cases, but they were never produced and future citations of these leases referred only to the Chancery Roll. In 1579 a decree of the Council of the North regarding tenant right said that counterparts were the required proof of leases and noted specifically that exemplifications under Bishops' seals were not sufficient proof.[27] In February 1513 a last effort was made by Ruthall in the enrolment of a supposed five year lease of a third of Westramshawell (Windiside) at 8s. 4d. per annum to Anthony Richardson in place of Agnes Blackburn at 11s. 11½d.[28] Richardsons remained at Windiside another eighty years, but as customary tenants. Weardale rents continued to be delivered to the old collector in the dale not individually to Durham Exchequer. In 1508 Cuthbert Tunstall, later Bishop of Durham, had become Rector of Stanhope and the galling results of Ruthall's attempts to impose his will on Tunstall's parishioners, would not have been lost upon him.

Most of the 'lessees' of 1511 were familiar with copyhold tenure, as regulated in the Bishop of Durham's Halmote Courts held two or three times a year in Wolsingham. As practised in this manor the tenure meant that a copyholder's widow, then children or kinsmen, succeeded to the holding in turn, almost automatically, save that the admittance had to be made in the Halmote Court. The court which regulated the Forest grazing grounds had been the Forest Court. If that court failed to act, it was to be expected the last people to be allocated grazing would continue to hold it and pass it to their heirs in the same way as they did their other, their copyhold, land.

Sir Richard Lumley, Master Forester, died about May 1510 and almost at once Ruthall ordered his son John to deliver the keys of Westgate tower and the Forest Court Rolls to John's uncle William Hilton, whose patent as Master Forester during pleasure was dated June 10 1510.[29] Despite John's protestations and his patent, Ruthall kept Hilton in office until 1512, over the period of the leases. After Hilton, Roger Lumley was made deputy to John who quarrelled with violence with them both and spent most of the rest of his life at variance with his Bishop.

From 1511 to Ruthall's death Forest Courts were held only in 1516/17 and probably 1519/20, but no record survives of business.[30] It is not known if Ruthall relented and if the courts held in 1516/17 handled Forest grazing according to John's patent, but it is unlikely. Perhaps it was just coincidence that these courts took place when the 1511 lease periods would have been expiring and perhaps further measures were planned. The perquisites in 1519/20 were recorded as nil, 'quia in manus Domini Lomley'. After 1513 no renewals of the leases are to be found in Ruthall's Chancery Rolls, nor was it ever claimed that they were renewed. Although he was unwelcome in administration, Lord John Lumley was useful in mustering the Weardale men against the Scots in 1522. However in January 1523, just before Ruthall died, Lumley complained to the King that the Bishop had prevented him from holding his Forestership for four years.[31] He was to receive even shorter shrift from Wolsey with whom his account was usually in arrears.

Cardinal-Bishop Thomas Wolsey (1523-29) took detailed interest in his Durham affairs (though rarely there,) as his letters show. He disallowed Lumley's fee as Master Forester and directed business included in his patent to other channels. The Forest Courts' perquisites were recorded as nil for Wolsey's years 1523-5 and 1526-9.[32] Weardale men suspected of taking game were bound by recognizance to appear at Durham Assizes.[33] In 1523/4 Lumley rendered account at Durham Exchequer, but the Forest rent collection was given to a new Receiver, Richard Pemberton, responsible to the Exchequer not to the Forester. As Lumley already felt aggrieved because he considered his own collecter of Park and Forest rents, Henry Emerson, had been defrauding[34] him between May 1 1523 and May 1 1525, it would be in character for him to act precipitately to upset Wolsey's policy of not admitting Forest tenants in Forest Courts, by doing just that in 1526, as his patent empowered him.[35] For Lumley the result of his various ill conduct was the further denial of his fee by mandate of the Cardinal and a summons in summer 1529 to Durham Place, the Bishop's London residence, to do as he was bidden there. He had received a similar summons in 1519.[36]

Wolsey's successor, Cuthbert Tunstall (1529-59), at least allowed Lumley the fee of £6. 13s. 4d. per annum which went with his empty title, for no Forest Courts were held by Lumley and Pemberton continued in office.[37] In 1536 Lumley joined the Pilgrimage of Grace, was pardoned and disgraced and his son executed, marking the end of the dynasty of Lumley Master Foresters which had begun in 1436. In February 1538 Tunstall appointed his nephew Brian Tunstall, Chief Forester for life, with power to hear and determine all Forest cases according to ancient use (despite a clause in an Act of 1536 forbidding the Bishop of Durham to commission justices).[38] In Tunstall's ninth, eleventh and twelfth years only, were perquisites of Forest Courts in Weardale recorded and in 1553 a special court was held in the 'prince's name' i.e. Edward VI, before Robert Hindmers (Chancellor of Durham since March 1530 and sometime Rector of Stanhope) probably between the Dissolution of the see in March and Mary's accession in August.[39]

What other evidence of landlordly attitudes to the Forest tenures in 1510-36 is there besides the virtual suppression of Forest Courts which had regulated them? To the absentee Wolsey, Weardale tenure merited little attention, he paid more to the mineral rights (which had been included in the Lumley's patent). Hugh Whitehead, Prior of Durham, had his licence to exploit Weardale iron.[40] Wolsey had a clerk of mines, William Bulmer again, and the Chancellor, William Frankelyn, also invested. In February 1529 Wolsey granted to Thomas Winter, Dean of Wells and Archdeacon of Richmond, his reputed son, a furnace and all the mines of metals and minerals in all the Bishopric and the 'country called Weardale' for thirty years at a mere £5 per annum.[41] Any further definition of the tenants' rights to the surface would have complicated this exploitation and not been in Wolsey's interests. Apparently his only land grant in Weardale was of Eastgate in Stanhope Park to George Emerson, already farmer there, for sixty years on May 10 1527, of which the Emersons were to enjoy twenty-three without interference.

In January 1530 in the vacancy between Wolsey and Tunstall a spurt of long leasing occured which must have been the initiative of those left in charge, Tunstall not being provided to the see until February 21 1530. Those in charge were William Frankelyn, Chancellor, John Bulmer, Sheriff, Robert Bowes, Escheator and a man who had had much concern with land transactions on the episcopal estates, Thomas Tempest of Holmside, Steward since 1510 and aware of the Weardale situation since Ruthall's abortive leases. (His brothers Roland and George had keeperships and a long lease of Wolsingham Park). The Weardale grants were all of premises in Stanhope Park for twelve years and took place between January 8 and 11 1530.[42] One was New Park, which went from Frankelyn to Bulmer, the Clerk of the Lead Mines. Langlee went to Lancelot Trotter and Westernhopeburnshield and Whitwellhouseshield to John Emerson. The Trotters and the Emersons were for decades to provide Keepers of Stanhope Park and it may be that these grants, at smaller rents than for the same properties at other times that century, were both conditional on accepting offices and intended to quieten prominent local residents who might have provided leadership in resisting other attempts to alter customary holdings. Langlee remained leasehold, but despite later episcopal efforts, the premises granted to the Emersons persisted as customary.

Bishop Tunstall's attitude to his tenants and his own rights in Weardale was ambivalent.[43] He saw advantages in not holding Forest Courts in Lumley's time but had them held thereafter in his ninth to twelfth years after he had been deprived of the right to commission justices. In 1546 occurred the problem of Dirtpot, a holding which in 1439 had consisted of seasonal grazing for thirty sheep and fifteen cattle let that year to John Dixon for 20s.[44] After a succession of occupants, Anthony Dobynson, Isabel Dobynson, John Simson and Thomas Collingwood were there in 1511. In 1520 it sheltered at least Alexander Dobynson and John Simson, yeomen, who were indicted at Durham Court of Pleas but declined to attend. In about 1526 Margaret, Alexander's widow, was admitted at a Forest Court in widowright. Despite her young son, she sold her right to William Nattress for £6 13s. 4d. Margaret's son William waited until he was twenty-one and petitioned Tunstall to restore Dirtpot to him.[45] Tunstall could no longer ignore the situation or equivocate. A decision either to support the claimed hereditary right or to arrange a lease with someone, had to be made. Tunstall passed the problem to Hindmers whose pronouncement showed that Tunstall was then tolerating the claimed custom of Weardale rather than a provocative policy of attempted resumption. Hindmers referred the case to a Forest jury which met in Stanhope parsonage. Complications emerged.

Widow Dobynson had been daughter of Thomas Wardale, whose name occurred as holding Dirtpot in 1503/04 and 1505/06 and she had inherited her father's share before she married Dobynson with his share. However, on the grounds that she sold to Nattress without the heir's consent, the sale was judged void, Nattress and his family raised at Dirtpot were expelled and Dobynson put in by Master Forester Vaux as in times past. A Forest holding had been shown to have been inherited and tenant right according to the Weardale custom had been supported on this occasion.

Tunstall's policy of increased leasing in the dale continued conservatively for a while. Some premises leased had already been let for terms of years or were park lands, or had otherwise been recently in hand. On October 15 1548 Sunderland in Stanhope Park was let to William Hilton Esquire of Biddick for twenty-one years for rent and services including provision of a light horseman or two footmen to serve in Scotland or elsewhere.[46] Hilton had been paying regularly for Sunderland for at least twenty years previously. Eastgate, granted for sixty years in 1527 to George Emerson, was on July 26 1550 granted by Tunstall to Anthony Tunstall of Stockton for thirty years. This was enrolled twice, one copy including the provision that Alice, widow of George Emerson, should not be disturbed in her widowhood, either a promise or a threat suggesting that old Alice had not agreed to surrender or renew her lease, granted for an inordinate length by Wolsey to the disadvantage of his successors.[47] Tunstall apparently made a lease of Burnhope frith to Anthony Tunstall the text of which does not survive.[48] This area had been reserved frequently for episcopal stock or red deer and there could be no question of the Bishop's right to make a lease of it.

The efficacy of tenants' tenacity and the Bishops' further attempts to reduce tenant right to the terms of leases were illustrated in events relating to several key holdings, Pinfold House, Windiside and Lintzgarth in Forest, Brotherlee and Westernhopeburn in Park and at Westgate. On April 12 1551 a lease (not enrolled) was made of Pinfold House, a customary holding, to John Vasey for twenty-one years at a rent of 20s. per annum and service of one soldier. On May 15 1551 Tunstall's political troubles had increased to such a pitch that he was summoned to London, leaving a virtual vacancy and as Steward, Robert Meynell, who had followed Tempest in 1546. In Tunstall's absence the pace warmed for the customary tenants. On June 20 1551 was granted to Gabriel and Henry Emerson a lease, not enrolled, of Brotherlee for thirty years and on November 10 Westernhopeburn was let to William

Cornforth a Forester of Weardale, for twenty-one years from the death of the present occupant Emmot Emerson, for rent and service to the King and Bishop with one able horseman. The same day (and also enrolled) a holding at Windiside was granted to John Foster for twenty-one years at 20s. per annum after the death of occupants Robert Gibson and his wife.[49] These grants will be considered in turn. Tunstall, aged about seventy-seven, was too preoccupied to stir up trouble in Weardale. Perhaps conditions of non-disturbance were put in by his officials to please a relatively kind-hearted Bishop, known in Weardale and who was to make no martyrs in Durham in Mary's reign. These leases to run after the deaths of present tenants, otherwise known as concurrent or reversionary leases, could well have been used to blackmail the existing tenants into coming into some agreement with the landlord e.g. accepting a lease. That these two such rareties were made in Tunstall's absence, the duration of which for such an old man might have been permanent, suggests that the episcopal officials were anticipating the policy of a new Bishop, based on policies seen elsewhere. There was no legislation regulating such leases till 13 Eliz. c.11.

At Pinfold House William Richardson and his ancestors had been customary tenants 'time out of mind'. (In fact they first occupied it between 1506 and 1511). They had paid their rent, suit of court and border service. Bishop Tunstall appointed some Spanish mercenaries to serve in the Bishopric about 1550 and four were billetted in Weardale on Richardson. Being 'doubtful of their good behaviour' he offered to pay cash instead and local people believed Tunstall's consequent anger to be the reason for his lease of Pinfold House to John Vasey, one of the four Foresters, on April 12 1551. Vasey, helped by other of the Bishop's officers (some of whom had similar leases of customary holdings), ejected Richardson by force. Richardson took immediate action, but his untimely death on a journey back from London left Vasey in possession for the full twenty-one years, as Richardson's son Cuthbert was a simple man and did not continue the case.[50] Simple Cuthbert, however, had a son in about 1560, of whom more will be said later.

The unenrolled Brotherlee lease of June 20 1551 to Henry and Gabriel Emerson also failed to take hold. Brotherlee's tenurial status was investigated by the Council of the North following Bishop Pilkington's further attempt to convert it in the 1570s. Evidence then showed that this Gabriel was son of Henry who had been admitted to Brotherlee by John Lumley at a Forest Court.[51] These witnesses of 1579 remembered no interruption to the customary tenure of Brotherlee, Gabriel Emerson and later two younger brothers, Thomas and William, being admitted at Forest Courts. Gabriel Emerson was given the office of one of the four Foresters of Weardale on July 1 1551.[52] Perhaps acceptance of a lease had been a condition of receipt of office.

The issue of Westernhopeburn lay dormant as Emmot Emerson lived long. About twelve years after the lease, when neither Cornforth nor the Bishop's officers were alert, Emmot appeared at a Forest Court with her daughter and son-in-law Ann and Arthur Neville, formally gave her consent and Neville was admitted tenant![53] Neville was a direct descendant of Ralph Neville, first Earl of Westmorland.[54] In 1578 perhaps it was he who took the initiative in encouraging his neighbours as that year, after Cornforth had begun a suit in Durham Chancery, he took the case of Westernhopeburn to the Council of the North and soon after the tenants of Brotherlee and Lintzgarth also claimed tenant right. On August 12 and 17 1579 and June 8 1580 came the Council's three decrees for Brotherlee, Westernhopeburn and Lintzgarth, all in favour of the customary tenant.[55]

Windiside, by 1595, consisted of both customary and leasehold land and it is hard to know if this lease of 1551, to follow the Gibson's, refers to land there which became leasehold in 1551 or which remained customary in spite of the lease.[56] One concludes that this attempt to create leasehold at Windiside failed, but not immediately. In 1625 John Gibson of Windiside paid a customary rent of 26s. 8d.[57]

These four leases, attempted when Tunstall was under pressure, produced no eventual conversion to leasehold despite initial success. Once free, Tunstall authorised two more Weardale leases,[58] one of uncontroversial New Park to Cuthbert Layton in succession to Richard Pemberton, Receiver, for thirty-one years on November 22 1556 at £5 per annum and the other (unenrolled) on May 16 1556 of Over Horsley in Stanhope Park, already leasehold, for twenty-one years to Nicholas Maddison, whose family had lived there before and were, in Stanhope, second in social standing to the Featherstonhaughs of Stanhope Hall.[59] The latter family seem deliberately to have avoided Bishop's leaseholds after the 1511 fiasco.

Elizabeth deprived Tunstall on September 28 1559 and he died that November aged about eighty-four. He had known Weardale and the North in general better than any other Tudor Bishop of Durham and his policy towards the rights of the Weardale tenants was to leave the vast majority of such holdings well alone. Tenant right worked in

Northumberland and Cumberland without registering the change of tenant in court (as did occur in Weardale if a court were held), but by payment of a fine on the death of tenant or landlord. No fine was paid by the Weardale customars beyond the tack penny into the May Forest Court which had distributed the summer grazing. ('*Taka*' means 'tenure' in Old Norse.) This payment was similar to the 'God's penny' which changed hands at biannual servant hirings in many parts of England as an earnest of an oral agreement. Had the Bishops begun by trying to enforce fines of several years rent on succession in this inflationary period, as other landlords did, rather than the more difficult problem of enforcement of leaseholds, it might have profited them more. Tunstall saw the failure of both wholesale and piecemeal attacks on tenant right. After 1541, no Forest Courts were held, apart from the Dirtpot inquiry, until 1553.

It is unfortunate that Tunstall's long episcopate was disjointed by the Act of Supremacy, the Divorce, the Dissolution, the legal and political after-effects of the Pilgrimage of Grace, and Edward's and Mary's contrasting religious policies. He neglected to clarify an already anomalous situation in Weardale. The continued disruption and insufficient replacement of the Master Forester's duties of rent collection and control and oversight of tenants, foresters and parkers in the Forest Court lost Tunstall official contact. Having been resident in Weardale, doubtless he had his own contacts and was perhaps unaware of the ignorance of his officials in Durham. This loss of contact, which Tunstall bequeathed to his successors, is vividly illustrated in the way the record keeping changed under Richard Pemberton, Particular Receiver of the Forest rents. Before Pemberton, Weardale, in charge of the prominent Lumley family, had always been considered worthy of a new clean page in the transumpt book each year. In Pemberton's time this mark of esteem died away and the High Forest of Weardale often appeared in whatever space remained after the preceding coal mining section. Pemberton, after John Lumley's death, began, in 1537/8, a new and simplified way of accounting for his responsibilities which was inserted into the transumpt books on an extra sheet.[60] The Exchequer, however, continued with the old, detailed list of expected Forest income and expenditure, side by side with the new for thirty more years(!) The customary holdings became subdivided with scarcely any note of it in the episcopal records. The old way covered four pages, the new scarcely one. Pemberton condensed his charges into uninformative round figures which did not allow the Exchequer clerks to annotate their list of expectations with names of tenants or officers. He was not often in arrears, thereby escaping investigation, but his office was virtually at farm.

After Tunstall's death the guardian was Robert Tempest, Sheriff. As he had shown no support for tenant right in Weardale, it must have been on royal orders that the Forest Courts met in 1559/60.[61] In September 1561 William Fleetwood of the Middle Temple was made Steward of the Swainmote Courts in the Forest of Weardale to execute the Forest Laws of the Queen of England, as well as the local customs, and an Indian summer began for the courts.[62] Fleetwood had no familiarity with the situation of the regular courts of over fifty years before. He saw an irregular situation in the Park and Forest with episcopal tenants going their own way, with no local court enforcing good neighbourhood, no landlordly forum in an area where in the course of the century the holdings of 1510 had been subdivided without any trace of episcopal authorisation to about seventy-seven in 1578 and where year-round occupation had become the norm.[63] Weardale was a distant, somewhat disreputable area where, apart from mineral lessees and clergy who were not permanent residents, the Bishops had had no good sources of information on local affairs and feelings for many years.[64] The patent of John Vaux, Bailiff of Stanhope, as Chief Forester for life in 1549 contained no reference to holding courts or demising in Park or Forest.[65] Gone the sweeping powers of the aristocratic Lumleys, leaving lawyer Fleetwood's hands free. His attitude towards these Forest Courts of the new foundation, held in Stanhope, shows in the occasional reference to them as 'Halmotes'.

Like the Wolsingham Halmotes, the Forest Courts continued regularly throughout Elizabeth's reign, twice yearly, in fact held by the Vaux family.[66] Surviving court rolls are few, but show suit enforced by fines and essoins. (Some leases laid down suit at the Forest Court, such as Horsley Head.) Juries from Park and Forest, Bolihope, Stanhope, Wolsingham Park and Roughside presented for the same offences as Halmotes for other areas, plus the old forest offences. The fine for building a deer-proof fence of any sort was 6s. 8d., for hunting with hounds, greyhounds, gun or crossbow 10s. (6s. 8d. extra if the dog were unlicensed). The penalty for hunting deer was still higher than for drawing a man's blood, which was only 6s. 8d., or half that for an affray without blood.[67]

As regards succession to Forest holdings, the damage had been done in 1510/1559, a period of general movement into old forest areas throughout England. The Weardale Forest Court had then lost its place as the link in the transfer of the holdings. On other estates the payment of a fine, not a Forest Court appearance with its tack penny payment, was the landlord's point of intervention in the inheritance of a customary holding, as the Halmote was for a copyholding. Tenant right, a demand in 1536 from the Pilgrims of Grace from outside Durham Bishopric estates, became established in Weardale through the Bishop's default. The relatively few holdings considered in this paper are almost all those known to have been subject to disputes over tenure. The remaining majority were inherited unquestioned. The new Forest Courts, in surviving proceedings 1598-1607, made only technical admissions, no more than noting inheritances, as they occurred according to the custom of Weardale which allowed a widow right before her children, inheritance by a younger son if the elder agreed, sale by heir's agreement etc.[68] The new courts supplied a needed local court for matters of neighbourhood. In keeping the power of punishing deer poachers, they retained one of the powers of the old Weardale Forest Courts, whereas royal Forest Courts only prepared cases and the royal Forest Justices meted out the punishments at intervals.

In the absence of a manorial court, certain local matters could have been settled by the tenants themselves at the byrlaw court alias burlaw, byerlea or plebiscite, found in the Borders and Scotland. Documented in Weardale and other parts of the Bishopric estates c. 1590-1610, including Wolsingham which had a Halmote too, it is likely to have existed earlier. It was an unofficial assembly of neighbours which settled disputes about boundaries, cattle etc. without recourse to law. In 1602 the earlier practice of using the Forest Courts to strengthen byrlaw agreements was repeated.[69] The existence of the byrlaw kept disputes within the dale and reduced opportunities for outside intervention. The Dirtpot jury, so readily available when the Forest Court was in abeyance, illustrates this local readiness to settle their own affairs, as do the meetings of stintholders in Weardale today.

Pilkington, the first Protestant holder of the see, a Marian exile and zealous reformer, was very careful of the rights and privileges of Durham and had trouble in obtaining the gradual restitution of the temporalities upon payment to the Queen. After 1561 no leases of Weardale property appear on the rolls of Durham Chancery for the rest of the century and no counterpart leases survive earlier than this episcopate. His concern with Weardale took note of its heavy involvement in the 1569 Rising and took other forms than an immediate attack on tenant right, such as non-payment of officers implicated. He continued to lease out Burnhope frith and in 1572, when the lease of Pinfold House expired, he let it again peacefully to Richard Marley for twenty-one years. Young Cuthbert Richardson was then only about eleven years old. Also to Marley he leased a Windiside holding, which had reverted to customary by 1595. Pilkington also introduced leaseholding to Lintzgarth, possibly when it was derilict.[70]

Bishop Pilkington afforded the only case of the attempt to convert a customary holding into a copyhold. To the Halmote Court held at Wolsingham on September 23 1572, before Thomas Calverley, Esq., Steward, came George Pilkington and others, the governors of Rivington School, Lancashire, and were granted Lodgefield at Blackdean, then or late in the occupation of George Emerson and now in the Bishop's hand, to hold according to the custom of (this Halmote) court paying 1d. per annum if asked, with subletting permitted.[71] The entry is countersigned in manuscript by Calverley, who became Steward also of the Dean and Chapter's Halmotes. Three separate George Emersons were pardoned for implication in the 1569 Rising, so the availability of Lodgefield is probably a result of forfeiture following 1569, of customary land, the only such forfeiture found so far. Why this land was not granted through the Forest Court, which certainly met that year, or by a conveyance, is not known. It reflects the confused attitude of the episcopal administration towards the customary holdings. However, this grant must have been inoperative, as in 1576/77, one Ralph Emerson was noted as owing the Bishop, not the governors, 5s. rent for Lodgefield.[72] Much later it became leasehold, the earliest surviving counterpart being a renewal of 1669.[73] It was not among the leaseholds listed in the Parliamentary survey of 1647.[74]

Brotherlee was only one of many customary holdings from which tenants bought pardons in 1570.[75] Richard Watson senior and junior and John Emerson, all of Brotherlee, did so. On October 20 1574, when William Emerson, admitted in one of Pilkington's Forest Courts, was tenant at Brotherlee, the Bishop issued to Gregory Butler, holder of several episcopal offices, a lease of Brotherlee for twenty-one years. Butler received also land at Sedgefield, late of Robert Tempest, attainted after 1569. Emerson described Butler as 'very covetous and of insatiable desire'![76] Thus began events which continued into the next episcopate. At first the 'Lord Treasurer' helped Emerson, showing some sympathy for the customary tenants among the Bishop's council, but when Emerson petitioned the Queen, pressure on him was increased. In the vacancy after Pilkington's death, Butler obtained an Exchequer writ to remove the Emersons. Physical violence, six men with daggers and guns, having failed, Butler assigned his lease on July 4 1578 to Francis Conyers, on purpose to try the title at common law. Despite Conyers' objections, that summer Emerson's case against him began before the Council of the North. The decree in Emerson's favour came on August 12 1579. A week later came the Council's decree that Westernhopeburn was held by tenant right and the following June, Lintzgarth in the High Forest similarly. The issue at Lintzgarth had not at first involved the Bishop.[77] Roland Emerson, a tenant there, once kidnapped by Scottish raiders, had four daughters, the eldest and heir named Alice. Ann, a younger daughter, married Alexander Vasey, perhaps a relation of the Forester. John Barnes and Cuthbert Layton (both lessees in Stanhope Park) abetted the Vaseys in claiming that Lintzgarth was not customary, in order that the Vaseys might obtain a lease of it. The Council of the North upheld Alice's customary title on June 28 1580. Episcopal opportunism in using a family quarrel to introduce a lease had failed. However, Barnes did perhaps have some success at Lintzgarth. In 1595 besides two customary tenants there, Alice Emerson at 10s. and Robert Lawe 3s. 4d., there were two leaseholders, Richard Whitfield and Roland Pattinson at 13s. 4d., named as 'of Lintzgarth' at Forest Courts in 1599 and 1600. In 1592 when John Phillipson (whose ?grandson obtained a 6s. 8d. leasehold at Lintzgarth in 1604) accused Alice Emerson of being a witch and a whore, Roland Pattinson in evidence mentioned that he had known Alice about twenty years, which suggests his arrival at Lintzgarth in Barnes' time or Pilkington's.[78]

From 1580 survives the only copy found so far of the text of an apparent admittance to a customary holding. When asked for evidence of title, customary tenants would produce neighbours who had either been present at an admission at a Forest Court or who could testify that an heir had actually inherited after the death of father, husband etc. Most probably copies were not given by the Forest Court. None survive nor were mentioned. In the fifteenth century when grazing was let for the year or half year, copies were unnecessary and this practice would continue. The 1580 indenture of admittance was of Agnes Emerson, daughter of Richard Emerson deceased, to the tenement called (Westgate) Castle Nook in Stanhope Park for life.[79] It contained no reference to the Forest Court. The conditions included the forbidding of harm to red or fallow deer, harbouring or meeting suspicious persons and keeping goats and hounds. Military service, hue and cry, watch and ward were specified. This document may well have been yet another attempt to impose new restriction on a customary tenant. This admittance was not strictly a lease but contained a voidance clause, if the rent were twenty days late. Customary tenants were often in arrears and the remedy taken was distraint of stock, no example of re-entry having been found. In 1579 the Council of the North had upheld tenant right in Weardale and this sole survivor of 1580 may have been an experiment to alter tenure in a subtler way. No mention is made of the consent of Jenett Emerson, widow, in possession in 1580 and probably Agnes's mother. According to Weardale custom she had prior right. Agnes was therefore in a difficult position to avoid conditions if she wanted admission. No male members of the family were mentioned, the armed horseman would have to be hired. Her father Richard was dead and some relation, William Emerson of Castle Nook, had been involved in the 1569 Rising. This admission cannot then have been at all typical. The text states that Agnes set her hand and seal to the indenture. Vestiges of a seal remain although no signature nor recognisable mark, but by 1595 no Emerson held any of the 28s. 4d. holdings at Westgate.

In 1581 Cuthbert Richardson came of age. His grandfather had died after eviction from Pinfold House, 'cast . . . forth with his wife and family and all his stuff with all extremity that might be showed' as a witness put it.[80] Marley's lease had been assigned to William Walton and R. Peart and then to Christopher Walton and Percival Lee, whom Richardson sued in his Bill of Complaint to the Council of the North dated November 25 1581. The decree for the plaintiff came in August 1582. The tenement ought to have descended to his father and to Cuthbert who was to enjoy it unhindered. Despite this decree and those of 1579/80 it was only three years before Barnes sanctioned a return to the struggle for Pinfold House.

After 1569 pacification of the North had been carried out partly by Elizabeth's cousin Henry Carey, Lord Hunsdon, and his son George, who doubtless visited Weardale then and later, on his employment about the Borders. Barnes agreed to make George Carey a lease on January 25 1583 of the South part of Stanhope Park, containing Brotherlee and also Westernhopeburn even though William Cornforth junior, inheritor of his father's lease of 1551, was, despite the Council of the North's decree, still from 1579, pursuing the Nevilles of Westernhopeburn in Durham Court of Pleas. There he was eventually nonsuited in 1584, the year in which in desperation Neville had petitioned the

Court of Requests.[81] Perhaps it was deliberate policy of Barnes in the 1580s to inflict on Weardale the punishment it missed largely in 1570. The decade is full of litigation. Barnes, once Bishop of Carlisle and therefore aware of the complications of Northern tenures, had been appointed by Elizabeth to the Council of the North.

On March 1 1583 Carey wrote a letter to the tenants of the South part of the Park, from the Court, to emphasise his powerful connections.[82] It was threatening. He urged them to take leases from him and not stand upon tenant right or he would let the holdings to strangers who would pay more. They were more stout than wise, more stubborn than well counselled. He would force them to pay dearly for the least trouble they put him to in law or otherwise. They would pay for their folly with their repentance. One can guess the reaction to this fighting talk in Weardale. Carey achieved nothing in 1583/84. At Durham Court of Pleas in January 1585, declarations of ejectment were made by Carey against each tenant individually.[83] The tenants' attorney was Henry Cressy who had represented the Nevilles when Cornforth's case against them over Westernhopeburn had been nonsuited. A day was set for hearings but it passed with no action.

Carey then apparently obtained a further lease from Barnes on December 24 1585, of the same holdings and repaired again to Durham on January 11 1586, represented by his attorney Michael Calverley, which was probably to his advantage, as that day the tenants were moved to arrive there in their proper persons. Apparently Carey dropped all cases but one, against Richard Watson of Brotherlee. A jury was empanelled in July 1586, Carey was nonsuited and took his leave of the Weardale scene.[84]

Barnes' next accomplice was Gilbert Tall or Tawlle, an old soldier of Berwick garrison.[85] To him was leased on June 7 1584 and again on August 11 1584, four holdings at Westgate. Had the premises been confined to Westgate Castle which was undoubtedly the Bishop's, the lease might have stood, but to it were joined other lands in the Westgate quarter of Stanhope Park, last in hand for episcopal stock in the 1480s and 1490s since when customary tenants had become entrenched.[86] Tall's cases against the tenants, John and Ralph Emerson, Henry Robinson, came up at Durham in January 1585, the same day as Carey's. Disconcertingly Tall's defendants appeared in person and Tall did not proceed. Declarations in ejectment were repeated in the same court on July 21 1589, after Barnes' death.[87] Tall again failed to proceed and soon died. A further effort in 1586 or after, of which little is known, was over Billingshield in Stanhope Park, leased by Barnes to Edward Armstrong, whose case against the customary tenant, Peter Wright, was dismissed by the Council of the North.[88]

Other leases[89] in Weardale by Barnes were of New Park and Eastgate to his father John in 1583, two messuages at Burtreeford to Arthur Emerson and yet again Pinfold House and Windiside to George Gifford servant of the Bishop (whose first wife was a Gifford) in 1585, New Park to Robert Tailbois (Barnes' son-in-law) and Henry Appleton (his Steward), Horsley Head to Robert Walker (Bishop's servant) in 1587 all for twenty-one years and most important, thirteen tenements at Westgate in both Park and Forest, leased to the Queen[90] on January 17 1586 for seventy years, which she assigned to John Stanhope, Esquire.

Burtreeford in Forest had not apparently been leased before 1585 and the existing customary tenant was agreeable to taking a lease probably because a new land use was envisaged, the building of a lead mill, which would require the Bishop's co-operation for its supplies. The lease of 1585 safeguarded the lord's soil as well as the red and fallow deer. By 1595 Emerson and Sir William Bowes were partners in the mill there, but in 1604 the lease was renewed to Emerson only.[91] Pinfold House was leased to George Gifford in 1585 and again in 1592 and 1609 (at the ancient rent of £1 per annum) which last counterpart mentions his expensive efforts in previous years to obtain possession.[92] Cuthbert Richardson had sold it in 1582 and two subsequent owners were admitted at Forest Courts, showing more bad liaison among the Bishop's officers. The 1609 lease was the last. By 1616 Pinfold House was accepted as customary and remained so.[93]

Matthew Hutton, Dean of York and later Bishop of Durham (1589-95), had the significant case of the Queen's lease pending. Before it, he again tried to lease Billingshield to Arthur Wright who was taken to the Council of the North by the customary tenant Peter Wright. The verdict went against Arthur, who had stolen Peter's conveyance.[94] Hutton made leases of New Park, and Kilhope and Welhope in 1590, and Pinfold House in 1592, all of which had been leased before, however questionably.[95]

The most important of all these test cases was brought by John Stanhope in 1592, over thirteen tenements at Westgate, in London at the Exchequer, even farther for the defendants than York.[96] Stanhope's case was carelessly prepared, some defendants having died before the lease to the Queen or before the suit began. He claimed he had entered the premises and been ejected, but depositions showed that heirs had been admitted to the holdings in the Forest Courts since the lease to the Queen and that neither this lease nor Tall's had interrupted succession. Stanhope took his time. An undated petition from the tenants to Sir John Fortescue, Chancellor, requested a speedy hearing, Stanhope's attorney having failed on the day set. Eventually on November 14 1594 William Cecil, Lord Burghley and his colleagues, upheld the case of Messrs. Stobbs etc., yeomen of Westgate, dismissing the case of the Queen's friend and Master of the Posts, based on the Queen's assignment of a lease from the Bishop of Durham. Stanhope had got no better result in London where he knew and was known to Exchequer personnel, than if he tried the Council of the North, where his brother Edward was a member. Perhaps Barnes made the lease to Elizabeth tongue in cheek. It was made after the Council's decrees of 1579/80.

This decision for tenant right cast doubts on the whole policy of lease-introduction over the last eighty years. To save further episcopal embarrassment, the tenurial situation in Park and Forest had to be clarified. After Hutton was translated to York in March 1595, the new Bishop, Toby Matthew, commissioned the survey of Weardale of 1595 which bears his name. He had been Dean of Durham since 1583 and on Durham Dean and Chapter estates the issue of claimed customary tenure had been decided first for, then against, in 1572 and 1577, by the Council of the North.[97] The survey was made the opportunity to investigate many aspects of Weardale life, property owned by or due to the Bishop, by whom and when, concealments, intrusions, types of tenure, alienations, tenants' names, delapidations, demesnes, minerals, timber, water, boundaries, courts, officials, game, services, watches, etc., twenty-seven composite questions. The sixteen jury, nine local men, all agreed and made one great verdict or presentment (except for one man demurring over one question of the Forestership of Roughside). The survey contained a rental of all the rents of whatsoever sort in Park and Forest and listed one hundred and fourteen names (and two anonymous) responsible for amounts of rent, most of them sharers of tenements and some names recurring, the total rent being £116 12s. 3d. per annum. Disputed holdings such as Pinfold House, Lintzgarth, Westernhopeburn, Brotherlee and Westgate were agreed as customary. The customary rents comprised £77 8s. 7d. and ninety names of the total. Matthew's Survey provides a detailed tenurial picture of Weardale at the close of the Elizabethan age, which remained the standard source for legal consultation even after the 1920s when customary tenure was abolished. Bishop Matthew renewed as continuing, successful leaseholds, Langlee 1595 and 1606, Horsley Head 1595, Burnhope 1596, the Parrock (Westgate Castle grounds) 1598, New Park in 1600 and 1606 and Lintzgarth two small leaseholds of 6s. 8d. each in 1604.[98] He considered another attempt on Billingshield in 1605 (which Bishop James pursued), but the Wrights were still paying rent as customary tenants in 1625.[99]

On March 24 1603 Queen Elizabeth died. The end of the Tudor period in Weardale left the tenants with peace for a few years, Bishop Matthew tolerating the findings of 1595 in an uneasy truce.[100] The sixteenth century had seen the development of the tenants' position in Weardale from a well-established privilege to a legal right. In different circumstances the Bishops might have dictated the terms, for some tenants were in favour of leases, but their activity was intermittent, unsustained and often ill-prepared. During vacancies royal or Priory policies might be introduced, despite continuity among officials. There were ambivalent attitudes within episcopacies, let alone from one to the next, not helped by bad record keeping and bad liaison among episcopal officers. Ruthall's initiative towards resumption was followed too late by the persistence, energy and opportunism of Barnes in fighting customary tenure by trying to introduce leases in so many ways. The neglect and caution of Wolsey and Tunstall in declining to replace the outgrown system of the Lumleys with a positive, well-considered alternative policy, had given the tenants the chance they were too perspicacious to miss, for all Carey's blustering, to manoeuvre the Weardale situation by degrees to their own advantage by tenacity in their running battle with the Bishops. Although they were the Bishop's men, his nepotism and blackmail were to be expected as often as his good will, nor were court decisions to be long respected.

The succession of James VI and I marked the beginning of a new phase for Weardale, as James set his face against tenant right, an integral part of which had been service on a border which in theory no longer existed. The next unsuccessful campaigns against tenant right in Weardale were to come from Bishop Matthew's successors, William James and Richard Neile, the sides now armed with Matthew's survey and James I's measures, and even later during the Commonwealth.[101]

NOTES

1. For discussion of tenant right in Northern England and its relationship to leasehold tenure see: R. Fieldhouse and B. Jennings, *A History of Richmond and Swaledale* (1978), C. B. Phillips ed., 'Lowther Family Estate Books 1617–1675.' S.S., 191 (1979), J.M.V. Bean, *The Estates of the Percy Family* (1966), S. J. Watts, 'Tenant-right in Early Seventeenth Century Northumberland,' *N.H.*, 6 (1971), pp.64–87, R. R. Reid, *The King's Council in the North* (1921), D. Marcombe, 'The Dean and Chapter of Durham, 1558–1603.' (unpub. Ph.D. thesis, Univ. of Durham 1973).
2. In 1381 Bishop Hatfield had 936 cattle and 258 horses in the Forest. 'Historiae Dunelmensis Scriptores Tres', S.S., 9 (1839), p.cliii. By 1515 there were only 91 cattle and 589 sheep divided between the Forest and Stockton Park. D.D.R., Church Commissioners' Deposit, Durham Bishopric estate papers (CC) 190191 Instaurer's account.
3. P.R.O., Durham Palatinate Records, Chancery roll, Durh 3/36 mm. 11 and 14. This demising was theoretically subject to the supervision of the Bishop's Steward, but the writer has failed to find any evidence of supervision. It is unlikely that Stewards would provoke argument with the Lumleys, the 'Cocks of the North' over an area so little valued as Weardale. Occasional consultations with the Chancellor over finances did occur. D.D.R., CC 220198 f. 292 c.1490, CC 220197 f. 376v 1501, transumpt books. The Bishops of Durham exercised Forest jurisdiction, see J. L. Drury 'Durham Palatinate Forest Law and administration, especially in Weardale up to 1440,' *A.A.*, 5th Series, 6, 1978 pp.87–105.
4. D.D.R., CC 190040 draft of Master Forester's account c.1492–3. They were not shown in 1509–10 either, CC 220124 f. 170 transumpt book.
5. Elizabeth, daughter of Edward IV by Elizabeth Lucy of Southampton is said to have married Thomas Lumley, only son of the third lord. W. Hutchinson, *History and Antiquities of the County Palatine of Durham*, (1794) with pedigree inset at the end of Vol. III. The writer has seen no contemporary evidence for this marriage, but two early seventeenth century sources give it, B.L., Add. MS 27423 p.220, Harleian Ms 710 f. 38v.
6. The use of the half year was an indication of transhumance in upland areas as far apart as the Pennines and the Pyrenees. E. Le Roy Ladurie, *Montaillou* (1978) chap. VI 'The life of the shepherds' and p.278.
7. D.D.R., CC 220198 f. 246. 1519 was a particularly bad year for raids by Cumberland and Northumberland men into County Durham. P.R.O. Durh 3/239, Durham Palatinate Records, judgement roll. The information on the 1530s is contained in a deposition of 1578 by George Gray, D.D.R., W.Ch. 94/3, see note 27.
8. P.R.O., Durh 3/54 m.3 and D.R.R., CC 190031, Master Forester's account 1484–86.
9. D.D.R., CC 220198 f. 124.
10. *Ibid.*, CC 220197 f. 95 transumpt book.
11. P.R.O., Durh 3/61 m.6 Nicholas Morton's patent.
12. P.R.O., Durh 3/19, 1493–1501.

13. *Ibid.*, Durh 3/64 m.4.
14. D.D.R., CC 220200 demises in Chancery 1501–07. These demises of 1502 made briefly in the King's name in the vacancy were not entered in the Durham Chancery rolls where past Bishops had entered their relatively few grants for terms of years. The detailed conditions could suggest Henry VII's personal interest.
15. The perquisites of the Forest Courts were recorded in D.D.R., CC 189559, 190035 and 190037, Master Forester's accounts.
16. *Ibid.*, CC 220200 Demesnes at Chester-le-Street and Heighington were let for three and five years, Bedlington water mill (a copyhold responsibility of the Bedlington collector) for seven years and Fatherless Field (Boldon) for eighteen years.
17. P.R.O., Durh 3/67 m.4 and /73 m.36.
18. *Ibid.*, Durh 3/20–21 Halmote Courts before and during Bainbridge's episcopacy.
19. *Ibid.*, Durh 3/68 m.10. 20 August 1508.
20. *Ibid.*, Durh 3/71 1510–22 m.1. The leases were enrolled following the patent.
21. R. A. Lomas, 'Developments in land tenure on the Prior of Durham's estate in the late middle ages,' *N.H.*, 13 (1977) pp. 27–43.
22. P.R.O., Durh 3/68 m.10.
23. In 1497 a group of copyholders in Stanhope lost all their holdings of the Bishop for failing to follow Lumley against the Scots and these men were probably not even Forest tenants. P.R.O., Durh 3/19 f. 74. Fox's Halmote Court Book.
24. There are references to the surnames and to a few identifiable individuals in the Wolsingham entries in the Halmote Court Books 1502–11, P.R.O. Durh 3/20-21. The total population is harder to assess. Stanhope parish, with about 55,000 acres, the largest in the county, contained in 1548 only about one thousand 'howsling' people, that is communicants, which then would include most of the adult population. 'Ecclesisastical Proceedings of Bishop Barnes,' S.S., 22 (1850) app. vi p. lxviii. Stanhope parish comprised St. John's Chapel serving Park and Forest, Frosterley (which had belonged to St. Giles' Hospital, Kepier) Stanhope and Bishopley. Of the rest of Wolsingham Manor, the townships of Wolsingham, Greenwellside and Wigside lay in Wolsingham parish, Lynesack and South Bedburn in Hamsterley chapelry, parish of Auckland St. Andrew and North Bedburn in the chapelry of Witton-le-Wear in the same parish.
25. P.R.O., Durh 13/231–3. It is remarkable that for the Weardale men produced in court in Durham, few convictions were made. Arrest may have been a policy to intimidate. Ibid., Durh 13/229, 1494–1502.
26. D.D.R., CC 188771. Receiver General's account.
27. *Ibid.*, W(eardale) Ch(est) 94. Neville v. Cornforth over Westernhopeburn before the Council of the North, 1578–9.
28. P.R.O., Durh 3/71 m.2d.
29. *C.S.P., 1509* no. 291 and P.R.O., Durh 3/70 m.5.
30. D.D.R., CC 220219 f. 23 and CC 220222 f. 28, transumpt books.
31. *C.S.P., 1519–23* nos. 2531 and 2806.

32. D.D.R., 1523–24 CC 189839, 1524–25 CC 189840, 1526–27 CC 199841, 1527–28 CC 189842, 1528–29 CC 189556, Receiver General's accounts. The one for 1525–26 is missing but the transumpt book that year records the usual blank, for the perquisites, (CC 220224 f. 177v.) although there is evidence for a court held that year, see note 35.
33. P.R.O., Durh 8/78 pp. 87–88 book of accounts, demises and recognizances.
34. *Ibid.*, 3/77 m.2 and Durh 13/253.
35. The evidence for such an admittance is as follows. In 1578 William Dobyson or Dobynson aged about 53, in sworn evidence said that when he was a year old his father died and his mother was admitted at a Forest Court in widowright, i.e. about 1526. In 1579 Thomas Fetherstone aged about 76, born therefore about 1503, described how Lord Lumley admitted Henry Emerson to Brotherlee at a Forest Court in Thomas's presence. As courts were held only in three years, 1516–17, 1519–20 and 1526 (Dobyson) the last, in view of Thomas's age, would seem the most likely to be the one he attended. D.D.R., W.Ch. 94/1 also W.Ch. 93/2, Emerson v. Conyers over Brotherlee before the Council of the North, 1579.
36. P.R.O., Durh 3/76 m.49 (1529) and Durh 8/78, loose sheet at p. 123 (1519).
37. In 1532 a jury at a Halmote Court in Wolsingham held by Sir Thomas Tempest, Bishop's Steward, made a presentment about the building of a shieling and were told that this was a matter for the Master Forester's Court (which was not operating hence this attempt to enlist the Steward's help). D.D.R., HC I 6 f. 93.
38. William Hutchinson, *The History and Antiquities of the County Palatine of Durham* (1785), Vol. 1, p. 421. Brian Tunstall's patent D.D.R., Durh 3/77 m.16.
39. *Ibid.*, 1537–38 CC 189579, 1539–40 CC 189847, 1540–41 CC 190270 Receiver General's accounts. 1553, W.Ch. 94/3.
40. *Ibid.*, CC 189840 Receiver General's account.
41. P.R.O., Durh 3/74 m.2 enrollment of deed.
42. *Ibid.*, Durh 3/76 m.3.
43. In 1531 was murdered Patrick Makdell, chaplain, at St. John's Chapel, Weardale, who might have been Tunstall's curate from his own Stanhope days. P.R.O., Durh 13/253.
44. D.D.R., CC 190030 Master Forester's account.
45. *Ibid.*, W.Ch. 104/8–13 Emerson v. Neville etc. over Westernhopeburn before the Council of the North, c. 1599–1603.
46. P.R.O., Durh 3/77 m.41.
47. *Ibid.*, Durh 3/78 m.23d and 3/80 m.8.
48. D.D.R., CC 277863 (Bishop) Matt(hew's) Survey of 1595).
49. *Ibid.*, Pinfold CC 190172 f. 9 book of leases by indenture, Brotherlee ibid., f. 7, Westernhopeburn P.R.O., Durh 3/80 m.7, Windiside ibid., m.11. Leases at Cassop and Whickham, operable after the deaths of the current occupants were also made.
50. D.D.R., Matt. Surv. and W.Ch. 97. Richardson v. Walton and Lee over Pinfold House before the Council of the North, 1581–2.
51. *Ibid.*, W.Ch 93.

52. *Ibid.*, CC 184957a pp. 18 and 201 book of leases and appointments.
53. *Ibid.*, W. Ch. 94.
54. Pedigree, W. H. Smith, *Walks in Weardale* (1885) p. 132 also *Wills and Inventories, II*, S.S., 38 (1860) pp. 336–37.
55. D.D.R., Brotherlee W.Ch. 93/1, Westernhopeburn W.Ch. 94/1, Lintzgarth W.Ch. 96/3 Emerson v. Vasey over Lintzgarth before the Council of the North, 1579–80.
56. There had been Gibsons and Richardsons at Windiside since 1513 at least and in 1585 a John Gibson was there. In 1586 two holdings at Windiside, one sometime occupied by Robert Gibson and lately demised to John Foster were leased for twenty-one years to George Gifford, Bishop's servant, with Pinfold House. (D.D.R., CC 405/185593 counterpart lease.) Guy Bainbridge also leased a holding in 1586 at Windiside for 16s.8d. per annum. (D.D.R., CC 221645 f. 106v. book of leases granted.) In 1592 Bishop Matthew demised Pinfold House and other things to Gifford for twenty-one years and it seems probable that these 'other things' were the two Windiside holdings. Yet in 1595 the Windiside leaseholders were given as only Emerson and Bainbridge, and the customary ones, Widow Gibson, Roland Richardson and George Jackson. (D.D.R., Matt. Surv.) As Gifford was having trouble enough over Pinfold House, it may be he decided not to contest the Windiside holdings occupied by long-standing families whose case for tenant right might stand up well in court.
57. D.D.R., (Durham Bishopric) H(almote) C(ourt Records) 192461 Weardale customary rental, 1625.
58. P.R.O., Durh 3/79 m.2 and D.D.R., CC 190172 f.5v.
59. The relationship between the two families in about 1599 was illustrated nicely in a case, over a pew in Stanhope Church, in both the religious and civil courts. The Maddisons claimed a family pew, time out of mind. The Featherstonhaughs claimed it was their pew, but that they kept it for gentlemen of the family of meaner degree! D.D.R., V 7 Consistory Court Deposition Book, 1599–1604 and P.R.O., Durh 13/5, 1601.
60. The inserted brief *onus* appeared first in 1537–38, D.D.R., CC 195705/7 f. 293.
61. Perquisites 28s.4d. D.D.R., CC 190249 Receiver General's account.
62. P.R.O., Durh 3/82 m.2.
63. In 1539 Christopher and Matthew Harrison agreed to divide the farmhold of Swinhopeburn between them. D.D.R., W.Ch. 2. In 1578 George Gray deposed that there were 76–77 customary holdings. W.Ch. 94/3.
64. Homberston's survey of 1570 talks of 'the great wastes called fens, fells and Weardale which begin within two miles of Raby and so continue to Hexham, a great waste country and nothing so well inhabited as the East part of the Bishopric and few gentlemen of any lands or living inhabiting there for the most part.' P.R.O., E 164/37.
65. P.R.O., Durh 3/80 m.13.
66. The perquisites appeared regularly in the Receiver General's accounts.
67. D.D.R., W.Ch. 45 Orders by the jury and the officers of the Weardale Forest Court, 1602.
68. *Ibid.*, W.Ch. 44 The custom of the Forest of Weardale, 1601.

69. *Ibid.*, W.Ch. 45.
70. Pinfold House see note 50. Windiside, Matt. Surv. and Lintzgarth, W.Ch. 96/2.
71. *Ibid.*, HC I 33 f. 49 Halmote Court Book.
72. P.R.O., Durh 20/125/20 m.2. Receiver General's account.
73. D.D.R., CC 406/185622/1 counterpart lease.
74. *Parliamentary Surveys of the Bishopric of Durham* ed. Kirby, Vol. 1, S.S., 183 (1968) pp. 160–166.
75. *C.P.R.*, *1569–72*, pp. 97–98, 103, 105, 107 and 109, pardons.
76. D.D.R., W.Ch. 101 Petition of William Emerson and his son Arthur to Queen Elizabeth concerning Brotherlee. c.1578 and W.Ch. 93. Gregory Butler also acted as steward of the Rectory Manor of Bishopwearmouth. D.D.R., HC III B 7.
77. D.D.R., W.Ch. 96.
78. *Ibid.*, V 6, 1592–95.
79. *Ibid.*, CC A. 13.2 Admittance to Castle Nook, 1580.
80. See above, note 50.
81. *Ibid.*, W.Ch. 95. Cornforth v Neville over Westernhopeburn before Durham Court of Pleas, P.R.O., Durh 13/292 m.7d. and REQ 2/246/16, proceedings in the Court of Requests, 1579–84.
82. D.D.R., W.Ch. 98. Sir George Carey's letter.
83. P.R.O., Durh 13/297 and D.D.R., W.Ch. 99/1–11 (copies).
84. D.D.R., W.Ch. 99/16–25, copies, the original roll does not survive for 1586.
85. *C.B.P.*, I, pp. 273–77, 1587.
86. D.D.R., CC 220198 f. 124v and also CC 190034 Master Forester's account.
87. *Ibid.*, W.Ch. 99/12–15 and 26–29, P.R.O., Durh 13/297 and /299.
88. D.D.R., W.Ch. 145/3 (i) f. 5. Sir Arthur Hesilrige v. Stobbs etc. over thirteen tenements at Westgate before the Committee for removing obstructions in the sale of Bishops' lands, 1655–56. Peter had bought Billingshield in 1586.
89. New Park and Eastgate 1583 D.D.R., CC 406/185614/1, Burtreeford 1585 CC 406/185605/1, Pinfold House and Windiside CC 405/185593, Horsley Head 1587 CC 406/185616/1 and New Park 1587 CC 407/185636/1, counterpart leases. There was trouble over the last later that year. P.R.O., REQ 2/104/57.
90. D.D.R., CC 54137 f. 88. Copies of Barnes' leases.
91. *Ibid.*, 1594 Matt. Surv. and 1604 W.Ch. 12 certified copy of lease.
92. The 1609 counterpart, D.D.R., CC 405/185594, quotes the 1592 lease.
93. *Ibid.*, W.Ch. 6 schedule of writings relating to Pinfold House.
94. *Ibid.*, W.Ch. 102 Wright v. Wright over Billingshield before the Council of the North, c.1592.
95. New Park 1590 D.D.R., CC 407/185636/2, Kilhope and Welhope CC 406/185620/1.
96. *Ibid.*, W.Ch. 103 Stanhope v. Stobbs etc. over thirteen tenements at Westgate before the Exchequer, 1592–94. W.Ch. 145/2 summary of suits. P.R.O., E134 35–6 Eliz. Mich. 14 Exchequer Depositions and Commissions.

97. See above, note 1, Marcombe's thesis.
98. Langlee 1595 and 1606 D.D.R., CC 407/185629/1–2, Horsley Head 1595 CC 406/185616/2, Burnhope 1596 CC 221645 end folio, book of leases c.1595–96, Parrock 1598 CC 407/185642/1, New Park 1600 and 1606 CC 407/185636/3–4, Lintzgarth 1604 CC 406/185618/1–2.
99. *Ibid.*, CC 221562 f. 2v. leases to be renewed 1605 and CC 405/185590 counterpart lease 1609.
100. Matthew greatly increased his supervision of the Wolsingham Manor copyholders. In May 1596 the Wolsingham Halmote Court produced three pages of lists of fines for unlicensed subletting and encroachments on the lord's waste. D.D.R., HC I 41 f. 126v–27v. Other forest areas such as Bedburn, Lanchester and Evenwood were treated similarly.
101. J. L. Drury, 'Sir Arthur Hesilrige and the Weardale Chest.' *Transactions of the Architectural and Archaelogical Society of Durham and Northumberland*, New Series, 5 (1980) pp. 125–137. In the preparation of this paper the writer is grateful for advice from and discussions with Dr. R. Britnell in particular, Mr. J. Fagg, Prof. D. Loades, Dr. R. Lomas and Mr. P. Mussett, all now or once of the University of Durham and Dr. W. Childs of the University of Leeds.

The Dissolution of the Diocese of Durham, 1553–54

David Loades

For just over a year, from March 1553 to April 1554, the diocese of Durham had no legal existence. This strange interlude is normally dismissed by local historians as being of no significance, since the shortness of its duration and the national political situation at the time enabled the whole administrative machinery to continue without any break which is now discernible in the records. Cuthbert Conyers, Sheriff of Durham and Sadbergh, blithley accounted 'from the feast of St. Michael the Archangel in the twenty-third year of the pontificate of Cuthbert, by the grace of God Bishop of Durham, to the feast of St. Michael in the twenty-fourth year of the same pontificate' (1552-3) and again in the same terms for the following year.[1] This not only ignored the brief statutory Dissolution of the see, but also the fact that Tunstall had been deprived by royal commission on October 14 1552, so that the diocese was technically vacant for six months before the statute came into effect.

When the *status quo ante* was restored by Mary, the whole process was explicitly retrospective, Tunstall being granted all issues, profits and jurisdiction from October 14 1552,[2] so that the continuity preserved by the diocesan officials was formally sanctioned and approved. At the local level the whole episode is indicative, not only of legal and administrative conservatism, but also of the dilatoriness and reluctance with which the radical interventions of the Edwardian Council and Legislature was received in the North. However, at the national level it has a much more positive significance and provides some very interesting indications of the ways in which policy was being shaped and implemented during the last two years of Edward's reign.

By the summer of 1550 Cuthbert Tunstall, Bishop since 1530, was in deep disfavour with the Council in London. In spite of his acceptance of the Royal Supremacy and his great skill and experience in the administration of the North, he had become a liability to a regime which was concerned to impose a Protestant religious settlement.[3] At the beginning of September he was summoned to London to answer charges of concealing a treasonable plot against the government. The details of this alleged plot never emerged,[4] but the Earl of Warwick took advantage of Tunstall's presence with him at Ely Place to question the Bishop about his failure to send certain letters to the Council and concluded a brief report to Cecil with the significant words:

> the matter will touch him wonderfully and yield to the King as good a return as the B(ishop) of Winchester is like to do if the cards be true.[5]

The Bishop of Winchester, Stephen Gardiner, was in the Tower at the time, having refused subscription to the Act of Uniformity. In December he was to be deprived by royal commission and the revenues of his see, the wealthiest in England, taken into the King's hands.[6] When a Protestant bishop, John Ponet, was appointed to Winchester in the following year, the unprecedented step was taken of paying him a stipend of two thousand marks, the King retaining lands and profits amounting to almost twice that sum.[7] The explicit connection between the cases of Gardiner and Tunstall made in Warwick's letter is thus a clear indication of what was in the Earl's mind at that time. Durham was the second wealthiest see in England and, although Tunstall's conservatism was much more cautious than that of Gardiner, a pretext of a different kind had arisen to justify a similar course of action. Nevertheless, the process against him was slow and in many respects obscure. For over a year he remained under house arrest at his own residence, Cold Harbour in Thames Street, while attempts were made, first to compel him to testify against Gardiner and then to extract an explicit submission to the Protestant settlement. According to a report which reached the Imperial ambassador, Jehan Scheyfve, in January 1551, Tunstall had offered to renounce his see and submit to the Council, but that this offer had not been accepted.[8] Warwick seems to have been determined to secure a conviction for treason, but lacking adequate means to accomplish his purpose. An interrogation of Tunstall by the full Council in May 1551 having failed to produce a satisfactory result, a formal commission to investigate the case was set up in October, but again no conclusive evidence was found.[9] Only after the second arrest of the Duke of Somerset was this *impasse* broken; perhaps (as it was claimed) because his papers yielded the vital testimony,[10] or perhaps because the removal of his restraining influence had made the Council more amenable to Warwick's wishes.

On December 20 1551 Tunstall was finally committed to the Tower 'to abide there such order as his doings by the course of law shall appear to have deserved'.[11] By that time Warwick had been created Duke of Northumberland and Scheyfve drew the obvious conclusion – that the attainder of the Bishop of Durham was intended to clear the way for the establishment of a new secular Palatinate which would give the Duke overwhelming power in the North of England.[12] In the event, however, Tunstall was not attainted. No formal charges were brought against him in any court and although a Bill of Attainder for misprision of treason passed the House of Lords at the end of March 1552, it disappeared in the Commons and was not revived.[13] It seems that, despite his ingenuity and possible unscrupulousness, John Dudley could not produce enough evidence against Tunstall to make even a charge of misprision stick. On the other hand he may have come to realise that such draconian methods were not necessary. Gardiner had not been attainted, merely deprived, but the temporalities of Winchester had been effectively sequestered. It may have been felt that the resumption of a Palatinate jurisdiction by the Crown needed greater legal certainty, for there was no precedent for the dissolution of an ecclesiastical franchise and with or without an attainder such action could only have been based upon the Royal Supremacy and the overriding authority of statute.[14] After the failure of the Bill of Attainder no further attempt was made to press charges under the common law and the commission which was finally issued to Sir Roger Cholmeley the Chief Justice of Kings Bench and six others on September 14 1552 was almost certainly an *ad hoc* commission to exercise the Royal Supremacy, similar to those which had already been used against Bonner, Gardiner, Heath and Day.[15]

The commissioners sat twice at the Old Whitefriars, on October 4 and 14, and after the latter session declared the Bishop to be deprived of his see and sent him back to prison during the King's pleasure. Two weeks later Scheyfve reported that he had been found guilty of 'minor treason', but he was presumably describing the substance of the charges and not the legal verdict.[16] The Bishopric, its revenues and jurisdiction thus passed into the hands of the Crown, as would have been the case during a normal vacancy; but for the time being no attempt was made to make a new appointment and those who believed that more drastic action was intended were soon justified by events. Nevertheless, the traditional view, expressed by Burnet and Strype (and foreshadowed, as we have seen, by Scheyfve) that the whole process was part of a deep laid plot 'to add another title to the ambitious Duke of Northumberland, viz. Earl of Durham', will hardly stand up to close examination. There is no evidence prior to the Parliamentary session of March 1553 that Dudley sought autonomous power for himself in the North, in spite of a thoroughly misleading entry in the *Calendar of State Papers, Domestic, 1547-1580*. A letter from Northumberland to Cecil, there dated April 7 1552, is summarised as containing a request that the Palatinate jurisdiction of Durham be conferred upon the writer.[17] The original document presents a number of problems: it is slightly damaged and only one part of it consists of a note signed by Northumberland. However, the relevant passage runs

> Che (sic) as now the jurisdiction of the County Palatine of . . . oprike (sic) of Durham is in the King's Majesty's hands . . . it is thought good that the same be used still as . . . Palatine like as Chester is at this day. I . . . therefore in my absence to move Mr. Vice Chamberlain . . . also to be means to the King's Majesty that . . . his Highness Chancellor and Steward of the same . . . to me and my sufficient deputies with such fee . . . office as shall be thought meet to his Majesty to appoint to the . . . whereof I shall be the better able to serve . . . in those parts.[18]

This corresponds very closely to the scheme which was eventually implemented in two patents which passed the Privy Seal early in May 1553. One of these created 'the King's County Palatine of Durham' in place of the Bishop's County Palatine;[19] the other granted to Northumberland for life 'the Office of Chief Steward of all the King's lands . . . which belonged to the late Bishopric of Durham' with 'the rule and leading of all the King's men and tenants . . . and all profits . . . as amply as Thomas Tempest Kt., Richard Bellasis Esq. and John, Lord Lumley deceased, or any other had them.'[20]

Had time permitted these patents to come into effect, Northumberland's position in the North would certainly have been strengthened. However, the traditional terms in which the Stewardship was granted conferred no kind of Palatine authority upon the Duke himself. Nor was there any intention to dissolve the Palatinate and convert Durham into ordinary 'shire ground'. The jurisdictional structure would have remained intact, although the county would have sent members to Parliament.[21] The main effect would have been to divorce the County Palatine completely from the Bishopric and it is in terms of ecclesiastical rather than secular policy that the main purpose of the scheme has to be viewed. Burnet was quite wrong to conclude that only Edward's death prevented Northumberland from establishing himself as 'a Prince in the North'.[22]

Recent historians, notably Barrett Beer, have recognised the strict limitations of the grant which was actually made and have tended to conclude that this demonstrated the limited nature of the Duke's power – the fact that he could not dominate the Council, which had the last word in all such matters.[23] It would, however, be more in accordance with the evidence to conclude that, in this respect, Northumberland obtained almost exactly what he set out to achieve and that he was concerned rather to carry further the policy which had been represented by the Franchise Act of 1536 than to establish a satrapy for himself.

Before the patents expressing this policy could be drawn up, however, the ground had to be more thoroughly cleared. The vacancy created by Tunstall's deprivation could have given an adequate opportunity to make a stipendiary appointment, as at Winchester, but could not, in itself, give the Crown sufficient legal grounds to alter the nature of the Palatinate. Nor did it allow the King to divert a significant proportion of the endowment for the creation of a new Bishopric. For these purposes the greatest certainty lay in an Act of Parliament and on March 21 1553 a Bill was introduced into the House of Lords, for the dissolution of the see of Durham.[24] This was read a second time on March 22 and committed. After a week's delay, which probably reflects some dissension,[25] it was approved and sent to the Commons on March 29. There it was rushed through three readings in twenty-four hours and passed without any recorded debate. Although somewhat misleadingly described in the Commons Journal as being for 'the erection of the two bishoprics of Durham and Newcastle', this Act in fact accomplished no such thing. A long preamble declared that

> for as much, as the circuit and compass of the ordinary jurisdiction of the said Bishopric is large and great and extendeth into many shires and counties . . . the charge thereof may not conveniently be supplied and well and sufficiently discharged by one ordinary . . .[26]

and because the area was backward and deficient in godly preaching and ministry, the King 'of his most godly disposition' had decided

> to have two several ordinary sees of bishops to be erected and established within the limits bounds and jurisdictions of the said Bishopric of Durham. Whereof the one shall be called the see of the Bishopric of Durham and the other the see of the Bishopric of Newcastle-upon-Tyne . . .

Each of these sees was to be endowed with 'manors, lands, tenements and other hereditaments', Durham to the value of two thousand marks and Newcastle to the value of one thousand marks.[27] At the same time

Newcastle was to be elevated to the status of a city and provided with a Dean and Chapter, similarly endowed but to an unspecified level. However, none of these intentions were implemented by the Act, which merely authorised the King to carry out his godly purposes by Letters Patent.[28] The operative clause of the statute ran

> Be it therefore enacted by the authority of this Parliament that the said Bishopric of Durham together with all the ordinary jurisdictions thereunto belonging and appurtaining shall be adjudged from henceforth clearly dissolved, extinguished and determined. And that the King our sovereign Lord shall from henceforth have, hold possessed and enjoy . . . all and singular honours, castles, manors . . . etc.

Only the establishment and endowments of the Dean and Chapter of Durham Cathedral were specifically exempted and preserved.

Had the plan outlined in this preamble been put into effect, there would have been very little direct financial benefit to the Crown, as Burnet noticed.[29] The total value of the see was not much in excess of £2,800 in peacetime and a good deal less during intermittent warfare with the Scots. If £2,000 of that was to be allocated to the new bishops and a further endowment provided for the new Cathedral at Newcastle, a profit of no more than £300 or £400 a year would be left in Augmentations. This did not at all correspond with the expectations which Northumberland had expressed to Cecil at the end of October 1552, when he was calculating the benefits of Tunstall's deprivation.

> His Majesty . . . (may) resume to his Crown £2,000 a year of the best lands within the North parts of his realm, yea I doubt not it will be 4,000 marks a year of as good revenue as any is within the realm . . .[30]

he had written optimistically. This great profit could be realised, he claimed, and still leave '. . . all places better and more godly furnished than ever it was from the beginning until this day . . .' His 'plan', if it can be called such, was to promote Robert Horn, the Dean of Durham, to be Bishop and shuffle round the other senior diocesan officers.[31] In doing this he blandly ignored the fact that the Bishopric and Chapter were separate institutions, apparently regarding their funds as interchangeable. This may indicate a tacit hope that the Chapter would be sequestered as well, but too much should not be read into a single hasty letter. What does seem clear is that Northumberland's priorities had not changed since he had written to Cecil in September 1550; and although he envisaged the creation of a Bishopric of Newcastle, there was no mention of endowment, or of a second Chapter. A few days after writing this letter he was urging Cecil to keep a vigilant eye upon the Bishopric accounts and to summon the Bishop's auditor to London 'otherwise it is impossible to have any profit or true knowledge . . .'[32] The Council took the same view and instructed Lord Wharton to seek for the same accounts and to send them up as a matter of urgency.[33] In fact the proprieties seem to have been very correctly observed and Robert Hindemers, Tunstall's Chancellor, continued to administer the temporalities of the see until after the Act of Dissolution, at which point the responsibility was taken over by the Court of Augmentations[34] – although this fact does not seem to have been noticed in Durham!

In the light of this evidence it seems very unlikely that Northumberland was responsible for drawing up the generous scheme described in the Act. Nor is it surprising that Horn refused promotion upon the disadvantageous and legally uncertain terms upon which it was actually offered to him.[35] Although it is possible that the concern and indignation which Northumberland expressed about the Durham situation in January 1553 was the result of genuine anxiety about the pastoral neglect of the diocese, that would not be consistent with his earlier attitude.[36] His criticism of Horn, as a man unwilling to serve and too much concerned with 'great possessions', suggests rather that he was indignant because the Dean's unco-operative attitude seemed likely to frustrate a financial 'killing' on behalf of the Crown – as indeed turned out to be the case. However, the battle over the see of Durham was never fought to a conclusion and we do not know how it might have ended. The Act of Dissolution may have been a direct consequence of Northumberland's failure to persuade Horn, or it may have been simply the result of more informed thinking. The preamble may have been no more than a device to disarm opposition and facilitate the passage of the Act or it may have represented the serious intention of someone other than Northumberland – perhaps the King himself, whose religious priorities were perfectly genuine. The one positive achievement of the Act was to lift the threat to the Durham Chapter which had certainly been implied in Northumberland's letters. Ridley was named for the reconstituted see of Durham and William Bill for the new see of Newcastle,[37] but neither was appointed because the Letters Patent creating and endowing the sees were never issued. This may have been because of the King's death early in July, but as we have already seen, the corresponding patents relating to the Palatinate were issued in early May. It was certainly not the case that, as Burnet declared, the lands, revenues and jurisdictions were granted to Northumberland instead, but the conflict between religious and fiscal priorities may well have remained unresolved to the end.

The ancient Bishopric of Durham, although legally dissolved, was not, therefore, plundered in the same sense that the great abbeys had been. Its endowment suffered no more than a few chips around the edges. One of these was the loss of the Bishop's London residence. Henry VIII had retained Durham Place in the Strand after Wolsey's fall and in July 1537 Tunstall (in a weak position after his performance in the Pilgrimage of Grace) formally conveyed it to the King, together with certain lands and tenements in Westminster. In return he had received the reversion of Cold Harbour and eight messuages in London, a transaction which was confirmed by the statute of 28 Henry VIII c.33.[38] On June 30 1553 the Cold Harbour and its attendant messuages were granted to the Earl of Shrewsbury and valued at £66 16s 1½d.[39] Only one other formal grant of Bishopric property was made, but that was the substantial one of all lands in Howdenshire to Sir Francis Jobson. These lands had a clear annual value £284 19s 8½d. but since Jobson was required to pay a rent of £200 a year into Augmentations his own profit was relatively modest.[40] Other grants were of a less straightforward nature. One, as we have seen, conferred on Northumberland the office of Chief Steward, a position which carried with it formal fees of about £40 a year, together with many perquisites and opportunities for influence. Another assigned the profits of the Bishopric lands in Norhamshire (£163 6s 8d) to the Captain and garrison of Norham Castle.[41] A third conferred the Mastership of Sherburn Hospital, worth £135 7s 0d, upon Sir Richard Rede.[42] Sherburn was not a parcel of the Bishopric, but the Mastership was in the Bishop's gift. The most serious depredation however, was contained not in a grant, but in another statute. At the same time as the Bill of Dissolution was going through Parliament a second Bill, sponsored by the burgesses of Newcastle-upon-Tyne, sought to detach the town of Gateshead from the Bishopric and annex it to their own jurisdiction. This expressed a long standing ambition on the part of the larger town, which regarded its Southern neighbour as a nuisance and a refuge for delinquents.[43] Officially, Gateshead was only worth about £35 a year to the Bishop, but in practice its revenues were probably a good deal more and well worth the expense of legislation. On March 30 1553, the same day that saw the passage of the Act of Dissolution, 'An Act for the uniting and annexing of the Town of Gateshead to the Town of Newcastle-upon-Tyne' (7 Edward VI c.10) was also completed.[44]

At the time of Edward VI's death, therefore, there was no lawfully constituted see of Durham (let alone of Newcastle); but there was a secular Palatinate in the hands of the Crown, co-extensive with the former ecclesiastical franchise except for Gateshead; and about 75% of the property of the Bishopric remained under the control of the Court of Augmentations. In Durham itself, although some leases had been approved in Augmentations, both the diocesan and the Palatinate administration continued without interruption, presumably awaiting the attentions of the royal commissioners who would sooner or later have appeared to 'take further order' for the whole organisation.

With the accession of Mary after a brief period of uncertainty, any possibility that that might happen rapidly disappeared. The new sovereign had many preoccupations and it was not likely that the settlement of Durham would be given a very high priority, but her initial actions served to make the situation even more anomalous and confused. Cuthbert Tunstall, now seventy-nine years old, but still active, was released from the Tower on August 6, and was sworn of the Privy Council as Bishop of Durham, on August 14.[45] He promptly appealed against his deprivation and on August 23 a commission was established under the Earl of Arundel to hear the appeal.[46] In the circumstances the result was a foregone conclusion; the commissioners declared the earlier sentence void upon the specious grounds that those pronouncing it had all been laymen.[47] By the beginning of October Tunstall was again functioning officially as Bishop of Durham; on November 18 he instituted the new Dean, Thomas Wastson,[48] and was summoned to the House of Lords in Mary's first Parliament by that title. On November 27 a Bill was introduced into the House of Commons '. . . for the confirmation of the Bishopric of Durham and Durham Place, to Cuthbert Tunstall, Bishop there, and his successors'.[49] The use of the word 'confirmation', and the reference to Durham Place, were both significant of the Council's attitude. Legally, Tunstall had no standing apart from that conferred by his episcopal orders and the main purpose of the Bill must have been to repeal the Edwardian Act of Dissolution. However, the whole process of repealing her predecessor's ecclesiastical legislation was extremely distasteful to Mary, who preferred to regard it as invalid *ipso facto*, and the word 'confirmation' suggests a formula which tried to avoid recognising the authority of the earlier Act.[50] Similarly, Durham Place had, as we have seen, been conveyed to the Crown in 1537 in exchange for the Cold Harbour. In April 1551 it had been granted, along with other properties, to Princess Elizabeth, who was still in possession in 1553.[51] Whether any compensation was offered in the original draft Bill we do not know, but when it came back for a second reading on December 1, a proviso was inserted 'for the Lady Elizabeth's Grace, for Durham Place'.[52] Even with this amendment the Bill failed on its third reading, on December 5, without the necessity to count a division.

Mary's first Parliament was, in other respects, reasonably co-operative and had repealed the Protestant Act of Uniformity, together with several other measures of the previous regime, without a great deal of acrimony.[53] These measures did not, however, affect particular property rights and it seems likely that the burgesses of Newcastle (striving to retain their newly won control over Gateshead) succeeded in persuading their fellow M.Ps that the restoration of Durham would create a precedent for reversing the whole process of statutory acquisition, going back to 1536.

Monastic and Chantry lands were soon to be an extremely sensitive and important issue and it looks as though the first shots were fired over this abortive Bill.[54] In any case its failure was a serious embarrassment for the government and left Tunstall himself in an even more ambiguous position than he had been at the beginning of the session. If a remedy were not found quickly, local opponents of the Bishop or those with grievances against his administration, would be bound to challenge the whole legal basis of his authority in the royal courts and the result might well be further and worse embarrassment. Consequently, upon January 18 1554 in response to a further petition from Tunstall, the Queen issued Letters Patent erecting a new Bishopric in Durham

> with ordinary episcopal jurisdiction to extend throughout the said city and the county and precincts lately called the Bishopric and royal liberty of St. Cuthbert of Durham between the waters of Tyne and Tees, throughout the whole county called Norhamshire and Bedlingtonshire . . .[55]

This patent recited the whole story of Tunstall's deprivation, the annulment of that sentence and the passage of the Act of Dissolution. It also 'nominated and elected' Tunstall to this new Bishopric '. . . he and his successors to be from henceforth a body corporate with perpetual succession by the name of the Bishop of Durham . . .'[56] and proceeded to grant him the temporal and spiritual possessions of the previous see. Contrary to what is sometimes claimed, this patent did not pretend to repeal or annul the Act of Dissolution; rather, it took advantage of the empowering clause in that Act to re-erect the ancient see instead of the two new sees which had been envisaged. What it did annul, implicitly rather than explicitly, was the patent of May 1553 establishing a secular Royal Palatinate. Since the Palatinate jurisdiction and the bulk of the possessions of the former see were in the Queen's hands, however, the patent was in no sense *ultra vires*.[57]

Nevertheless, it was not a satisfactory solution to the problem. The grants of Cold Harbour and Howdenshire and even more the annexation of Gateshead to Newcastle were bound to create thorny legal problems unless the two relevant Edwardian Acts were repealed. Whether this was clear to the Queen's legal advisers all along and the patent never intended to be more than a stop-gap measure, or whether the new creation was challenged almost at once, we do not know. However, on April 7 1554 a Bill of Repeal was introduced into the House of Lords of Mary's second Parliament.[58] This covered both the offending measures, which were roundly (and characteristically) described as having been

> compassed and brought to pass in the tender years and minorities of our said late sovereign Lord the King by the sinister labour, great malice and corrupt means of certain ambitious persons then being in authority, rather for to enrich themselves and their friends with a great part of the possessions of the said Bishopric than upon just occasion or godly zeal . . .[59]

The preamble then went on to recite the whole story, up to and including the patent of January, concluding

> Yet the said Reverend Father in God, Cuthbert, now Bishop of Durham, notwithstanding the repeal of the said sentence, cannot by virtue thereof, nor by force of the said Letters Patent, have, possess and enjoy to him and to his successors all and singular honours . . . etc . . . for the said two several estates remain yet in their perfect force and effect . . .

The Lords passed this measure without demur, but the Commons, once again, were recalcitrant. This time we know that the burgesses of Newcastle led the fight, calling legal counsel to their aid.[60] As the debate went on, various provisos and amendments were introduced; protecting the interest of the Earl of Shrewsbury in Cold Harbour, that of Sir Francis Jobson in Howdenshire and, more generally, that of all grantees of Bishopric property.[61] Eventually only the first of these was incorporated in the Act of Repeal, but the city of Newcastle had to be bought off with leases and grants which were very disadvantageous to the Bishopric and the House made its feelings clear by instructing '. . . that Mr. Speaker in their names, shall require the Bishop of Durham to show favour to Sir Francis Jobson in his suit.'[62] On April 19, after an intervention by Tunstall himself, the Commons passed this extremely controversial measure by two hundred and one votes to one hundred and twenty – a measure of the strong feelings which it had aroused and a marked contrast to the passage of the original Bills just over twelve months earlier.

Once the Edwardian Acts were repealed, since all the relevant grants had been made retrospective to October 14 1552 the episode was, as far as Durham was concerned, closed. Its implications were certainly grasped by those most concerned and written large in terms of the struggle to restore Papal jurisdiction which occupied the latter part of 1554; but there was hardly a shadow of a weapon left to use against the Bishop of Durham, should anyone have wished to do so. Nevertheless it was not forgotten. In 1559 Tunstall was again deprived and in appointing Robert Tempest to be Sheriff of Durham during the first year of his episcopate the new Bishop, James Pilkington, was careful to recite the rights of the Crown over the Bishopric, including his own appointment.[63]

In spite of its brief duration, and somewhat theoretical nature, the Dissolution of the see of Durham was an interesting and significant development. Northumberland, the villain of the piece to generations of church historians cannot, I think, be exonerated from the charge of placing secular priorities (particularly financial ones) ahead of religious – although we cannot be entirely sure of his final attitude towards the 'statute scheme'. There is, however, no evidence to support the charges that he intended primarily to enrich himself or to give himself autonomous power in the North of England. It would be fairer to conclude that the Duke's true concern was to strengthen the position of the Crown, and that in placing Palatinate jurisdiction and extensive ecclesiastical revenues in the King's hands he was acting in the true spirit of the Cromwellian tradition in which he had been trained. Mary, in spite of her profound distaste for what had been done and her willingness to ignore technical impediments in the path of justice as she saw it, was nevertheless forced to recognise the immovable obstacle of an unrepealed statute. In spite of the strict legality of her patent re-creating the see, there could have been no peaceful possession for the restored incumbent until that obstacle had been removed. This was in several ways a very useful 'trial run' for the policy of ecclesiastical restoration and clear proof (if that was needed) of the extent to which the capacity of statute had developed during the previous twenty years; a capacity which could in no way be dimished by charges of unworthy motivation, however heartfelt – or justified.

NOTES

1. P.R.O., Durham Sheriffs' Accounts, Durh. 20/51, 52.
2. *C.P.R.*, *Mary*, I, p 378, P.R.O., c.66/877 m.32.
3. C. Sturge, *Cuthbert Tunstall*, pp. 281–296. D. M. Loades, 'The last years of Cuthbert Tunstall, 1547–1559'; *Durham University Journal*, 66, 1973, pp. 10–21. Tunstall had consistently opposed every step in a Protestant direction, short of actually defying the law. The latest issue in 1550 was over the reformed Ordinal.
4. Tunstall was accused by Ninian Menville, a former dependant of the Nevilles, perhaps on a personal grudge. Sturge, p. 288.
5. P.R.O., SP/10/10/31. Warwick to Cecil, September 16, 1550.
6. The troubles of Stephen Gardiner are examined at length in J. A. Muller, *Stephen Gardiner and the Tudor Reaction*, pp. 183–203.
7. *A.P.C.*, III, p. 231; March 8 1551. Ponet was admitted to the office on condition of surrendering the revenues.
8. *C.S.P. Span*, X, p. 214.
9. *A.P.C.*, III, p. 381; Loades, op. cit.
10. A letter from Tunstall to Menville was alleged to have been found in a casket, which the Bishop confessed to the Council that he had written when interrogated on December 20, Sturge, pp. 289–90. *A.P.C.*, III, p. 449.
11. *A.P.C.*, III, p. 449.
12. *C.S.P. Span*, X, p. 425; December 27 1551.
13. *L.J.*, I, p. 418; *C.J.*, I, p. 21.
14. The main precedent for altering the status of franchises was the Act of 27 Henry VIII c.24, which had not only deprived the Bishops of Durham of the right to issue writs and appoint Justices in their own names, but had also affected the Bishop of Ely's liberty in the Isle of Ely and that of the Archbishop of York in Hexhamshire.
15. P.R.O., SP/10/13/49. *C.P.R.*, *Mary*, p. 76.
16. *C.S.P. Span.*, X, p. 582; October 29, 1552.
17. 38 'April 7; Chelsea; Northumberland to Cecil. To remember the Dean of Worcester's licence. Desires a grant to himself of the Palatine Jurisdiction of Durham. Lady Magaret Douglas wishes to return home, being pregnant.'
18. P.R.O., SP/10/14/18. The first paragraph, relating to the licence, is dated 'from Chelsea this vii....ell 1552' and signed 'your assured loving friend, Northumberland.' The other two paragraphs follow the signature in the same hand (a clerk's), but it is not clear whether they are intended to be part of the letter, or are memoranda subsequently written on the blank page. The jurisdiction of Durham was not in any sense 'in the King's hands' in early April 1552, since Tunstall was not deprived until October. The reference to Lady Margaret Douglas is not much help, since the birth date of her second son Charles (subsequently Earl of Lennox) is given only as 'about 1556'; *Complete Peerage*, VII, p. 600. Since he was admitted to Grays Inn in 1572, he could have been born in either 1553 or 1554.
19. *C.P.R.*, *Edward VI*, VI, p. 177; May 4 1553. P.R.O., C66/858 m.20.
20. *C.P.R.*, *Edward VI*, V, p. 175. P.R.O., C66/858 m.17.

21. P.R.O., Chancery, Patent Rolls C66/858 m.20 It may be significant that the office of Chancellor was not conferred along with that of Chief Steward, as Northumberland had suggested. The terms of the creation of the new Palatinate made the office of Chancellor a very powerful one. The Chancellorship was not bestowed before the King's death. According to the terms of the creation, Durham County would have been represented by one Knight and each town by one burgess, on the model of the new counties created in Wales by 27 Henry VIII c.26. P.R.O., C66/858 m.20.
22. G. Burnet, *The History of the Reformation of the Church of England*, II, pp. 194, 216.
23. B. L. Beer, *Northumberland*, pp. 142–3.
24. *L.J.*, I, p. 436.
25. The Bill was committed to the Bishop of London, the Lord Chief Justice, the Attorney General and the Solicitor General, which suggests legal snags rather than objection of principle. *Ibid.*
26. P.R.O., Parliament Roll, 7 Edward VI, C65/161 item 12.
27. *Ibid.*, It is quite clear that this plan did not envisage Durham and Newcastle as stipendiary sees on the lines of Winchester.
28. 'And for the better corroboration and perfecting of the erections and establishments of the said two new Bishoprics ... which the King's Majesty mindeth presently to do and accomplish by his most gracious Letters Patent and to appoint them severally by the said Letters Patent their episcopal and ordinary jurisdictions, circuits and authorities. Be it therefore enacted by authority of this present Parliament that the said Letters Patent ... shall be good and available in the law to all intents, constructions and purposes ...' *Ibid.*
29. Burnet, II, p. 216.
30. P.R.O., SP/10/15/35. October 28 1552.
31. '... if His Majesty make the Dean of Durham Bishop of that see and appoint him one thousand marks more of that which he hath in his Deanery and the same houses which he now hath as well in the city as in the country will serve him right honourably ... and the Chancellor's living to be converted to the Deanery and an honest man to be placed in it, the Vice Chancellor to be turned to the Chancellor, the Suffragan who is placed without the King's Majesty's authority and also hath a great living, not worthy of it to be removed ... and the same living with a little more to the value of a hundred marks will serve for the erection of a Bishop within Newcastle ...' *Ibid.*
32. P.R.O., SP/10/15/57: November 15 1552.
33. *A.P.C.*, IV, p. 155: October 31 1552.
34. On March 7 1553 the Council wrote direct to the Chancellor of Augmentations to grant a lease of Bishopric property at Northallerton. Presumably Hindemer would not have been permitted to commit property in this way, since the dissolution of the ancient see had already been decided upon. *A.P.C.*, IV, p. 232.
35. Horn, an advanced Protestant, had been appointed to the Deanery only in November 1551, after the death of Whitehead, and Northumberland presumably thought him to be as amenable as Ponet. His refusal to accept the see becomes easier to explain if he was expected to be a party to the plunder

of both the Bishopric and the Cathedral and was offered a mixed package of revenues without any secure title. There is no reason to suppose that Horn doubted the legal validity of Tunstall's deprivation. J. Strype, *Ecclesiastical Memorials*, II, ii, p. 22. It is important to realise that Horn was not offered the see on the terms later outlined in the Act.

36. The Duke always professed great zeal for 'God's service' and wrote frequently to Cecil about the situation in Durham, but by the beginning of 1553 sincere Protestants as diverse as John Hooper, John Knox and Thomas Cranmer had ceased to believe his professions. Beer, *Northumberland*, pp. 141–3.
37. P.R.O., SP/10/19/28. Burnet, II, p. 216. Nicholas Ridley was Bishop of London and William Bill a Royal Chaplain.
38. *S(tatues of the) R(ealm)*, III, pp. 687–8.
39. *C.P.R.*, *Edward VI*, V. p. 230.
40. *Ibid.*, p. 133; June 22 1553.
41. *Ibid.*, p. 6; grant of the office of Warden of Norham Castle to Richard Bowes.
42. *Ibid.*, p. 134; February 5 1553. Rede, described as 'the King's councillor', received this grant for his services with the Duke of Northumberland. He had also been a member of the commission which deprived Tunstall.
43. 'Where the quiet order regiment and governance of the corporation and body politic of the town of Newcastle-upon-Tyne hath been not a little disturbed and hindered ... by reason that the said town of Gateshead is parcel of the said County Palatine of Durham and without the liberties of the said haven town ...' Statute 7 Edward VI, c.10.
44. *SR*, IV, i, pp. 173–4.
45. Loades, 'Last days' p. 18. Mary accepted Tunstall as Bishop of Durham without hesitation or enquiry, Sturge, p. 297.
46. *C.P.R.*, *Mary*, I, p. 76.
47. *Ibid.* This was one of the main grounds for Tunstall's appeal, the other being that he had had inadequate time to prepare his defence. In fact there was no established legal procedure for these commissions under the Royal Supremacy, which were a new development in Edward's reign. Precedent, in the shape of Thomas Cromwell's Viceregency in Spirituals, suggested that there was no valid objection to laymen exercising the Royal Supremacy, provided that they were properly commissioned. Mary, of course, objected to the whole exercise of the Supremacy, but could not use that as a ground of nullity, since her own commissions had to sit by the same authority.
48. Loades, 'Last days', p. 18. Horn had fled, one step ahead of arrest, C. H. Garrett, *Marian Exiles*, p. 188.
49. *C.J.*, I, p. 31.
50. Mary's conscience, prompted by Reginald Pole, urged her to regard all heretical (and schismatic) legislation as invalid, but she quickly became convinced of the necessity for Parliamentary repeal. '... it was first necessary to repeal and annul by Act of Parliament many perverse laws made by those who ruled before her', as she told Henry Penning in August 1553. For a full discussion of Mary's attitude to the Royal Supremacy and its consequences, see D. M. Loades, *The Oxford Martyrs*, pp. 104–8.

51. *C.P.R.*, *Edward VI*, VI, p. 91.
52. *C.J.*, I, p. 31. Elizabeth's interests were not touched by the successful Bill of the next session.
53. Resistance to the government's religious policy in the House of Commons was determined, but limited in scale – about 80 members out of 360. It was clearly property, not doctrine, which provoked opposition in Parliament. Loades, *The Reign of Mary*, pp. 154–7.
54. The issue over these lands was one of legal title. Did the Henrician statutes confer a valid title to confiscated ecclesiastical property upon the Crown? If so, then the Crown could convey that title to the purchasers, and the church's interest ceased. If not, then the purchasers had no secure title in return for an investment almost twenty years old in many cases. The settlement of December 1554 was ambiguous; English common lawyers interpreted it as a concession of title by the church, but Pole clearly regarded it as a *de facto* concession only, dependant upon the will of the Pope for the time being. B.L., Add. MS 41577, f. 1661; J. H. Crehan, 'The return to obedience; new judgement on Cardinal Pole', *The Month*, n.s. 14, 1955, pp. 221–9; Loades, *Oxford Martyrs*, pp. 144–5, *Reign of Mary*, pp. 327–9.
55. *C.P.R.*, *Mary*, I, p. 377. P.R.O., c66/877 m.32.
56. *Ibid.* This wording makes it clear that the new Bishopric would have had no legal continuity with its predecessor, and corresponds with the terms of the Bishop's petition, as cited '... Cuthertus Tunstall nuper Dunelmensis Episcopus nobis humilitate supplicavit ut Episcopatum et sedam Episcopaleum apud Dunelmensis praedictam de novo erigere et stabilire...'
57. As I formerly argued; 'Last days', p. 19.
58. *L.J.*, I, p. 450.
59. 1 Mary, st.3 c.3. *SR*, IV, i, pp. 226–8.
60. *C.J.*, I, p. 34. Counsel was called on April 16, and appeared on April 17.
61. *Ibid.* April 18 when the Newcastle Counsel also appeared again.
62. *Ibid.* There is no evidence that Tunstall paid any attention to this representation.
63. P.R.O., Durh. 3/82 m.1.

A Rude and Heady People: the local community and the Rebellion of the Northern Earls

David Marcombe

When the North of England erupted into serious rebellion in November 1569 Cecil may well have taken the precaution of searching his files of correspondence to seek out references to a region he had been, at best, only half aware of during the problematical years since the Queen's succession. Had he done so he would have discovered at least two letters which in the light of current events seemed uncannily prophetic in tone. In October 1561 the new Bishop of Durham, James Pilkington, had written to him in unusually distraught terms –

> I am afraid to think what may follow if it be not foreseen. The worshipful of the shire is set and of small power, the people rude and heady and by these occasions most bold.[1]

The warning had been ignored, as indeed had an equally impassioned plea from the Bishop in the following month –

> for the nature of the people I would not have thought there had been so forward a generation in this realm . . . I am grown into such displeasure with them . . . that I know not whether they like me worse or I they. So great dissembling, so poisonful tongues and malicious words I have not seen . . . where I had a little wit at my coming, now have left me almost none.[2]

Such mutual detestation between governor and governed in a region far removed from the direct supervision of central government should have registered a clear warning in the Secretary's mind, but it does not appear to have done so. Cecil doubtless rationalised the Bishop's rantings as an over-reaction to a situation which would settle with time and anyway there were always more important problems nearer to home. However, in these two letters – and in the government reaction to them – we see a mirror image of the Northern Rising eight years before the event. The mutual dislike between Pilkington and the people of the North and the failure of the central government to come to terms with the problem until it was too late were to be critical factors in the shaping of the final conflict. Pilkington's grim warning in *A Confutation of an Addition* – 'so will God's good bishop . . . pull down the unbridled stomachs of the people' – was to have a special significance in the religion and politics of the Tudor North.[3]

One point which seems to be generally accepted by historians is that the revolt did not have its origins in the North but developed chiefly out of the factional squabbles of the Elizabethan Privy Council so well documented by Professor Wallace MacCaffrey.[4] Indeed, the Rebellion is a classic example of an historical phenomenon traditionally approached from the point of view of central government rather than from that of the people actually involved in it, and because of this it is an instance in which the 'national' historian can learn much from the regional and local specialist. Basically Professor MacCaffrey describes a conspiracy on two levels, linked – to a greater or lesser extent – with the proposal for a marriage between Mary Queen of Scots and Norfolk. The 'inner ring' of the conspiracy comprised courtiers and privy councillors keen to safeguard the succession and at the same time limit the influence of Cecil in government. The 'outer ring' comprised a group of Northern nobles, headed by the Earls of Northumberland and Westmorland, who shared the broad aims of the courtiers but often showed a marked hostility to individuals in the first grouping. The plotters were indeed strange bedfellows, and when the 'inner ring' collapsed due to the defection of Leicester and Norfolk late in 1569 the disgruntled Northerners went ahead with a rash and ill-timed project of their own. This continuation 'when all good hope was passed' is a difficult question to resolve, yet it is critical to our understanding of the Northern Rising. As early as September Westmorland received warning from Norfolk telling him not to stir, yet in spite of this and a general recognition of the hopelessness of their position the Earls went ahead with their venture.[5]

Professor MacCaffrey places the blame on 'extremists' which he identifies with a 'knot of ardent Catholic gentry' and in taking this line he follows the view of most well informed contemporaries.[6] Sussex and Sir George Bowes thought that Westmorland was less to blame than a group of 'close conspirators' or 'wicked councillors' who had corrupted him with their 'false delusions'.[7] Northumberland in his confession stated that Westmorland had been 'encouraged by many gentlemen out of the Bishopric' and that he 'was ever unwilling . . . but only pressed and sore urged by others'.[8] The spearhead of this militant group of Durham gentry was made up of Christopher Neville, John Swinburne and Robert Tempest whose crimes were considered so heinous as to exclude them from the general pardon issued by Sussex in November 1569;[9] these were some of the 'headstrong and reckless partisans' described by Sir Cuthbert Sharp, the 'Northern hotheads' pilloried by Professor MacCaffrey.[10] Sadly, neither of these historians comes close to understanding the grievances which caused a section of the Durham gentry to risk all in a desperate and ill-timed insurrection.

To link the Northern Rebellion too closely with the London-based conspiracy – as Professor MacCaffrey and others have tended to do – is a dangerous over-simplification: to take refuge in clichés such as the 'wild men of the North' neglects the political and religious complexities of the region.[11] In fact, the Rebellion of the Northern Earls – while upholding a vague sympathy for the cause of Mary Stuart – was basically the result of a *regional* crisis rather than a national one. In the North Mary was regarded more as a catalyst whereby local grievances might be amended than as a panacea for a national ill. The strength with which these local grievances were held helps explain why the Earls – acting out of a sense of duty to their following – ignored pleas for moderation and charged headlong to ruin when they might have been saved.

One of the few things the Earls were agreed upon was the way in which they and their followers had been systematically slighted by the Tudors and their 'new set up nobles' who 'go about to overthrow and put down the ancient nobility of this realm.'[12] This was already a well established grievance in 1569 and to understand it fully we must look back to the early sixteenth century. The Percys, Nevilles and Dacres had traditionally enjoyed key positions of authority in the North, a pre-eminance which was first seriously challenged by Henry VIII who, by way of courtier Bishops such as Ruthall, Wolsey and Tunstall, exerted pressure on magnates he considered to be unreliable.[13]

One result of this pressure was the Pilgrimage of Grace in which most of the ancient Northern families were involved to a greater or lesser extent. Under Mary the Henrician policy was reversed and the old families once more stood in high favour, the Percys being restored to their sequestered Earldom – lost after the Pilgrimage – and the Earl of Westmorland receiving the prestigious accolade of Lieutenant General of the North.[14] But none of this was to last long. Elizabeth's return to her father's policy meant that after 1558 new Protestant courtier families such as the Russells, Dudleys and Careys began to move into positions of prominence in the North, positions traditionally held by Percys, Nevilles, Dacres or their clients: as always a section of the gentry was to concur with these changes while others were to feel alienated and angry.

Examples of this shift in influence and control can be seen both on a regional and county basis. After 1560 the Council of the North was headed successively by Rutland, Warwick and Archbishop Young of York, all of them Protestants and relative newcomers to the region. Only in 1568 did a Lord President appear who was in any sense amenable to the old families in the person of the Earl of Sussex, whose presence at York and generally ambivalent attitude may well have given some encouragement to the rebels in 1569.[15] In the sensitive Border region the story was the same. The Earl of Northumberland was removed from the semi-hereditary post of Warden of the East and Middle Marches and eventually replaced by such anti-Percy stalwarts as Sir John Forster and the Earl of Bedford who stood in high favour at Court.[16] The important Governorship of Berwick – the strongest garrison in the land – was held by Bedford and later Lord Hunsdon, the Queen's cousin. Factors such as these helped to ensure that when the Rebellion did come the support from Northumberland was minimal, the vast bulk of the Percy following being drawn from North Yorkshire.[17]

Away from the potentially explosive Borders administrative changes were slower but equally relentless, slower because the government had no wish to alienate the ruling Marian shire oligarchies before it had had a chance to establish firm control. Thus, in Durham Henry Neville, fifth Earl of Westmorland, was appointed Lord Lieutenant in 1559 which office he was permitted to keep until his death in 1564 when he was replaced by the more amenable and reliable Sir George Bowes.[18] Similarly, following the fall of Bishop Tunstall in 1559 the government was quite content to permit his officials to continue in office during the long vacancy of the see.[19] During 1560 the Palatinate was ruled by an oligarchy which comprised Robert Meynell, the Bishop's Temporal Chancellor, Christopher Wandisford, his Steward, and Robert Tempest, the Sheriff. Hints of things to come were given by the early restoration of Dean Horn, who fought a lone battle for Protestantism in the early months of the new reign, and occasional exclusions of particularly unreliable individuals from the Commission of the Peace.[20] The perpetuation of the Catholic administrative oligarchy for almost two years after Elizabeth's accession was the result of unwillingness to alter the balance of power, a preoccupation of government with problems elsewhere and a desire to keep the wealthy Bishopric of Durham vacant as a source of revenue for the Crown. Short term political expediency in London was to leave a lasting legacy of resentment in the North in that in the first two years of the reign the precedent was set for a conservative and traditional administration under the auspices of a reforming and innovative Queen. Until 1561 the diocese had been shielded from the full blast of Reformation change: the next few years were to provide a rude awakening for those whose conception of Protestantism had been shaped by the moderate and conciliatory man who had been their Bishop for almost twenty years.

The political situation in the North was eventually changed by the death of Lord President Shrewsbury in September 1560 and a letter from Archbishop Parker to Cecil in the following month urging the appointment of Bishops to the vacant Northern sees –

> they be a rude people of their own nature and the more had need to be looked to for retaining them in quiet and civility. I fear that whatsoever is now too husbandly saved will be an occasion of further expense in keeping them down.[21]

Within seven months of this warning the four Northern sees had been filled with worthy Protestant incumbents and the Earl of Rutland had been sent to York as the first Protestant Lord President.

Pilkington, the new Bishop of Durham, arrived in his diocese in May 1561 and at once began a Visitation during which the Supremacy Oath was administered to officers and the clergy. It proved to be the critical device in clearing the decks of the old Marian oligarchs. Meynell, Wandisford and Tempest were all removed for religious irregularities or hints of corruption, Pilkington lamenting that Meynell 'has ruled this country alone above twenty years with the evil report of all men'.[22] Suitable replacements were not always easy to find, and although there was never a complete exclusion of the older families from the Commission of the Peace and from Palatinate offices there was a significant shift in emphasis.[23] William Fleetwood became the Bishop's principal legal advisor, Thomas Calverley his Temporal Chancellor and Robert Bowes, Sheriff, an administrative phalanx which displayed a traditional blend of alternative-faction county gentry and 'new' talent brought in from outside the Palatinate.[24] What was remarkable about the situation was not that such a shift in the local political balance had taken place, but that it took place under the auspices of a clerical hierarchy which was probably unique in its indiscretion: it was this factor which in Durham gave the political changes of the 1560s an explosiveness which they might not otherwise have had.

The centre of the opposition to the old families in Durham was the clerical establishment. This was to be expected. Bishops of Durham had always been appointed by the Crown and certainly since the time of Ruthall had been regarded as necessary counterweights to the power of the local nobility: indeed, Mervyn James tells us that

> Tension between the Bishop, often supported by the Crown, and the leading Durham lay magnate, supported by a powerful gentry faction, was a traditional feature of Palatinate politics.[25]

Thus a united Protestant clerical establishment, comprising Bishop and Dean, was the major source of support which the Crown looked to in the diocese and the Bishop was a more potent ally then he might have been elsewhere because of his possession of *jura regalia*.

In the 1560s it is not surprising to discover that the clerical hierarchy of Durham came to reflect the political and religious views of those courtiers closest to the Queen in London. Bishop Pilkington and the new Dean, William Whittingham, were both nominees of the Dudleys, as was a fair proportion of the Durham Chapter, replacing those Catholic prebendaries who had been deprived as a result of the 1559 Visitation.[26] Bishops of Durham invariably came from outside the Palatinate, but for the *Cathedral* to become a centre of 'alien' influence was a new departure. Traditionally the monks of Durham had been drawn from the middling ranks of local society and had stood in a relationship of deference to the gentry, a situation which was perpetuated in 1541 when the last monks became the first prebendaries and minor canons of the new foundation Chapter.[27] In view of this the 1560s were doubly alarming to the Durham gentry, not just because the new clerics were considered to be placemen of their political opponents, but also because as outsiders and gentlemen themselves they looked on the resident gentry of the shire as social equals and indeed as possible competitors. Moreover, these incoming churchmen invariably mirrored the radical brand of Protestantism so popular at Court, yet distasteful to the Earls and the priests and gentry associated with their households.[28] Birth, patronage and doctrinal belief combined to make the new clerical hierarchy suspect from the very start.

This fundamental mistrust was compounded by the incoming Protestant clergy who appear to have made little effort to make themselves amenable to the old conservative oligarchs. In the highly charged religious atmosphere of the decade it would perhaps have been surprising had they done so, and there was certainly a popular belief that Pilkington and his sort had been sent as far away from London as possible to blunt the edge of their radicalism in a land of papists and malcontents. Certainly Durham was unique as a stronghold of puritanism during this period, and Professor Collinson has commented that 'here alone the puritans had unfettered control'.[29] Their mentality had been heavily influenced by recent events. Many of the incoming clerics had been exiles during the Marian period, an experience which gave them a strong sense of their own righteousness and a lasting antipathy to papists. Most of them had little or no experience of office in church or state and some of them had senior Palatinate offices cast upon them at a surprisingly early age: Robert Swift was still less than thirty when he became Pilkington's Spiritual Chancellor in 1561 and Thomas Calverley, the Temporal Chancellor, was still considered 'a young man' in 1570.[30]

For these reasons some of them were perhaps not as diplomatic as they might have been, a fact which has special significance when we bear in mind that the Bishop was frequently ill and forced, of necessity, to delegate important matters to his officers from time to time. There was also an important contrast in attitude between the Protestant clergy and their new gentry neighbours, a contrast which is central to Mervyn James's concept of a transition from a 'lineage' to a 'civil' society in sixteenth century Durham. The Catholic/knightly concept of life, with its honorific connotations, had no more vehement champion than that latter-day crusader Charles Neville, sixth Earl of Westmorland, while the Protestant/meritocratic code, upheld by the Tudor parvenus, found dour and stalwart upholders in Bishop Pilkington and his Lancastrian compatriots Thomas and Ralph Lever. The Calvinist ethic persuaded these men to speak their minds openly at all times, their self-conscious identification with prophets and patriarchs causing them to be insensitive to criticism offered up against them: Pilkington likened himself to Jacob and St. Paul, Ralph Lever to Elias and John the Baptist struggling manfully against a world full of sin and wickedness.[31] In the course of their bigoted tirades the Protestant clergy sometimes hit out at concepts held dear by the 'lineage' groups in local society –

> And to rejoice in ancient blood, what can be more vain?' asked Bishop Pilkington. 'Do we not all come from Adam our earthly father? . . . How can we crack then of our ancient stock, seeing we came all of one earthly and heavenly father.[32]

Ralph Lever endorsed the same point –

> you stand so much upon your honour and high estate which in these matters have no pre-eminence at all . . . in these matters of conscience never care what man sayeth but fear and obey the Lord's commandment.[33]

Not only were the new clerics sometimes outspokenly provocative, they also had economic ambitions and did not flinch from using the law as a means of bringing their ideas to fruition. From the debates at the Court of Edward VI, to which Pilkington and Thomas Lever had been notable contributors, came a passionate belief that the Reformation had substantially weakened the economic position of the clergy and that it was a moral duty to redress the balance so far as was possible.[34] Pilkington and his friends, in their first flush of power, were determined to put these godly principles into operation. Preaching at Court in March 1560 'his matter went much to maintaining Oxford and Cambridge scholars and the bishops and clergy to have better livings', and in the following year, as Bishop of Durham, Pilkington resisted the retention of episcopal land reminding Cecil that 'such plucking away defaces the doctrine of Christ'.[35]

This sort of attitude sometimes led the Protestant clergy into conflicts with their own patrons whose expectations were not always as altruistic as they might have been, but in an area like Durham, long under the influence of well-established families of *Catholic* gentry, it was more likely to provoke confrontation with the established local community which had already profited from the changes in land ownership and occupation initiated by the Reformation.[36] It should not be forgotten that in the 1560s the possibility of a restoration of Catholicism was a real fear for the Protestant clergy, hence a belief on their part that a continuing 'Catholic' interest in church lands and resources should be undermined to make such a restoration more difficult and perhaps impossible. Pilkington knew only too well the shifts that his predecessors had gone to hedge their bets against premature retirement –

> Divers of these holy prelates . . . had so leased out their houses, lands and parks, that some of the new bishops had scarce a corner of a house to lie in and divers not so much ground to graze a goose or sheep . . . and yet have these holy fathers provided that if they be restored . . . they shall have all their commodities again.[37]

Despite his exaggeration Pilkington makes an important point. By attacking the landed interest of Catholics the Protestant clergy would not only improve their own financial situation but would also be guarding against a possible popish restoration. The law was their only weapon in this, and in 1560 Dean Horn set the tone of what was to be an acrimonious and legalistic decade by commencing a suit against some of the deprived prebendaries to recover books and goods allegedly taken from him when he was forced to leave Durham in haste in 1553.[38] There were those who suspected that this economic activity had less to do with the improvement of the ministry than the needs of married Elizabethan clerics to maintain their families and 'desire to make their sons gentlemen'.[39]

This policy of bolstering the economic fortunes of the clergy against secular encroachments found no more staunch upholders than Bishop Pilkington and Dean Whittingham. 'I love not law', warned Pilkington ominously, 'and yet I praise God law never went against me.'[40] The rapidly expanding coal industry provided one early point of friction for the Bishop who soon discovered that the vacancy of the see had led to encroachments on coal producing lands at Ryton and Chester-le-Street. At Chester-le-Street the antagonist was Richard Gascoigne, a relation of the Earl of Westmorland: Pilkington wrote to Cecil in 1562 complaining that Westmorland had 'made a great ado of late to recover it' and that the Bishop and his officials were 'misused . . . with very big and uncomely words'. However, with characteristic determination he added 'I cannot leave so great a piece of ground for brags'.[41] Violence also erupted at Ryton where John Swinburne, lord of the neighbouring manor of Chopwell, had encroached on the Bishop's common and had sunk pits there, taking away and selling coal: in the course of the dispute it was alleged that Pilkington's servants had been 'sore beat and hurt'. An arbitration of 1563 recommended that the land should be restored to the Bishop and leased to Swinburne as a gesture of 'goodwill', but the pious hope that there would be 'faithful friendship' between the two protagonists thereafter was never to be realised.[42]

If Pilkington was keen to maintain his control over the rich deposits of coal in the Palatinate he was also determined to preserve the ancient Hospital foundations of the diocese against improper use. These had been among the saddest victims of the Reformation, with Kepier in a state of total collapse and Greatham and Sherburn on the brink of ruin.[43] The Bishop's plan to revive Kepier in 1561 by challenging John Heath's title to the property came to nothing, and he had little success at Greatham where the reactionary Master, Thomas Sparke, ruled the roost until 1572 dispensing favours to the local gentry.[44] Even so the

Bishop tried. In 1569 he made efforts to have Robert Tempest's lease of the Hospital cancelled commenting to Leicester that he 'kept a good house for gentlemen but not so many poor, nor so well used as the foundation requires'.[45] But it was at Sherburn, Durham's largest Hospital, where the stakes were highest. Here the Henrician and Edwardian Masters, Thomas Legh and Anthony Bellasis, had conveyed away most of the endowment in a series of reckless and irresponsible leases. Reform was attempted by the Marian Master, Anthony Salvin, who struck on the idea of invalidating the old leases because they had been made by the Master without the consent of the brethren.[46] However, when his own deprivation for Catholicism was imminent in May 1559 Salvin proved himself to be no better than his predecessors by leasing extensive tithes to his nephew, Gerard Salvin of Croxdale, for forty years, 'the said master, brethren and sisters' having agreed to the act 'by their whole and mutual assent, consent and agreement'.[47] Salvin's removal at least opened the way for the appointment of two Protestant Masters, Ralph Skinner and Thomas Lever. Lever, in particular, tackled the job of reform with energy and determination, irritating not only the Salvins but a long list of other leaseholders in the process. In 1568 suits were pending before the Assizes, King's Bench and Court of Requests, and Pilkington, his stalwart friend and ally, wrote to Cecil asking for support – 'you know how unfit he is for troublesome suits', he reminded the Secretary, 'yet the miserable state of that poor house forces him to follow it for conscience sake'.[48] Conscience was the yardstick against which almost any act, however indiscreet, could be justified.

But once more it was the Cathedral which was to prove the centre of the most widespread and disruptive innovations. After the Bishop the Dean and Chapter was the biggest landowner in the county, yet Dean Whittingham felt that the estate was badly run down due to lax administration and a tendency to regard the endowment almost as a 'social service' for the gentry and yeomanry of the shire.[49] Backed by both puritan and conservative members of the Chapter, Whittingham initiated a policy of administrative reform characterised by a marked increase in legal activity and the construction of a new Exchequer over the old abbey gatehouse in 1568/69.[50] The policy had many manifestations, but in every instance it won the Chapter enemies rather than friends amongst the established local community. Perhaps the most provocative issue amongst the gentry was the question of Corps lands.[51] At the foundation of the Dean and Chapter in 1541 most of the old demesne lands of the priory had been allocated to the Dean and individual prebendaries as personal estates, or Corps, which were regarded as part of their capitular income. These lands comprised many of the choice properties of the Cathedral, such as the manors of Elvet and Finchale and the Rectory of Billingham. In the years between 1541 and 1559 almost all of these lands had been let out on long leases by the first prebendaries to their relations, friends or trustees who were often members of prominent local families – Thomas Tempest, Robert Dalton, Lancelot Hodgson, Percival Lambton and Roger Booth had all been beneficiaries.[52] However, the leasing of Corps – without a proviso that they should be vacated on the death of the prebendary – was against the meaning of the Cathedral statutes, and in practice it meant that the Protestant prebendaries of the 1560s found themselves in possession of preferments greatly reduced in value.

Between 1565 and 1567 the Chapter undertook a campaign to recover these lands in a series of suits prosecuted before the Council of the North: the argument was that all leases made before 1565 were technically invalid because the title of the Cathedral corporation had not been stated in correct form, a similar device to that envisaged by Salvin at Sherburn.[53] These suits were generally successful, and a high proportion of Corps property passed from the hands of the established gentry into those of the relatives and friends of the new Protestant prebendaries: indeed, one of the last formal acts of the Dean and Chapter prior to the Rebellion was to seal many of these new leases in September 1569.[54] The situation with regard to Corps land was made even more complex and contentious when in 1567 the Chapter passed an Act which decreed that the tithes of various townships, hitherto in lease to the laity, should be annexed to the twelve prebendal stalls as Bye-corps as the current leases expired.[55] Even though there were not the sudden changes in occupation that there were on the landed estates, it soon became clear to many of the lay tithe farmers that they were in occupation of non-renewable assets – gentlemen such as William Parkinson, William Smith and Robert Tempest added their voices to the growing chorus of protest.[56] But the complaints were not always simply vocal, and the old tenants sometimes registered their disapproval with legal action of their own. In 1569, for example, the Hodgsons and Tempests, farmers of the Rectory of Lanchester, challenged the traditional exemption of Corps land from the payment of tithe, and Ralph Lever's tenants at Muggleswick were forced to defend a suit in the Exchequer.[57]

By the mid 1560s it seemed plain that the new Protestant élite was attempting to establish a permanent niche for itself in county society on the strength of episcopal and capitular patronage and that this rapid expansion of the 'church interest' was to be at the expense of – rather than alongside – some of the established families of the shire. Each wave of Reformation change brought new economic beneficiaries as well as doctrinal innovation, and by the 1560's the law of diminishing returns had begun to apply to such a degree that the new Elizabethan hierarchy could only establish its own fortunes by seeking to deprive others: with only crumbs left in the larder Peter had to rob Paul to enjoy the semblance of a feast. The struggle for the Corps lands, and the eventual victory of the new order, forms a microcosm of the conflicts and tensions in the Palatinate at large.

The collection of debts owing for rent was another issue which brought the Chapter into conflict with the gentry. Gentlemen tended to be the worst offenders here because they were not dependent on leases for their livelihoods and before 1559 tended to regard the prebendaries as social inferiors anyway. After 1563 a determined effort was made to recover old debts and a test case was brought against the executors of the fifth Earl of Westmorland following his death in 1564. The Chapter claimed arrears of rent for property at Staindrop totalling £71. 3s. 4d., a sum which indicates that the Earl had paid no rent for almost twenty years.[58] A successful outcome probably encouraged the Chapter in its dealings with lesser men. In 1567 and 1568 letters of attorney were issued to the Receiver to sue for any arrears of rent owed since the foundation of the Dean and Chapter.[59] However, the most tactless and provocative economy made by the Cathedral in the 1560s concerned a fee of £10 per year traditionally paid to the Nevilles for leading the Chapter tenants in war.

On the death of the fifth Earl this payment was suspended and despite protests was never restored. It may well have been felt that the office was obsolete and archaic and that the task was better done by the Lord Lieutenant anyway, but that did not take account of the honorific connotations of such a position and the loss of face involved with its cancellation. When the matter was taken up with Cecil by Christopher Neville in 1568 the Dean and Chapter pleaded poverty as its excuse and pointed out that 'such grants were not made to bind the successors thereunto'.[60] Neville, who was 'sore offended' by the whole matter, was not to be hoodwinked and regarded the incident as a deliberate slight to his family –

> sure I am that at this present they are in as great wealth as ever they had since the suppression of the house. Their greedy covetousness is such that ten times so much as they have may not suffice themselves.[61]

He was probably about right in his assessment of the Chapter's wealth. It is difficult to accept the defence of poverty when the real income of the Dean and Chapter was rising steadily, especially from fines, and it was capable of replacing the Neville fee with an annuity of £6. 13s. 4d. to one of its own henchmen, Thomas Calverley.[62] The cancellation of the fee was another indication of the changing direction of policy rather than a practical economy.

The tenantry too suffered as a result of these administrative changes. A minor irritant was the revival of obsolete feudal obligations initiated in some of the Dean and Chapter manors. When John Hawkins leased a tenement in Westoe in 1563 he was bound to pay 'bowl corn' to the keeper of Haining Wood 'as of old antiquity hath been accustomed', and in the following year a new lease to Godfrey Toft, one of the Dean's servants, authorised the collection of 37½ quarters of 'rent corn' from the tenants of Billingham.[63] At Westoe the total rent of the township rose by £1. 9s. 4d. between 1564/65 and 1574/75, the extra income coming from payments for 'court oats' and capons, geese and hens.[64] But the most fundamental assumption on the part of the Chapter tenants challenged by Dean Whittingham was the belief that they held their farms by 'tenant right' which assumed an inalienable right to renew their leases and pass on their holdings to their heirs on payment of a minimal fine.[65] The Chapter argued that the tenants had no special rights and were merely 'tenants at will', and to endorse the point they embarked on a policy of issuing concurrent leases to their own nominees of lands already occupied by ancient tenants. The process is illustrated by the case of John Swinburne of Chopwell. In 1558 Swinburne occupied the Chapter Rectory of Bywell St. Peter under the terms of a pre-Dissolution lease made by the Prior and Convent to John Allanson. In 1560 the Chapter leased the property in reversion to John Horn, a relative of the Dean, on the expiry of the lease to Allanson. Swinburne, wishing to remain in possession, approached Horn and bought his lease for a cash sum: a comparable case in Northumberland involved a payment of £20. Finally, to put the whole matter above board the Dean and Chapter issued a new lease of the Rectory to Swinburne in 1567 to take effect after the expiry of the original indenture.[66]

Money, in the form of entry fines or bribes, was the motive behind this policy rather than eviction, but the implications were extremely disconcerting for the tenants. Their security of tenure was threatened at the very moment their traditional 'leader', the Earl of Westmorland, was deposed from office. As it happened alternative leaders were to emerge from the ranks of the tenants themselves, two of whom, at least, were to be active in the Rebellion, and the grievances over concurrent leasing were to continue long after 1569.[67] However, there is a clear link between the policy of concurrent leasing and the Rebellion. The townships most affected by this aspect of Chapter policy between 1564 and 1569 were in South Durham, Aycliffe, Merrington and Billingham being especially badly hit. In the pardons issued to rebel sympathisers in 1570 Chapter manors in the South of the county are generally well represented, but the overwhelming majority of Cathedral tenants suing for pardon came from these same three manors. Merrington produced a total of twenty-four, Aycliffe twenty-seven and Billingham a startling sixty-one, this latter manor having been uniquely unfortunate in having been the victim of concurrent leasing, the feudal revival, and part of it, at least, belonging to the Corps of Dean Whittingham.[68]

Clearly some of the prosperous yeoman farmers who swelled the ranks of the rebel army as light horsemen in 1569 had grievances such as these very much to the forefront of their minds.[69] The new policies had thoroughly alarmed the tenants and had exposed the new prebendaries as self-seeking and avaricious in the popular imagination. On this point, at least, gentry families such as the Tempests and the farmers of East Merrington would have been agreed. However, the fact that the grievances which existed in the Palatinate in the 1560s were sectional – and sometimes purely individual – is well borne out in the Rebellion. Several historians have commented that the movement was dominated by the gentry, and this is hardly surprising since the gentry – or at least a section of it – saw itself as most threatened. The confusion which was one of the major hallmarks of the movement stemmed from the fact that individual participants were motivated by individualistic grievances which were only linked by some general sense of injustice – as Northumberland said there was a vague and pervading hope amongst his gentry following that 'all would come as they would have it'.[70] There were very few truly 'popular' grievances evident in 1569 outside of the religious sphere. Those rank and file who did join in as activists appear to have been swayed by false promises of pay, confusion over the mustering process and in some cases by compulsion. Sir George Bowes summed it up well – 'By fear, fair speech and money . . . they draw away the hearts of people'.[71] Clearly no movement could endure for long with its foundation built on such shifting sand.

Unsavoury reputations stuck with the new churchmen partly because in the first decade of the reign they had little opportunity to implement their religious ideas in the way in which they would have wished. This was partly due to the intransigent nature of the area in which they were working and partly due to practical administrative and financial difficulties. By 1565, despite a conservative element still within the Chapter, the Cathedral was approaching the godly ideal of the reformers with public sermons and fasts, an outstanding array of preachers and an active involvement in the spiritual affairs of the region at large.[72] Outside the Cathedral, although Protestants were injected into some of the wealthier livings of the diocese and the Bishop's administration waged a relentless war against pluralists and non-residents, progress was slow.[73] Many of the upland parishes in both Northumberland and Durham were affected by sporadic disorder, the average value of Northumberland livings according to the *Valor Ecclesiasticus* was only £12 a year and although Durham livings by comparison were quite wealthy – an average of £24 a year – the county had some large impropriate parishes such as Chester-le-Street and Lanchester which were only served by poorly paid curates.[74]

The national shortage of reliable clergy in the 1560s was probably more acute in the North than elsewhere. In 1565 Pilkington commented pessimistically – 'the parishes be great, the people many, the wage small, priests bad and very few to be had and fewer to be hoped for'.[75] Placing Protestant clergy presupposed the old incumbents being removed by death or deprivation, but neither of these factors could be relied upon. A high proportion of crypto-Catholic clergy had survived the 1559 Visitation and the purge of 1561, such as William Watson, Chaplain to the Prior of Durham, who was Vicar of Bedlington from 1557 to 1575 and nostalgically turned up to hear mass in the Cathedral in 1569.[76] Advowsons in the hands of Catholic laymen meant that even death was not always the end of the old beliefs. In 1564 John Swinburne presented Thomas Brown, an ex-canon of Blanchland, to the Vicarage of Bywell St. Andrew under the terms of a grant from the dissolved Abbot and Convent. In view of the dubious nature of the case – the Abbey had been dispensing blank pieces of parchment under the Convent seal prior to the Dissolution – Pilkington initiated an enquiry, but Swinburne's nominee won the day.[77] Several contemporaries commented on the conservative nature of the region. In 1560 Norfolk reported many altars still standing around Newcastle, and in 1561

Pilkington informed Cecil of a young priest who had stood up at his Visitation and refused the oath 'rejoicing much in his own doings' and stating that 'none other temporal man or woman could have power in spiritual matters but only the Pope in Rome'.[78] Open outrages such as these became less common as the decade progressed and Knollys was probably quite close to the truth when he stated in 1568 that 'The Bishop of Durham has his diocese well instructed, though there be obstacles in his way'.[79]

Although the Bishop and Dean worked hard to reform the diocese along the lines they thought best they were never popular figures and soon developed unsavoury reputations stemming from their personal behaviour, and some of the attitudes popularly supposed to be 'puritan'. Covetousness and contentiousness displayed in their dealings with the laity were compounded by a hypocrisy which allowed their own relatives and friends to get away with things which were not considered acceptable for others: Pilkington, who was not unusually dishonest by the standards of the Elizabethan episcopacy, consistently connived at Protestant non-conformity and the non-residence of associates such as Leonard Pilkington and Richard Longworth.[80] And this might have been considered particularly reprehensible in face of the harsh moral code imported into the area in the 1560s. In 1560 Dean Horn suggested 'severe discipline' to prevent 'licencious living' and in the following year moral offenders were being punished in the pillory as a supplement to the more usual sanction of penance.[81]

But punishment depended sometimes on who you were. In August 1561 the Queen wrote to Archbishop Young on a matter of some delicacy –

> we find it strange that in your diocese or province the Earl of Westmorland is permitted to keep the sister of his former wife in manner as his wife, being as we think contrary to the law of God and of man . . . We therefore will you take order . . . that neither this nor such like disorder be suffered uncorrected.

Young stated in mitigation to Cecil that the Earl was 'marvellously affected' to the lady in question and that 'many lawful husbands in England be not in such love with their lawful wives'. Wisely Pilkington did not want to become involved and after an informal conversation with Westmorland commented that 'I had rather other men be judges openly lest he should think me an evil neighbour'. Yet the prosecution proceeded, and Westmorland was in no doubt from whence the malice stemmed. 'There cometh a rumour all over the country . . .', he complained to Cecil, 'that the Queen's Majesty should . . . be my heavy lady and mistress which is my greatest grief and doth most trouble me'. The upshot, he believed, was inevitable; he would be 'defaced' in his country, an intolerable slur for any Elizabethan magnate and a humiliation which might have contributed to his premature death.[82] And this was not an isolated case. Following a midnight raid on a brothel in Bishop Auckland in 1567 George Swinburne was apprehended for fornication with a prostitute called Elizabeth Allanson. Swinburne was a Cathedral almsman and probably of the Chopwell family, and his exposure resulted in the cancellation of his pension. In the light of the statutes this seems wholly justified since almsmen were supposed to be 'oppressed with poverty . . . or crippled or multilated . . . or worn out with old age' and these criteria seemed directly at odds with what had been going on at Bishop Auckland.[83] The point was, however, that the moral offenders tried before the Church courts at York and Durham tended to be representatives of the same families who were at odds with the clergy for different reasons: in Durham the Bishop was uniquely placed to conduct a campaign of harassment using both his civil and ecclesiastical jurisdictions. Protestants presumably did not commit such indiscretions, or at least if they did there were ways and means of preventing public exposure.

However, the aspect of ecclesiastical policy which probably caused the most popular resentment was the opposition to images and in particular those connected with the Palatinate and its past. Pilkington shared the simple concept of worship of most of the Marian exiles –

> where the gospel is preached . . . they are content with an honest place to resort together in . . . with bare walls or else written with scriptures.[84]

This was all well and good at Basle or Geneva, but as a Bishop in England one had to adjust to the embarrassment of Cathedrals and collegiate churches, many of them still heavily overlaid with remnants of the Catholic past. In the old collegiate church of St. Andrew, Auckland, the Bishop

> burst in pieces the College bells . . . and sold and converted them unto his use, and in the lower part of the said College . . . he made a bowling alley and in the house above . . . he built a pair of butts, in which two places he allowed both shooting and bowling.[85]

In the Cathedral Whittingham vied with the Bishop for practicality but proceeded with even greater determination. Holy water stones were put to 'profane uses' in the Dean's kitchen, and most of the pre-Dissolution tombs with images on them were either broken up or used for building, 'for he could not abide any ancient monuments nor nothing that appurtained to any godly religiousness or monastical life'.[86]

Popular revulsion to these acts lived on in tales of ill fortune associated with houses incorporating this looted material, but this was nothing compared with the destruction of the last vestiges of the cult of St. Cuthbert. Cuthbert was more than a Saint. He epitomised the Palatinate and provided it with a social and political focus as well as a religious one: he was a reminder of all that was considered great in the region – the ancient Kingdom of Northumbria, the Mediaeval Priory Church, the victories against the Scots. Insensitive to all this, yet loyal to scriptural dogma concerning images, Whittingham took it on himself to finally wrench the inhabitants of the Palatinate from their Saint and their past. St. Cuthbert's banner, which had been displayed at the battles of Nevilles Cross and Flodden, was burned by Mrs. Whittingham 'in the notable contempt and disgrace of all ancient and goodly relics' and the Saint's statue was 'defaced and broken all in pieces, to the intent that there should be no memory nor token of that holy man St. Cuthbert'.[87] 'Our poor papists weep to see our churches so bare . . .' said Pilkington triumphantly, 'there is nothing in them to make curtsy unto, neither saints nor yet their old little god'.[88]

Even in an age when saint cults had lost some of their potency, all of this shows a hopeless incomprehension on the part of the Dean and his French wife of the emotional feelings of the people of the Palatinate: once again conscience and dogma had prevailed against compromise and understanding, and if the Dean was hated for anything in Durham it was surely for this. Revenge for these and other enormities came during the Rebellion, which was as much an anti-clerical movement as a Roman Catholic crusade. One of the earliest reports from Lord Eure on November 2 said that Pilkington's house had been sacked, and thereafter several informants recounted similar tales.[89] Sir George Bowes stated that 'they did wholly spoil from Mr. Dean of Durham all his household, cattle and corn and so did they from the rest and residue of the churchmen of Durham'; Archbishop Grindal commented that 'they ransacked the property of the Bishop of Durham and that of all the pastors and ministers'; Sir Thomas Gargrave said that 'there was none that was known to favour religion that they left unspoiled.'[90] When fresh stirs were reported around Brancepeth in February 1570 Leonard Pilkington went to Hunsdon to complain 'that the Earl of Westmorland has threatened to take certain prebendaries and others of Durham and hang them'.[91] Fortunately he never got the opportunity since all of the

Protestant clergy fled before the rebel advance, but one wonders what sort of treatment Leonard Pilkington expected. The frequency with which specific unpopular targets were singled out for spoliation by the rebels – the Bishop, the Dean, the Chancellor, for example – indicates that this was a movement of protest directed against predetermined objectives rather than a random and mindless series of attacks.

Yet to many people it must have seemed that there was still a credible alternative in the 1560s. Catholicism survived in virile pockets both amongst the gentry and the populace at large, and its popularity can only have been enhanced by the supposed outrages of the Protestant clergy. Catholic survivalism did not so much emanate from the patronage of the great families as from the rump of the Marian establishment. The Earl of Westmorland's ecclesiastical patronage was minimal, certainly less than was controlled by the Percys in Northumberland. The only living of any importance to which the Earl presented was the wealthy Rectory of Brancepeth, close under the castle walls, occupied between 1558 and 1571 by Nicholas Forster. Forster had no illusions about his position. In 1563 Westmorland described him as 'my chaplain' and during his period in office he demised the entire Rectory rent free to Cuthbert Neville.[92]

Although placemen like this were the exception rather than the rule in Durham, other clergy certainly did live in relationships of deference to prominent Catholic gentry and some families maintained private chapels where either the resident priest or some itinerant papist could say Mass. The Salvins, for example, appear to have maintained a chapel in their house at Croxdale, and in 1562 John Swinburne was fined a hundred marks by the High Commission for unlawfully keeping a priest.[93] But the architects of the Elizabethan settlement had foreseen problems such as these from the beginning, and it was hoped that isolated pockets of Catholicism would soon wilt and die. What they did not bargain for was a more sustained and orchestrated campaign, clear indications of which can be seen in Durham in the 1560s.

The Visitation of 1559 had only partially cleared the Cathedral of reactionary clergy. Eventually Dean Robertson and five prebendaries were deprived, while five more prebendaries – all ex-monks of Durham – survived into the 1560s. The minor corporation was barely touched at all.[94] Some of those prebendaries who conformed in 1559 undoubtedly harboured Catholic beliefs. George Cliffe, for example, had been emphatic that 'the Pope hath and ought to have the jurisdiction ecclesiastical and not the Queen,' and although he eventually submitted he maintained close links with the Nevilles and was watched carefully by Pilkington who had an 'evil liking' of him 'for certain disorders that he suspected him for'. Cliffe was, in fact, the only prebendary to be actively involved in the Rebellion.[95]

Similar suspicions were directed against Thomas Sparke, William Bennett and Stephen Marley: Sparke tried to resist Whittingham's iconoclasm and certainly had dealings with the Tempests, and Marley – the brother of a Louvain exile – was eventually deprived for Catholicism in 1572.[96] Of this group only William Todd proved to be incapable of keeping his reactionary proclivites within the bounds of decorum and in 1567 he was deprived of his stall by the High Commission for habitual drunkenness and because he

> hath used to say superstitious prayers with a loud and audible voice that the people dwelling nigh the places where he was might hear him.

Suspended from his priestly function he was sent to live with relations at Croxdale under a bond of £100.[97] By making this order the High Commission simply strengthened a well established cell of Catholicism. Under the Salvins Croxdale was a well known centre of recusancy, and it was presumably felt that Todd could do little damage there: certainly he could mutter his popish incantations to the local rustics without provoking the sharp reaction he evidently got on the Cathedral close.

Those prebendaries who had been deprived in 1559 had long ago merged into the sort of twilight zone inhabited by Todd after 1567. Although some had gone overseas, Robert Dalton and Anthony Salvin remained in the North and their efforts amongst the gentry were supplemented by those of at least two other senior Marian churchmen, Thomas Sedgwick and William Carter.[98] What evidence we have suggests that these individuals were both mobile and active proselytisers. Robert Dalton's case is perhaps the best documented. Dalton belonged to a wealthy family from West Auckland and was acknowledged to be 'stiff' in his popery: in 1559 he had stated that 'he that sitteth in the seat of Rome hath . . . the jurisdiction ecclesiastical over all Christian realms'. Deprived of his stall he became a semi-permanent houseguest of the nobility and gentry of the North. In 1561 he was with Lord Dacre and two years later he appears in company with the Earl of Westmorland. In 1564 he was prosecuted by the High Commission for making a pretence of conformity to conceal 'an evil and cankered heart' and the fact that he was forbidden from wearing clerical apparel indicates that he was given to performing service according to the old rites. When he made his will in 1569 he was still recalcitrant because he left every householder of St. Helen's, Auckland, a shilling 'to pray for my soul', which might have been a reflection of Dalton's optimism or the high level of survivalism in that part of the county.[99] The case is interesting in many ways. It reveals a mobile Catholic underworld with close links with the nobility and gentry: moreover, the implication in the High Commission records is that Dalton was not an isolated case, because he is bracketed with 'divers other of his sort'. Certainly the support from the gentry was widespread. In the bonds for appearance taken from the prebendaries in 1559 sureties were given by William Lawson of Washington, Gerard Salvin of Croxdale, William Hodgson of Lanchester and Thomas and Robert Tempest of Lanchester amongst others.[100]

One of the most alarming features of this movement, so far as Pilkington was concerned, was the help and support which it was likely to receive from abroad. The establishment of the Kirk in Scotland led to an influx of Catholic refugees into the North 'who mind to do no less mischief in England than they have done in Scotland'. In 1563 Randolph warned especially of John Black, a friar, who had been taken in by the dowager Countess of Northumberland there 'wealthily to lie lurking in corners working mischief':[101] it was an itinerant priest, Copley, a man of 'no certain abiding' who was responsible for the conversion of the Earl of Northumberland in 1567.[102] Soon after 1559 the most scholarly of the Marian prebendaries of Durham, George Bullock, had gone overseas to Louvain, and in the course of the following decade he was joined there by the deprived prebendary Nicholas Marley: young men from the Palatinate travelled abroad to seek Catholic ordinations and a regular traffic in correspondence and books developed.[103] Pilkington was especially concerned about the case of John Raymes, Master of the Blessed Virgin Mary Hospital, Newcastle. Raymes was the nephew of John Swinburne of Chopwell who presented him to the living in 1558 following a period as a fellow of St. John's College, Cambridge. Thus Raymes was both learned and well connected, and it was feared that the resources of the Hospital were being used to fund Catholic subversion. Newcastle, with its expanding coal trade to London and the continent, provided the perfect staging post for people and propaganda. Unsuccessful attempts were made to displace him in 1564 and 1567, latterly in spite of evidence of popery, non-residence and defective orders.[104] In sending Cecil some Louvain propaganda which had fallen into his hands in 1565 Pilkington commented that

> wise men do marvel that policy can suffer such seed of sedition . . . God turn all to the best, but surely evil men pick much evil out of such books.[105]

One possible disseminator of these popish tracts in the North was Thomas White, a Catholic schoolmaster apprehended in 1567. White, it was discovered, had been active in Barnard Castle and other places for about three years and had drawn up to sixty pupils. He rarely attended church and when he did so he 'sitteth far out of the hearing of service reading of other Latin and popish books'. These works were regarded as critical in his corruption of youth. He himself wrote books 'which lend to the subverting of true religion' and he was 'not only a keeper and reader of them privately and publicly, so far as he dare, but also a sender of them abroad in contempt of the Queen's laws'.[106] With contacts amongst the nobility and gentry, an intellectual base at Louvain and men like White prepared to work towards the conversion of young people, Pilkington's fears were not alarmist: long before the coming of the seminary priests and Jesuits he was encountering a Catholic underground which was both organised and militant. Its weakness was that its efforts were geared almost entirely to the propertied class, though in this it did not differ substantially from subsequent movements of Catholic evangelism.

On two occasions at least before 1569 reactionary forces came into direct and hostile conflict with reforming Protestant ministers. In September 1567 the Bishop's Spiritual Chancellor, Robert Swift, Rector of Sedgefield, personally supervised the removal of the communion table and stalls from the choir of Sedgefield church into the nave: in doing this he was obeying an episcopal order of August 1562 and it is puzzling why he should have waited so long to have complied. Perhaps it indicates Swift's lack of serious interest in his church, perhaps he calculated that local opinion needed all of five years to be prepared for such an alteration to the traditional geography of worship. In any event the incident provoked angry reaction. On Monday November 7 the churchwardens entered the church and 'very contemptuously and rebelliously' removed the communion table, calling Swift 'a hinderer and no furtherer of God's service'.[107] Protest continued in the parish. In November 1568 Brian Hedlam 'disturbed the church with talking', refused to take his hat off during service and denied to pay the shilling fine to the churchwardens: that Hedlam was not simply a crank but was a Catholic with a point to make is proved by his active involvement in the Rebellion.[108] Indeed, Sedgefield was to be an important centre of revivalism in 1569. The parish produced some prominent rebels such as Anthony Hebburn,

Ralph Conyers and William Clavering, and under the guidance of one of the churchwardens, Roland Hixson, altars and holy water stones were re-erected and the Protestant service books were burned on the village green: fifty-three men from Sedgefield sued for pardon in 1570.[109] It is tempting to suppose that this unusually high level of violent protest had something to do with the puritanical innovations of Robert Swift, his indifferent interest in his parish, and his intimate connection with the unpopular disciplinary sanctions of the new Protestant hierarchy.

By contrast Barnard Castle was a very different sort of community, a market town dominated by a royal castle and influenced by local families of Protestant gentry, notably the Bowes and Middletons. The town was a chapelry within the Vicarage of Gainford held by the Durham prebendary William Stevenson, and together these Protestant gentlemen concurred to see that the needs of the place were served by as worthy a minister as possible. Early on in the reign the cure was served by Ralph Bailes who in his will in 1566 looked forward to 'the most joyful resurrection of all true and faithful company of the select and chosen stock of Christ':[110] he was replaced by Thomas Clarke in whose appointment Pilkington was involved and who was thought by the Protestants to have 'used himself honestly there'.

However, it appears that not all of the townsmen of Barnard Castle shared this opinion and opposition seems to have been co-ordinated by Thomas Rolandson, Bailiff of the town. They objected in particular to the fact that Clarke did not use the sign of the cross at baptism, that he denied communion to certain parishioners presumably deemed unworthy and that he refused to undertake perambulations on Rogation Day. These breaches with tradition provoked a confrontation in 1567. The four churchwardens took the keys to the church from the parish clerk's 'wench' and barricaded themselves in the building early on a Saturday afternoon: in this they had the backing of Rolandson and three members of the Twenty-Four who 'thought it were good to shut up the doors . . . unto such things as was amiss were reformed'. Despite pleas from Thomas Clarke, Thomas Middleton and a large number of parishioners who came to hear service on Sunday morning the doors remained locked until late in the afternoon after a 'siege' of twenty-seven hours. Speedy retribution followed. Sir George Bowes seized the disobedient wardens and locked them up in the Tollbooth 'but not at the sitting of any Justice' and a case was brought before the Assizes. Meanwhile, Rolandson charged Clarke with puritanism before the High Commission at York, knowing full well he would receive no justice within the diocese.[111] The end result was that Pilkington removed Clarke to the Vicarage of Berwick, which had the double benefit of helping to defuse the situation in Barnard Castle while placing Clarke in an environment where his Protestant innovations would be greeted with enthusiasm rather than bolted doors.

Tensions such as these found open expression when central control temporarily collapsed in November and December 1569. Despite the vague hopes of a Catholic crusade, religious revivalism took the form either of a hostile reaction to Protestant innovation, as at Sedgefield, or an open performance of Catholic rites by conservative clergy, for which there had always been popular sympathy.[112] The Catholic 'underground' of the 1560s, with its élite connotations, had never had much effect on the populace at large which was motivated more by anti-clericalism and a revulsion to iconoclasm than by real hopes of a return to the Papal supremacy.

It is easy and tempting to lay the blame for the happenings of 1569 squarely on the shoulders of the Protestant clergy who followed an abrasive economic policy and arguably moved too quickly towards the standards of the continental reformers. However, that would be too simple and would not do them the justice they deserve. Pilkington's letters continually complain of the lack of support he received from central government and on occasion he goes so far as to suggest that certain policies were actually undermining his position in the North. Certainly it is true that having placed a nest of puritans in the diocese – for whatever reason – the government never had the courage or the inclination to back its representatives to the hilt.

Neither Pilkington nor Whittingham was popular with the Queen, and it is likely that even the support of their patrons – notably the Dudleys – eased when the extent of their opposition to further secularisation became evident. The growing divide also represented a genuine difference of opinion as to policy. For Cecil and others at Court the priorities were compromise and reconciliation, along the lines of the prevailing *via media* ethos, yet Pilkington and his officers favoured more decisive action against the old order and up to a point were able to achieve it because of the remoteness and jurisdictional independence of the Palatinate. Thus, the Durham Protestants were fighting a lone battle, and as time went on and their isolation became increasingly evident, potential opponents were encouraged: Pilkington himself understood that a Bishop in 'displeasure' did more harm than good in the region.[113] The truth of this was clearly born out in the first years of the new reign.

The long vacancy of the see following Tunstall's deprivation and the lack of any concerted action against Catholic officials until 1561 has already been discussed: even then Pilkington was dissatisfied with the scale of the purge because although Robert Meynell was removed from his Palatinate offices he was permitted to retain his seat on the Council of the North –

> such great authority makes many to think evil of my doings because I will not suffer him to rule here as he has done.[114]

The composition of the Commission of the Peace probably also irritated the Bishop because throughout the 1560s it included such well known papists as John Swinburne, Robert Tempest and Gerard Salvin –

> this boldness the people come into because they see that such as refuse to acknowledge their due allegiance escape not only punishment but are had in authority and esteem.[115]

More serious was the retention by the Crown of an important section of the episcopal estates. When Pilkington's temporalities were restored in March 1561 it was discovered that some important lands had been omitted: these were subsequently placed under the Bishop's custody, but not in his possession, in return for an annual rent of £880.[116] The Bishop was furious, and for the next five years he exerted an unrelenting pressure on Cecil for the full restoration of his lands. Firstly, he suggested that this action by the government had greatly weakened his authority –

> here needs authority and power to be given than taken away. They understand the taking away of the Bishop's living whereby his power is the less and so less he is regarded . . . who is there then to be afraid of?[117]

Secondly, he emphasised the practical difficulties of undertaking legal transactions in the detained areas and confided his fears about the ways in which these complications were viewed by the people. Writing to Cecil in 1565 he explained how they gave rise to

> great murmurings . . . and makes many intruders and usurpers . . . which I am sorry should chance in the time or by occasion of any that profess Christ's gospel: and surely, the people say, this is the fruit of our religion to procure such mischiefs.[118]

Whether these arguments had any effect on Cecil is uncertain. However, in 1565 he approached the Bishop for a lease of Craike for his son and since this was part of the detained lands Pilkington took the opportunity to tell him 'that I see not how I may make a good lease in law'.[119]

Thereafter things moved more quickly. By May 1566 restoration was under discussion and in June the Bishop received full possession of his temporalities in return for an annual rent of £1,000. Cecil's lease – the effective price of the deal – was sealed later in the year.[120]

Similar tensions were evident amongst the Protestant clergy themselves who were unable for very long to keep up a united front in face of opposition. Interestingly one of Northumberland's reasons for his disillusionment with the new faith was 'the disagreement and great dissention continually growing . . . amongst the Protestants'.[121] The wisdom of maintaining unity was endorsed early in the reign by the Council of the North which suspended a suit between the Bishop and Chapter because 'they would gladly have no controversy to proceed' between them.[122] But that sort of attitude was not to last long. In 1561 Archbishop Young announced his intention to visit the diocese of Durham as part of his primary metropolitan Visitation. Pilkington, who feared that the whole incident would cause a 'foul clamour', fell back on ancient precedent claiming

> that Archbishop Young had no right to visit him or his diocese nor shall not in his time . . . and . . . the Archbishop's Sumner bringing a letter, Bishop Pilkington said to him thus, 'If thy master will needs come to visit me bad him send me word and I will meet him in the midst of Tees.[123]

This sort of fighting talk was likely to win the Bishop friends in the Palatinate, but it put a strain on his relationships with his colleagues at York because Young was said to be 'grievously offended' by the failure of his Visitation.

The Archbishop got his revenge some years later. In 1566 and 1567 the Dean and five prebendaries of Durham were called before the High Commission Court at York charged with vestiarian offences. Some of the most influential individuals in the diocese were involved, including Robert Swift, the Chancellor, John Pilkington, Archdeacon of Durham, and Thomas Lever, men who had the full backing and support of the Bishop: indeed, Parker believed that Pilkington would give up his diocese rather than enforce the wearing of vestments amongst the clergy. In the end all agreed to conform except Thomas Lever and William Birche who were deprived of their prebends but permitted to keep their other livings.[124] The case was by any standard a startling one and it was the first serious challenge to Pilkington's policy in the Palatinate – a challenge, moreover, from his own side rather than the much vaunted Catholic 'opposition'. However, the two were more closely interlinked than at first glance may seem evident. As the Bishop and his officers became increasingly isolated from politicians and ecclesiastical colleagues at London and York, they became more vulnerable to attacks from those within the Palatinate who began to consider seriously the possibilities of change. Dean Hutton of York thought that the vestiarian controversy was 'a great occasion given to the adversary to rejoice' and Whittingham delivered a similar message to the Earl of Leicester in eloquent and aggrieved tones –

> Alas! my Lord, that such compulsion should be used towards us and so great lenity towards the papists . . . These misers laugh and triumph to see us dealt with, yea, not ashamed hereupon to brag that they trust that the rest of their things shall follow.[125]

And follow they did. The arrival of Mary Queen of Scots in England in 1568 and the appointment of Sussex as Lord President of the Council of the North provided the practical possibility of change which people in the Palatinate had looked to since 1561.

The 1560s had thus been a period of ferment in the North during which new ideas and attitudes had come into headlong conflict with the old – indeed, it was arguably the critical decade of the century. In the forefront of these new ideas had been the Protestant clerical establishment which assaulted the sensitivities of the local community on two fronts. First, by way of a campaign to recover alienated ecclesiastical lands which was seen as an unprecedented attack on the property rights of the gentry. Secondly, by way of doctrinal innovation which induced militant anti-clericalism and probably stiffened Catholic survivalism. Yet the effect of all this should not be exaggerated. Even though the 1560s was a decade filled with tension, the old order and the new co-existed side by side for much of the time. The Earl of Westmorland, who according to Professor MacCaffrey had 'fewer reasons for resentment of the Crown' than Northumberland, accepted the new regime and tried to work with it so far as he was able: in 1561 Pilkington expressed surprise that he 'finds more gentleness than he looked for or deserved' from Henry Neville, and in 1564 the Bishop commended Charles Neville's work as a Justice placing him in esteem even above his Spiritual Chancellor, Robert Swift.[126] There are some notable instances of cooperation, such as the founding of Darlington Grammar School in 1563, and during this decade Westmorland was building a large house in the Market Place at Durham in an attempt to shift his centre of influence away from the ancient castles of Brancepeth and Raby closer to the real administrative hub of the county.[127]

In the 1564 report to the Privy Council the Durham Justices were notable for their indecision rather than their active hostility to government policy.[128] This may seem surprising in the light of recent events, and from that same report it is clear that in other parts of the country there was more open opposition from the gentry than there was in the Palatinate. Poor Bishop Scory of Hereford, for example, was at his wits end with the local papists, and like Pilkington he felt the need of more resolute support from London.[129] However, Hereford differed substantially from Durham in the way in which the diocese was administered in the 1560's. At Hereford the Catholics had few real grievances because they were still effectively in control, despite the rumblings of Scory and Dean Ellis. Scory emphasised the critical role of the Cathedral in the process of Protestantisation and how his own establishment had failed –

> if the Cathedral church of Hereford were reformed . . . the whole diocese would soon be . . . in like manner reformed . . . this church which should be the light of all the diocese is very darkness.[130]

Amongst the English dioceses in the 1560s only Durham had a puritan Bishop who possessed *jura regalia* and was able to pursue a semi-independent policy: only Durham had a Cathedral dominated by militant Protestants and committed to an economic revival at the expense of its Catholic neighbours. The Durham gentry were indecisive in 1564 because of the scale of the task they were up against and their heavy dependence on ecclesiastical patronage: they had no love for their new neighbours, but they were sensible enough to see that there was very little they could do about it. The Protestant establishment might have won without a fight had it not been for events taking place in Scotland.

When an alternative seemed to present itself in 1568 potential leaders who had been lying low and smarting under supposed slights and insults came to the surface. Christopher Neville, guardian of the family honour and more incensed about the dealings of Dean Whittingham than the Earl, was one of them: Sir George Bowes had no doubt that he 'hath done more harm to that noble young Earl, his nephew, than can be thought'.[131] Others were John Swinburne of Chopwell and Robert Tempest of Holmside. Tempest had been displaced as Sheriff, had lost valuable leases and had others threatened and had been under constant scrutiny as 'evil in religion'. Swinburne's religious disorders were notorious, he had lost valuable coal producing land to the Bishop and he had had leases and rights of advowson challenged. All three of these individuals had more to complain of than most because of their treatment at the hands of the new hierarchy: all represented the first generation of Reformation change – Catholic recipients of monastic or dubious Henrician leases – under challenge from the buoyant and resurgent Protestant clergy of the 1560s. Places on the Commission of the Peace did not compensate for such blows to faith, family or fortune. There was therefore every reason why Neville, Tempest and Swinburne should have approached Westmorland as representatives of a disaffected element amongst the gentry, the 'wicked councillors' singled out by Bowes and others. The scenario is well known. Westmorland, though he had little inclination of his own to take drastic action, succumbed to the pressure exerted on him, partly because of his own weakness of character and inexperience, partly because of the notions of honour and *noblesse oblige* with which he was imbued.[132] When he took the field against the Crown in 1569 he reassumed *de facto* the position from which the Dean and Chapter had deposed his family in 1564: he rode to his ruin as the champion of the Reformation settlement of Henry VIII, rather than some latter day Kingmaker fixated by a name and a glorious past.

NOTES

1. P.R.O., SP/12/20/5.
2. *Ibid.*, SP/12/20/25.
3. *The Works of Bishop Pilkington*, ed. Scholefield, Parker Society (1842), p. 491.
4. W. MacCaffrey, *The Shaping of the Elizabethan Regime* (1969), pp. 199–246 (hereafter MacCaffrey). Less has been written on the Rebellion of the Earls than on the Pilgrimage of Grace. The two most important papers to date are R. R. Reid, 'The Rebellion of the Earls, 1569', *Transactions of the Royal Historical Society*, 2nd series, 20 (1906), and M. E. James, 'The Concept of Order and the Northern Rising of 1569', *Past and Present*, 60 (1973): neither pays much heed to the local situation prior to the revolt.
5. Even Northumberland conceded that the decision to go ahead was 'very strange'. C. Sharp, *Memorials of the Rebellion of 1569* (1840), pp. 195/6, 199 (hereafter Sharp).
6. MacCaffrey, pp. 205, 206.
7. Sharp, pp. 20, 28, 54.
8. *Ibid.*, p. 197.
9. *Ibid.*, p. 52. Also excepted from the pardon, apart from the two Earls, were Egremond Radcliffe, Richard Norton, Thomas Markenfield, Francis Norton and Thomas Gennye.
10. *Ibid.*, p. xiii, MacCaffrey, p. 206.
11. MacCaffrey, p. 222.
12. Sharp, p. 42.
13. For a general discussion of the political situation in the Palatinate during this period see M. E. James, *Family, Lineage and Civil Society (1974)*, pp. 41–51.
14. *A.P.C., 1556–58*, p. 250.
15. R. R. Reid, *The King's Council in the North* (1921), pp. 191–208.
16. C. H. Hunter Blair, 'Wardens and Deputy Wardens of the Marches', *A.A.*, 4th Series, 28, (1950), pp. 71–74.
17. Northumberland's usual residence in the 1560s was Topcliffe, Yorkshire, and his brother, the loyalist Sir Henry Percy, enjoyed considerable influence in Northumberland.
18. A. A. Luxmoore, 'The Lieutenancy of County Durham', *A.A.*, 4th Series, 30, (1952), p. 217.
19. *C.P.R., 1558–60*, p. 340.
20. *C.S.P.For., 1559–60*, No. 850. In March 1560 Meynell and Wandisford complained to Winchester that William Claxton, Robert Hebburn, John Swinburne and William Brackenbury had been left out of the Commission of the Peace and that Robert and John Conyers 'men unknown' has been included. By 1562 Brackenbury was back in the Durham Commission and Swinburne was included for Northumberland: there is no reference in this year to Robert or John Conyers. *C.P.R., 1560–63*, pp. 441, 445.
21. *Correspondence of Matthew Parker*, ed. Bruce and Perowne, Parker Society (1853), p. 124.

22. *C.S.P.For., 1561–62*, No. 371.
23. In 1562 Catholic sympathisers such as Gerard Salvin and John Swinburne were both represented on the Commissions of the Peace for Durham and Northumberland. *C.P.R., 1560–63*, pp. 441, 445. In 1562/63 Gerard Salvin replaced Robert Meynell as Steward of the Dean and Chapter Halmote Court. D.C.R., Treasurer's Book 3.
24. D.C.L., Sharpe Ms. 57 (Randall MS.), ff. 123, 127, C. H. Hunter Blair, 'The Sheriffs of the County of Durham', *A.A.*, 4th Series, 22 (1944), p. 49. Fleetwood, who had important Parliamentary connections, was a particularly valuable ally, *The House of Commons, 1558–1603* (1981), ed. Hasler, Vol. II, pp. 133–138.
25. M. E. James, 'The Sixteenth and Seventeenth Centuries,' p. 221, in *Durham County*, (British Association, 1970).
26. D. Marcombe, 'The Dean and Chapter of Durham, 1558–1603' (unpub. Ph.D. thesis, Durham University, 1973), pp. 56, 72–75.
27. D. Marcombe, 'The Durham Dean and Chapter: old abbey writ large', in *Continuity and Change* (1976), ed. O'Day and Heal, pp. 135–37, R. B. Dobson, *Durham Priory* (1974), pp. 58–60, 352.
28. Marcombe, thesis, pp. 181–90.
29. P. Collinson, 'The Puritan Classical Movement in the reign of Elizabeth' (unpub. Ph.D. thesis, London University, 1957), p. 31. Note in comparison the early development of Arminianism in the diocese in the early seventeenth century.
30. C. Garrett, *The Marian Exiles* (1938), p. 302, Sharp p. 186.
31. P.R.O., SP/12/20/5, *C.S.P., For., 1561–62*, No. 371, B.L., Lansdowne MS. 36, f. 138.
32. *The Works of Bishop Pilkington*, p. 125.
33. B.L., Lansdowne MS. 36, f. 136.
34. *Sermons and Society* (1970), ed. Welsby, pp. 66–72, Marcombe, thesis, pp. 88–90, D. Marcombe, 'Bernard Gilpin: anatomy of an Elizabethan legend', *N.H.*, 16 (1980), pp. 27–28.
35. *The Diary of Henry Machyn, 1550–63*, ed. Nichols, Camden Society (1847) p. 227, *C.S.P.For., 1561–62*, No. 371.
36. In 1561 Pilkington was already in conflict with Lord Robert Dudley over the leasing of Howden to Walter Jobson: in August he complained to Cecil that 'we may preach here and do what we will, but if we fill not their bellies all is in vain'. *C.S.P.For., 1561–62*, No. 371.
37. *The Works of Bishop Pilkington*, p. 595.
38. P.R.O., SP/12/11/16. John Watson of London, a relation of Dean Watson, had in his possession the Letters Patent of Henry VIII founding the Dean and Chapter, Edward VI's confirmation and various other important documents. P.R.O., C.3, Bundle 50, No. 105.
39. The accusation was made to Whittingham by his Genevan colleague, Thomas Wood, P. Collinson, *Letters of Thomas Wood, Puritan*, Institute of Historical Research, Special Supplement No. 5, pp. 6–9. For the effects of marriage on the clergy and their inclination to found landed dynasties, see Marcombe, thesis, pp. 25–30, 41–43.
40. B.L., Lansdowne MS. 8/87.

41. *Ibid.*
42. D.C.L., Hunter MS. 4b f. 377, P.R.O., Durham 7, 1 (Box 1), *37th Report of the Deputy Keeper of Public Records*, Appendix 1, p. 72.
43. For suspected misappropriation at the Blessed Virgin Mary Hospital, Newcastle, see below.
44. *C.S.P.For., 1561–62*, No. 371.
45. *H.M.C., Pepys MS.* II. 265.
46. D.C.L., Randall MS. 12 (Depositions concerning Sherburn Hospital), G. Allan, *Collectanea ad Statum Civilem et Ecclesiasticum Comitatus Dunelmensis* (1763–99): section relating to Sherburn Hospital.
47. D.C.R.O., D/Sa/D. 512.
48. *C.S.P. Addenda, 1566–79*, Vol. XIV, No. 14. According to Strype Pilkington 'had made a certain instrument for the disannulling of these leases ... but it wanted the Queen's confirmation'. J. Strype *The History of the Life and Acts of Edmund Grindal* (1821), p. 185.
49. For a general discussion of Dean and Chapter estate management during this period, see Marcombe, thesis, pp. 95–121, 122–60.
50. D.C.R., Treasurer's Book 6. Between 1558 and 1564 the Chapter issued only 2 letters of attorney: between 1565 and 1569 it issued 10. Chapter Register B, ff. 135, 139, 207/8, 211, 215, 235, 236, 239, Chapter Register C, ff. 1/2, 5.
51. See Marcombe, thesis, pp. 123–32.
52. D.C.R., Chapter Register A, ff. 45, 196, 201/2, 205/6.
53. Leases had been made in the name of the 'Dean of the Cathedral Church of Durham and the Chapter of the same' not in the name of the 'Dean and Chapter of Durham of the Cathedral Church of Christ and Blessed Mary the Virgin'. *Durham Cathedral Statutes*, ed. Thompson, S.S., 143 (1929), p. 234.
54. D.C.R., Chapter Register C, ff. 9–12.
55. *Durham Cathedral Statutes* p. 241, D.C.R., York Book, ff. 26–28.
56. D.C.R., Receiver's Books 9, 10.
57. D.D.R., DR. V. ff. 153–62.
58. D.C.R., Chapter Register B, f. 214.
59. *Ibid.*, f. 235, Register C, ff. 1/2.
60. P.R.O., SP/12/48/58.
61. *Ibid.*, SP/12/48/56. At about the same time as the Dean and Chapter suspended the Neville fee the Earl 'denieth to be bound to pay' a pension owing to the Chapter out of the Rectory of Staindrop. D.C.R., Receiver's Book 9.
62. Calverley received his first payment in 1568/9. D.C.R., Treasurer's Book 6.
63. D.C.R., Chapter Register B, ff. 187, 198/9, 221/1. The Chapter took the precaution of regranting Toft's lease incorporating the new preamble.
64. *Ibid.*, Receiver's Books 7, 10.
65. For a general discussion of the position of Chapter tenants see D. Marcombe, 'Church Leaseholders: the decline and fall of a rural élite', in *Princes and Paupers in the English Church* (1981), ed. O'Day and Heal, pp. 255–75.

66. D.C.R., Chapter Register B, ff. 125, 224/5, Consistory Court Proceedings, temp. Tunstall and Pilkington, f. 29. The payment of £20 had been made by Thomas Swinburne of Edlingham in respect of a concurrent lease of the Rectory of Edlingham.
67. Of the Chapter tenants who sued for pardon in 1570 William Thorpe of Wolviston and John Robinson of Mid Merrington became leaders of the protest movement: Thorpe especially was thought to be 'a great hinderer of others.' *C.P.R., 1569–72*, pp. 99, 114, Marcombe thesis, p. 154.
68. *C.P.R., 1569–72*, pp. 89, 94, 99, 100, 101, 103, 106, 108, 114. There are, of course, limitations in this sort of analysis, notably the fact that pardons were often regarded as an 'insurance policy' and that not all persons pardoned actually participated in the Rebellion. It is also interesting to note the heavy involvement of the Weardale men in the Rebellion: here too tenurial matters had been an issue for many years.
69. According to Sussex the major strength of the rebel army was in its horsemen, which implies that the strongest support came from the gentry and yeomanry. Sharp p. 49.
70. *Ibid.*, p. 202.
71. *Ibid.*, p. 44.
72. Whittingham gives a picture of the Cathedral at work in B.L., Lansdowne MS. 7/12. See also Marcombe, 'The Durham Dean and Chapter: old Abbey writ large', pp. 131–40.
73. Visitation material is non-existent for this period and the ecclesiastical court records are incomplete: however, an impression of the workings of the diocesan administration in the 1560s can be obtained from a book of precedents kept by Robert Swift, D.C.L., Raine MS. 124, and by *The Registers of Tunstall and Pilkington*, ed. Hinde, S.S., 161 (1952).
74. For the limitations of the *Valor Ecclesiasticus* see, Marcombe, thesis, pp. 387–89, where it is suggested that a multiple of four times the *Valor* figure might prove a more reliable guide for the later sixteenth century.
75. P.R.O., SP/15/12/108.
76. B. Wilson, 'The Changes of the Reformation period in Durham and Northumberland', (unpub. Ph.D. thesis, Durham University, 1939), pp. 192/3, *Depositions and Ecclesiastical Proceedings*, ed. Raine, S.S., 21 (1845), p. 147.
77. B. Wilson, thesis, pp. 196/7, D.C.L., Hunter MS. 6 f. 25. *Registers of Tunstall and Pilkington*, p. 146.
78. C.S.P. For., 1559–60, No. 572, P.R.O., SP/12/20/25.
79. *Calendar of Scottish Papers, Vol. II, 1563–69*, No. 829.
80. Marcombe, thesis, pp. 35, 185–89, D.C.L., Hunter MS. 12 f. 5.0. For a more general consideration of the charge of hypocrisy as applied to the Protestant clergy, see C. Haigh, 'Puritan Evangelism in the reign of Elizabeth I', *English Historial Review*, XCII (1977), pp. 34/5, D. Marcombe, 'Bernard Gilpin: anatomy of an Elizabethan legend', *N.H.*, 16 (1980), pp. 28–30.
81. P.R.O., SP/12/11/16, *C.S.P. For., 1561–62*, No. 371.
82. C.I.A. Ritchie, *The Ecclesiastical Courts of York* (1956), pp. 175–77, P.R.O., SP/12/20/5.

83. D.C.L., Raine MS. 124, f. 101, D.C.R., Treasurer's Books 2, 3, 4, 5, 6, *The Statutes of the Cathedral Church of Durham*, ed. Thompson, S.S., 143 (1929), p. 147.
84. *The Works of Bishop Pilkington*, p. 129. In 1568/9 the Chapter undertook repairs to several of is impropriate churches: these included 'washing' and 'whiting' the choirs at Aycliffe and Heighington, D.C.R., Treasurer's Book 6.
85. J. Raine, *Auckland Castle* (1852), p. 70, J. F. Hodgson, 'The Church of St. Andrew, Auckland', *A.A.*, New Series, 20, pp. 169/70.
86. *The Rites of Durham*, ed. Fowler, S.S., 107 (1902), pp. 60/1, 81/2.
87. *Ibid.*, pp. 26/7, 68/9, 75.
88. *The Works of Bishop Pilkington*, p. 129.
89. *C.S.P., Addenda, 1566–79*, Vol. XV, No. 8.
90. Sharp p. 186, *The Zurich Letters (1558–79)*, ed. Robinson, Parker Society (1842), p. 218.
91. *C.S.P., Addenda, 1566–79*, Vol. XVII, No. 76.
92. B. Wilson, thesis pp. 320/21, D.C.R.O., D/Sa/D. 1250.
93. *Wills and Inventories 1*, ed. Raine, S.S., Vol. 2 (1835) p. 348, *The Camden Miscellany Vol. 9*, ed. Simpson, Camden Society, New Series, 53 (1895), p. 67.
94. Marcombe, thesis pp. 164–69.
95. D.D.R., South Road, DR.V/6 (1594 Judge v George Cliffe: depositions), P.R.O., SP/12/10 ff. 32–38, *Depositions and Ecclesiastical Proceedings*, pp. 136/7. In 1571 Cliffe was presented to the Rectory of Brancepeth by Lady Adeline Neville, *Registers of Tunstall and Pilkington*, p. 170.
96. Marcombe, thesis, pp. 178, 204.
97. D.C.L., Hunter Ms. 18a f. 115, D.C.R.O., D/Sa/L 202 ff. 1–15, B.I., High Commission Act Book 1, f. 203, 3 ff. 116–118.
98. Sedgwick had been Professor of Divinity at Cambridge and Carter Archdeacon of Northumberland. *C.S.P., Addenda, 1547–65*, Vol. XI, No. 45.
99. *Ibid.*, P.R.O., SP/12/10 ff. 32–38. *A.A.*, 2nd series, 10, p. 83, Newcastle Reference Library, J. Raine, *Testamenta Dunelmensis*, B.3 (will of Robert Dalton of West Auckland, clerk), B.I., High Commission Act Book 1, f. 114.
100. P.R.O., SP/12/10 ff. 175–81.
101. *C.S.P. For., 1563*, No. 839.
102. Sharp, pp. 204, 213.
103. *C.S.P., Addenda, 1547–65*, Vol. XI, No. 45, D.C.R., Treasurer's Book 6, G. Anstruther, *The Seminary Priests 1, 1558–1603* (1968), p. 349.
104. *C.P.R., 1563–66*, p. 92, B.I., High Commission Act Book 5 f. 248, 6 f. 62, 'St. Mary the Virgin's Hospital, Newcastle', *A.A.*, New Series, 7 (1876), p. 203, A.L. Raimes, 'Shortflatt Tower and its owners', *A.A.*, 4th Series, 32 (1954), pp. 146/7, Wilson, thesis, pp. 412/13, *The Camden Miscellany Vol. 9*, p. 67.
105. B.L., Lansdowne MS. 8/87.
106. D.C.L., Raine MS. 124 f. 98.
107. *Depositions and Ecclesiastical Proceedings*, pp. 118–20.
108. *Ibid.*, pp. 111/12, 187, 190, 193.

109. *Ibid.*, pp. 183–93, *C.P.R., 1569–72*, pp. 101, 106, 111.
110. *Wills and Inventories 1*, p. 259.
111. D.C.L., Raine MS. 124, ff. 98/99, B.1., High Commission Act Book 4 ff. 28, 34/5, 56, D.D.R., DR V/2 f. 94–6.
112. Examples of the revival of old rites in 1569 are to be found in several parishes in the diocese with the areas around Durham City and Stockton and Darlington being best represented: see, for example, the case of John Brown, curate of Witton Gilbert, *Depositions and Ecclesiastical Proceedings*, pp. 174/5.
113. *The Works of Bishop Pilkington*, pp. ix/x.
114. P.R.O., SP/12/20/25.
115. *C.P.R., 1560–63*, pp. 441, 445, *1563–66*, pp. 25, 29, P.R.O., SP/12/20/25.
116. The exceptions were Norham, Norhamshire, Allerton, Allertonshire, Craike, Sadberge, Middleham, Easington Ward, Easington Coronator, Cotham Mundeville, Gateshead and a pension out of Howden. *C.P.R., 1560–63*, pp. 120, 167.
117. P.R.O., SP/12/20/5.
118. B.L., Lansdowne MS. 8/84.
119. *Ibid.*, 8/81.
120. *C.S.P., 1547–80*, Vol. XXIX No. 78, 81, *C.P.R., 1563–66*, p. 496/7, D.C.R., Chapter Register B, ff. 230/1.
121. Sharp p. 213.
122. P.R.O., Durham 7, Box 2 pt. 1 (Stevenson v Hutton).
123. *C.S.P. For., 1561–62*, No. 371, D.C.L., Hunter MS. 35A f. 40.
124. B.I., High Commission Act Book 3 ff. 54, 64, 71, 77–79, 83–84, 90, 93, 97–100, 108–20, 133–34, 146–55, 159–60, 163, 167–68, 4 ff. 8, 15–16, *Correspondence of Matthew Parker*, p. 237.
125. *State Papers, 1571–96* (1759), ed. Murdin, Oct. 6 1572, Matthew Hutton to Lord Burghley, J. Strype, *The Life and Acts of Matthew Parker* (1821), Vol. III, p. 83.
126. MacCaffrey, p. 226, *C.S.P. For., 1561–62*, No. 371, *The Camden Miscellany Vol. 9*, pp. 66–67.
127. *C.P.R., 1560–63*, p. 509, D.U.L., Mickleton and Spearman MS. 23 ff. 119/20.
128. *The Camden Miscellany Vol. 9*, pp. 65/67. Durham diocese had 34 undetermined JPs (the highest number in the survey), 11 favourable and 2 unfavourable.
129. *Ibid.*, pp. 11–23. Hereford had 43 'unfavourable' Justices.
130. *Ibid.*, pp. 20/21.
131. Sharp, p. 34.
132. The influence of his wife was clearly critical. Northumberland stated 'they could never get hold of him till the last hour and then by procurement of his wife'. Sharp, pp. 199, 207.

The Distribution and Use of Ecclesiastical Patronage in the Diocese of Durham, 1558–1640

Jane Freeman

From the mid sixteenth century the distribution of ecclesiastical patronage was wider and the variety of patrons greater than ever before. To the many individuals, officers and institutions whose right to nominate to ecclesiastical livings had survived the Reformation were added those who had acquired the patronage formerly held by monastic houses. To the nobleman or high official those rights were parts, although not unimportant parts, of a greater network of patronage; to the gentleman who was patron of his parish church, they offered the opportunity of shaping the religious life of his household and locality; to the great mass of the clergy they were the determinants of prospects and prosperity. From the time of taking orders the clergyman was committed to the system of patronage. To be ordained he required some title, some evidence that he could maintain himself without recourse to labour unfitted to his new profession. The monasteries had once provided the majority of titles but the post-Reformation clergy had to look elsewhere. For a favoured few the Universities or the households of great men provided the necessary security, but the majority could hope for nothing better than a parish curacy, a schoolmastership or some minor post in a Cathedral or charitable institution. Each of these places and any later preferment was in the gift of some person or body. The purpose of this essay is to identify those who held ecclesiastical patronage in the diocese of Durham and to examine the use they made of their rights in the eighty years after the accession of Elizabeth I.

The livings to which patrons presented and to which clergy aspired were chiefly those in the parishes. Most clergy held their first and many their only living as assistant or incumbent in a parish. In the diocese of Durham parochial livings ranged from Houghton-le-Spring Rectory, valued at £124 a year in 1535[1] and one of the most sought-after benefices of the English church, to assistant curacies in parishes where even the incumbent's income was meagre. In the 1560's there were about a hundred endowed Rectories and Vicarages in the diocese.[2] In another thirty parishes all the tithes had been appropriated and the minister who served the cure was a stipendiary, known variously as a Vicar or Curate. There were also some seventy-five dependent chapelries. Common throughout the diocese, these were found in greatest numbers in the large parishes of the North and West where they served the scattered settlements of the dales. Two changes only are recorded in the number and type of endowed livings before 1640; Kimblesworth Rectory and the neighbouring independent chapelry of Witton Gilbert were united as a single living in 1593 and Staindrop, formerly a stipendiary Vicarage, was re-endowed by Sir Henry Vane in 1635.[3]

Far greater changes took place in the dependent chapelries, especially in Northumberland. In 1563 many were vacant and some were never filled thereafter. No official clerical service is recorded at Belsay in Bolam or at North and South Charlton in Ellingham after 1563, or at Dishington in Newburn, Bednell in Bamburgh, Fenton in Kirknewton or Harbottle in Alwinton after January 1578.[4] James Pilkington, Bishop of Durham 1561-76, blamed the vacancies on the inadequate endowment of the chapelries and the consequent difficulty of finding clergy to serve them.[5] Lack of lay demand and the weak legal position of some chapelries after the Dissolution of the Chantries may have been equally to blame. Curates of dependent chapelries, even so, continued to form the largest group of unbeneficed clergy in the Northern Archdeaconry. In the Archdeaconry of Durham there were always fewer chapels and most unbeneficed clergy were assistants to incumbents. Beneficed clergy employed assistants because of illness or absence, but the chief cause of their employment was pluralism and almost half the parishes in which curates served were held in plurality. When the practice was at its height in the diocese, in the 1570s and again in the 1630s, the demand for assistant clergy increased in direct relation to the concentration of benefices in fewer hands.[6]

Livings outside the parishes were fewer but more various than those within. Many appointments were connected with the Cathedral or with the diocesan bureaucracy. The Marian statutes of the Cathedral provided for twelve prebendaries, twelve minor canons and a few miscellaneous officers including the Masters of the Grammar and Song Schools and the 'epistoler' and 'gospeller'. The prebendaries were senior clergy, usually pluralists with wealthy livings elsewhere in the diocese, but the minor canons and lesser functionaries rarely obtained higher preferment than a parochial benefice of moderate value. The two Archdeacons, of Durham and Northumberland, were parish clergy by virtue of the annexation to their offices of the livings of Easington and Howick. Other administrative posts were less closely married to the cure of souls and although the Chancellor of the diocese and the officials and deputies who presided over courts and visitations were often clergy, there was no rule or discernible pattern in their other appointments. The survival or refoundation of charitable institutions after the Reformation provided a handful of posts as Masters or Chaplains of hospitals and almshouses. Several schoolmasterships and some half dozen lectureships established during our period were the only new clerical posts, small compensation for the disappearance of so many minor clerical livings during and after the Reformation.[7]

Who then were the patrons of these various livings? Those whose identities are most easily traced are the patrons who presented to independent benefices to which the Bishop instituted their nominees; those presentations are recorded in episcopal registers and in the institution lists now in the Public Record Office.[8] The most striking feature of the distribution of advowsons of such livings in the diocese is the predominance of episcopal patronage. Owners of the advowsons of one hundred and seven parochial livings in thc 1560s have been identified; in thirty-one parishes the Bishop of Durham was patron. The livings in his gift were wealthy as well as numerous.[9] They included seven Rectories which had been valued at over £50 a year in 1535, among them Houghton-le-Spring, all in the Archdeaconry of Durham.[10] The Bishop's patronage in Northumberland was less extensive but still accounted for approximately one fifth of all benefices in the Archdeaconry, most of them of at least moderate value. The Bishop also presented to the two Archdeaconries and to the twelve valuable prebends of Durham Cathedral. If all these advowsons were kept in the Bishop's own hand, his control over his clergy was potentially much greater than that of most of his fellow diocesans.[11]

Even where the Bishop was not patron, ecclesiastical influence was strong. The Dean and Chapter of Durham presented to eleven benefices in Durham and seven in Northumberland.[12] All were in parishes where the Dean and Chapter held estates, usually the impropriated Rectory, and which were subject to their peculiar jurisdiction.[13] The Archdeacon of Northumberland held a single advowson, that of the Rectory of St. Mary in the North Bailey, in the City of Durham. He rarely presented to the living, which was a very poor one, and for much of the late sixteenth century and the early seventeenth it remained vacant. In Northumberland the Bishop of Carlisle was patron of four benefices, among them the Vicarage of Newcastle-upon-Tyne, the most important commercial centre in the North East of England, and the politically less significant but valuable Rectory of Rothbury. The Dean and Chapter of Carlisle presented to the Vicarages of Corbridge and Whittingham. A quasi-ecclesiastical influence was brought to bear by academic and charitable foundations. The Master and Brethren of Sherburn Hospital, the largest almshouse in the diocese, presented to three small parishes in South Durham, Sockburn, Bishopton and Grindon, and the Hospital at Greatham held the Rectory and advowson of that parish. Only one benefice in County Durham was in the gift of a University College, Gainford, to which Trinity College, Cambridge presented. In Northumberland two Oxford colleges, Merton and Balliol, held advowsons: Ponteland and Embleton in the former case and Long Benton in the latter.

The remaining benefices, just under half the total, were subject to lay patronage. The greatest lay patron in the diocese, as in the country as a whole, was the Crown.[14] Fourteen benefices in Northumberland and eight in Durham were in the monarch's gift. Although the majority were Vicarages of little value, in 1570 the Crown also held two Rectories, Middleton-in-Teesdale and Simonburn, for which there was fierce competition. The only other extensive block of patronage in lay hands was held by the Earl of Northumberland. In 1557 the Northumberland title and estates were restored to the Percy family. Among them were the advowsons of Long Houghton, Ellingham, Alnham, Chatton, Warkworth, Long Horsley, Kirkwhelpington and Newburn; all were in the Earl's own county but he presented only to four or perhaps five of them.[15] Three other noble families held advowsons. The Nevilles, Earls of Westmorland, presented to the Rectory of St. Mary in the South Bailey, in the City of Durham, and to that of Brancepeth. The Lords Ogle were patrons of Bothal and of the adjacent living of Sheepwash. Morpeth Rectory was in the gift of the Lords Dacre. Other lay patrons were gentry whose estates often lay in or near the parishes to which they presented. The advowson descended with the chief manor of a parish less frequently than might be supposed, but some examples can be found; the advowson and manor of Hurworth were bought by Sir Leonard Beckwith *c.* 1540 and sold by his son in 1607 to Henry Lawson whose family held them until after the Civil War.[16] In both

Archdeaconries, but more commonly in Northumberland, some advowsons were shared between two or three families. At Alston, a Cumberland parish within the Northern Archdeaconry, the living was in the gift of members of the Hilton, Archer and Whitfield families in turn and at Ingram the right of presentation was shared by Ogles, Dentons and Collingwoods. An unusual division of rights took place at Tynemouth, where the Earl of Northumberland and Sir Ralph Deleval were joint owners of the Rectory estate and advowson in the early seventeenth century. In 1623 a presentation was made to the living in both their names.[17]

Lay influence was proportionately stronger in donative livings than in endowed Rectories and Vicarages.[18] Most parishes where all the tithes had been impropriated were donatives, whose Curates and Vicars were required to obtain the Bishop's licence to serve but did not receive episcopal institution. The livings were thus more completely controlled by the patron, who was usually also the owner of the tithes. The largest group of donative livings was held by the Crown but both tithes and advowsons were often leased by local gentry. The greatest farmers of spiritualities belonging to the Crown in North East England were the Forsters of Bamburgh. In the late sixteenth century Sir John Forster appointed ministers to Bamburgh and its chapelries and to Carham as tenant to the Crown, and he was also farmer and patron of Hexham and its chapelries, a peculiar of York diocese within the County of Northumberland and a Crown impropriation.[19] The tithes and advowsons of five wholly impropriate parishes which were also subject to their jurisdiction belonged to the Dean and Chapter of Durham and appointments to the independent curacy of Ebchester were made by the impropriator, the Master of Sherburn Hospital.

The extent of patronage held by ecclesiastical officers and institutions changed little before 1640. There was no exchange between Crown and Bishop to increase the episcopal share of advowsons and impropriations at the expense of landed estates as at York, or to substitute less desirable livings for the wealthy benefices previously in the Bishop's gift, as at Worcester.[20] There was, however, some redistribution of advowsons held by the laity. Initially the patronage of the Crown was considerably increased by the forfeiture of the estates of those who took part in the Rebellion of 1569, including the advowsons held by the Earls of Westmorland and Northumberland and by Lord Dacre. The only permanent substantial gains made by the Crown were the advowsons of Morpeth and Brancepeth. Presentation to the church of St. Mary in the South Bailey, as to its sister church in the Archdeacon of Northumberland's gift, was a rare occurrence and the acquisition of its advowson was of little significance. Most of the livings in Percy's gift were restored, a process which was complete by the second decade of the seventeenth century, although it is impossible to trace the date at which each was returned. By then the Earl of Northumberland's patronage was even more extensive than it had been in the 1560s, since the advowson of Ilderton and a share in that of Tynemouth had been added to the total. Tynemouth had previously been a Crown living and a number of other benefices to which the Crown presented in 1570 had passed into the hands of local families by the mid seventeenth century. In Durham presentations to the Rectory of Cockfield were made by members of the Ewbanke family from 1629. When Sir Henry Vane bought the tithes of Staindrop to re-endow the Vicarage in 1635 he also acquired the advowson of the living. At Stranton a Yorkshire family, the Dodsworths, were named as patrons in 1650. In Northumberland, Tynemouth, Chillingham, Simonburn, Warden and Whalton all passed from the Crown's gift, some as early as the 1570s. When George Hume, Earl of Dunbar, was established by James I as a major landowner in the Anglo-Scottish Borders he was granted the advowsons of several Northumberland livings including the valuable Rectory of Simonburn.[21] Amongst the independent chapelries once in the Crown's gift, Alwinton passed through the hands of Dunbar and his Howard successors to the families of Widdrington and Selby while Castle Eden and Chester-le-Street were also granted to local gentry.[22]

Although the patronage of perhaps twenty benefices and independent livings changed hands by sale or grant during the period, in addition to those where rights were transferred by marriage or inheritance, there seems to have been little confusion over the *de iure* ownership of advowsons. Of the two known instances, one concerned Kelloe Vicarage, to which the Master and Brethren of Sherburn Hospital presented George Swallwell in 1580. Bishop Barnes refused Swallwell institution because he had already collated the Vicarage to Roger Wilson.[23] Four years later a note was added in the episcopal register beside the record of the institution of Humphrey Green, presented by the Crown to Long Horsley. At the last vacancy, it was recalled,

> the Right Honourable Henry, Earl of Northumberland, and Sir John Forster were the parties that severally made title and upon inquisition it was found then to belong to neither party. Immediately after Humphrey Green procured the said presentation from Her Majesty and after did resign the said Vicarage etc. doubting of the right for that the Earl prosecuted the trial.

Northumberland was apparently successful in his persistent claim and two years later his presentation of John Barker was accepted without objection.[24]

The procedure for appointments to livings which were outside the parochial framework but yet had some formal existence was often laid down at their foundation. Thus the minor canonries and other lesser appointments in Durham Cathedral were in the gift of the Dean and Chapter.[25] Schoolmasters elsewhere were appointed by local committees or by clergy according to the terms of the school's endowment. Lecturers were usually selected by those who paid their salaries; the Crown at Berwick-upon-Tweed in the late sixteenth century, the Corporation at Newcastle-upon-Tyne and Alnwick and local gentry in the remote chapelries of Barnard Castle and Belsay in the seventeenth.[26] In the case of more ephemeral posts, it must be assumed that those who were entitled to do so selected their own chaplains and that the beneficed clergy appointed the assistants whose stipends they paid. Such was probably the implication of a licence granted in 1624 to Christopher Burwell, as Curate in Sedgefield parish on the petition of the Rector, Marmaduke Blakiston.[27]

Incumbents' rights over dependent chapelries were apparently less secure, presumably because the Chaplains or Curates were often supported by small endowments. The lay impropriator appointed and paid the Curate of Beltingham chapel in the parish of Haltwhistle,[28] and in parishes where a complete impropriation had taken place both the mother church and the chapels were usually in the impropriator's gift. Even such minor appointments, which provided annual incomes of a few pounds only, were pieces of property to be valued and defended, just as the Earl of Northumberland had defended his rights in Long Horsley. So, at least, thought the Vicar of Gainford and two brothers, George and Percival Tonge, when they contested the right to appoint a Curate at Denton chapel in the early seventeenth century. Eventually the Vicar successfully asserted that the chapel was both a dependency of Gainford and rightfully in his gift.[29]

The identification of the long-term owners of advowsons provides no more than an introduction to the intricacies of the patronage system. Advowsons passed from their owners by virtue of grants of the next presentation or, more or less intentionally, by lapse to the Bishop and ultimately to the Crown, if the patron failed to present a satisfactory candidate within a certain period. Even when the final decision remained with the true patron and the presentation or nomination stood in his name, others sought to influence his actions. The friends and relatives of aspiring clergymen, as of other placeseekers, were active in making approaches and recommendations to those who had positions to give.

The incidence of grants of the next presentation to a living cannot be assessed with any precision without a full series of registers or presentation deeds, neither of which are available for Durham at this time. No presentation deed is known and the only complete registers to survive are those of James Pilkington (1561-76), Richard Barnes (1577-87) and Richard Neile (1617-27). In addition there are *sede vacante* registers for the years 1559-61 and 1576 and a fragment of the register of John Howson for the years 1630-33.[30] Of the two hundred and fifty presentations recorded in the registers, twenty-nine were made by someone other than the original patron of the living. Those made by the holders of grants of the next presentation to a living were most common in the diocese in the first years of Elizabeth's reign; eight of the forty-four appointments in the first nine years of Pilkington's episcopate were of this type. Only two were by virtue of grants made by the monasteries before the Dissolution, a major source of grants for a single turn elsewhere in the country at the time.[31] Under Barnes patrons for a single turn made two presentations only; the six such presentations made under Neile accounted for less than a tenth of the institutions recorded during his episcopate. Grants of turns of presentation were the principle cause of uncertainty over patronage rights and this too was most common at the beginning of the period. An illuminating case is that of Rothbury. In 1558 Owen Oglethorpe, Bishop of Carlisle, made a grant of the next presentation of the Rectory to William Gascoigne and Robert Thursby. In 1560 the grantees transferred their right to Roger Hollings, who in turn sold it to Francis Slingsby in 1565. Meanwhile, Oglethorpe's successor, John Best, had made another grant of a turn of the advowson in 1563 to William Baker and Oswald Metcalf and they had transferred it to Richard Tempest and Christopher Frothingham. When the living fell vacant late in 1565 both Slingsby and Frothingham presented candidates to the Bishop of Durham, who ordered an inquiry to establish the validity and precedence of their claims. The inquiry found in Slingsby's favour and he may later have acquired Frothingham's right to the following turn, since he also presented at the next vacancy.[32]

The major ecclesiastical patrons, the Bishop and the Dean and Chapter of Durham, made very few grants of the advowsons in their gift.

Only one episcopal grant is recorded, that by Bishop Barnes to his brother John and Richard Franklin, of Houghton-le-Spring, to which they presented in 1584. The canons of 1571 had forbidden Bishops to transfer rights of presentation within their gift and, although unconfirmed, the spirit of the ruling was apparently obeyed.[33] Grants made by the Dean and Chapter were usually to members of the Chapter. In the 1630s each grant specified the clergyman who was to be presented so preventing appointments passing entirely from their control.[34] The Dean and Chapter of Carlisle and, to a greater extent, the Bishop of Carlisle were more willing to dispose of their patronage in Durham; the Bishops' grants were largely responsible for the confusion over Rothbury described above. During Pilkington's episcopate all but two nominations to livings where the Bishop of Carlisle owned the advowson were made by grantees. Distance perhaps discouraged the senior clergy of Carlisle from a more active interest in the exercise of their Durham patronage. The same explanation may be given for the frequent grants of the advowson of Long Benton made by Balliol College; there the College authorities' lack of interest may have been reinforced by the poverty of the living. Other Colleges, however, kept advowsons in their own hands. Apart from one or two made by the Hospitals, the remaining grants were made by laymen. No pattern can be traced in their occurrence and no lay patron consistently granted away the advowson of a living with institution. The situation was different in the donative livings in the Crown's gift, where, as has been seen, both advowsons and impropriations were held by lessees.

The majority of those who received grants of presentations *pro hac vice* were laymen and most would otherwise have had no right of ecclesiastical patronage. Some came from social classes usually excluded from such influence; the few references to the status of grantees show yeomen presenting to livings. Merchants and tradesmen, however, were rarely attracted by such grants. In several towns, notably Newcastle-upon-Tyne, Alnwick and Berwick-upon-Tweed they already had considerable influence over the appointment of clergy as lecturers and schoolmasters and they were, perhaps, therefore less concerned with the selection of beneficed clergy.[35] Some grants were made, as might be expected, by people or institutions outside the diocese to local men. Such were the grants made by Balliol College and the Carlisle hierarchy. Occasionally the recipient was a member of the patron's family. Bishop Barnes's grant to his brother has been cited above; a lay example is that of Bothal Rectory, to which Ralph Ogle, a kinsman of Cuthbert, Lord Ogle, presented in 1564.

Grants within a family may have been made without payment, but in most instances the next turn of an advowson had a price, although it is difficult to discover now. The only contemporary reference to a purchase price which has been found among the Durham sources refers to Long Houghton Vicarage. On the death of the Vicar in 1617 the Archdeacon of Northumberland, John Craddock, approached Thomas Fotherley, an officer of the Earl of Northumberland, asking him to obtain the Vicarage for 'a poor scholar of his'. In April 1617 Fotherley wrote to the Earl:

> if your Lordship have not disposed of it already, I desire to have the preferring of this man to the same. It is a thing of small value, yet I could procure £20 for it, which I will pay . . . at the next audit.

Another servant, George Whitehead, had already begged the Earl to send down 'an advowson in my name', promising to be 'as good a husband to make a good bargain for your honour as I may'; the bargain would be the better the sooner the grant was forwarded. Unfortunately it is impossible to tell which, if either, petitioner was successful or what sum was paid. Fotherley was correct in his description of the value of the living; it was set at £9 9s. 4d. in 1535. Allowing for the increase in value by 1617 the suggested price of the presentation would probably have amounted to a substantial proportion of the Vicar's annual income.[36] If the general value of a single turn of presentation was as high, it is perhaps surprising that more patrons did not part with their rights.

Although there was obviously a market for advowsons, some patrons failed to use their rights and so allowed the presentation to lapse after six months to the diocesan and, if there were further delay, to the metropolitan and to the Crown in succession. No archiepiscopal presentation has been traced during the period and the Crown is only known to have presented to two benefices by lapse. The Bishops, however, found their patronage considerably augmented by this means. Especially remarkable was the extent to which the Dean and Chapter of Durham allowed their patronage to fall into the Bishop's hands. It has been suggested that in the early years of Elizabeth's reign this may have been the result of differences among the canons about the selection of candidates. While the Chapter still included a number of Marian survivors, enthusiastic Protestant prebendaries may have trusted Pilkington, rather than their colleagues, to present men of whom they could approve.[37] By the seventeenth century the Chapter showed no such hesitation and Neile only once presented to a capitular living. Pilkington also presented to livings in the gift of each of the University Colleges and Hospitals but these were also more careful of their rights in the later period. As with grants of next presentation, laymen were less willing to allow patronage to pass from their control than some of their clerical counterparts; only one lay advowson is known to have reverted to the Bishop on more than one occasion.[38]

Those who did not possess rights of patronage did not, of course, need to go to the length of purchasing grants of presentation in order to influence clerical appointments. Intercession on behalf of a particular candidate could be just as effective, although not necessarily less expensive, and there was often plenty of room for middlemen between the patron and the future incumbent. The Bishops, Chapters and University Colleges, patrons who had numerous candidates for livings to hand, were rarely open to recommendations from outside. Others, particularly those who were distant geographically or socially from the diocese, were more amenable. John Craddock's approach to Thomas Fotherley and through him to the Earl of Northumberland is one of the few glimpses we have of the interplay of local and outside influences. The Crown was both the greatest and the most distant of lay patrons and recommendations to many livings in royal gift were formalised and recorded. Most Crown livings in the diocese were at the disposal of the Lord Keeper, either because they were valued at less than £20 a year in 1535 or because they lapsed to the Crown during the vacancy of the see. Registers of the Lord Keeper's patronage for two periods, 1559-82 and 1596-1616, include the names of those who supported successful candidates.[39] The earlier registers list both those who petitioned the Lord Keeper on behalf of a clergyman and those who offered a recommendation, presumably of his talents and character, as a supplement to the petition; for the diocese of Durham the same person was usually named on both counts. The later records mention only the individual or institution offering the recommendation.

There is a marked contrast between those who put forward petitions and advice about Crown presentations in the diocese in the earlier and later periods. Between 1559 and 1582 ecclesiastical recommendations accounted for over a third of appointments. Episcopal influence was greatest in the three years before Bishop Pilkington's death, perhaps a little later than was generally the case; the episcopate as a whole intervened most frequently in Crown patronage in the late 1560's. Bishop Barnes, on the other hand, made no recommendation. Several appointments were made at the petition of a Mr. Lever, probably Ralph Lever, who was Archdeacon of Northumberland for part of the period and well placed to know of both candidates and vacancies. His brother Thomas, Master of Sherburn Hospital and sometime Prebendary of Durham, was also active in the disposal of Crown patronage, although his principal concerns lay outside the diocese.[40] Most of the remaining livings were assigned at the petition of local laymen, including prominent officials and gentry, such as Lord Eure, Sir Ralph Sadler and Sir George Bowes. Only three appointments were made on the recommendation of laymen who had no known connection with North East England. In the later period ecclesiastical influence was less strong. The Bishops of Durham and Carlisle each recommended a single candidate. Thomas Bell, Rector of Elton, put forward the name of Henry Bell, probably a kinsman, for the Vicarage of Stranton and 'certain preachers' supported Thomas Johnson's candidacy for Alnham Vicarage. Academic recommendations were more important; they came from the Universities and Colleges of Oxford and Cambridge and in one case from the Rector and Academy of Edinburgh. The proportion of presentations made on lay recommendation did not change but local families were rather less active. The Lords Eure continued to sponsor candidates and one unusual testimonial came from the burgesses of Alnwick. A number of livings, however, went to clergy recommended by influential individuals who had no ties with the diocese.

A different approach was necessary to influence appointments to the more valuable and desirable livings which remained directly in the monarch's gift and were not passed to the Lord Keeper. Grants of next presentation could be obtained, if the price was high enough and the request was made through the right channels. At Middleton-in-Teesdale, a large parish in the South-West corner of County Durham, the Rector received a substantial income, much of it from tithes levied on profitable lead mines. Leonard Pilkington, brother of the Bishop, was presented to the living by the Crown in 1561 and remained Rector until his death in 1599. Perhaps in view of Pilkington's advancing years, Clement Colmore, Chancellor of the diocese and one of his fellow prebendaries, had his eye upon the living as early as 1585. Colmore gained the support of the Earl of Rutland in his suit for a grant of the advowson and later sought that of Sir Francis Walsingham. Their efforts on his behalf were successful; the right of next presentation was invested in William Colmore, probably his brother, and Clement was presented to the Rectory as soon as it fell vacant.[41] To obtain such a prize it was necessary to have friends in the highest places.

The campaign carried out by Lord Eure, Warden of the Middle

March, between 1595 and 1597 to secure Simonburn, the richest living in Northumberland, shows a layman, rather than the prospective incumbent, taking the initiative. Eure first showed an interest in the living in September 1595, when he submitted to the Queen a petition for the reform of his March and included the suggestion that the advowson be permanently attached to the Warden's office. A precedent had been set by the exercise of the right of presentation by his grandfather when Warden. The incumbent of the moment was, he suggested, liable to deprivation as a pluralist; the way would then be open for an immediate appointment, this time of a preaching minister. The plan found no favour with the government but when the Rector of Simonburn died a year later, Eure immediately wrote to Lord Burghley, seeking the appointment for his son's tutor, Robert Crackenthorpe. When writing to Burghley on other matters, the Warden reminded him that no presentation had yet been made and at the end of September 1596, on hearing that there was competition for the benefice, renewed the pressure. Lady Warwick, it was reported, favoured the claims of Mr. Ewbanke, a 'young Bachelor of Arts'. Eure paid compliment to Ewbanke's ability, commenting that he would receive deserved advancement in time, but contrasted his age and standing with that of the Warden's own candidate, 'a Bachelor of Divinity . . . a worthy member of the church and necessary in this country'.[42] Eure's plans were disrupted the following month when it became clear that Crackenthorpe was unwilling to serve in Northumberland, 'deeming his body unable to live in so troublesome a place and his nature not well brooking the perverse nature of so crooked a people'. Another candidate was immediately forthcoming: George Warwick, an M.A. of six or seven years standing, known to Eure's son and well recommended. As the rival candidate had been satisfied elsewhere Lady Warwick was unlikely to continue her objections and soon Eure was able to assure Burghley that she favoured Warwick's appointment.[43] Eventually, four months after the vacancy had occurred and one year and four months after the Warden had first mentioned the appointment, George Warwick was presented to Simonburn by the Crown in January 1597. Within two years the place was again vacant and this time William Ewbanke was appointed on the recommendation of John Carey, one of Eure's associates in the government of the North East.[44]

Eure's negotiations for Simonburn not only reveal his anxiety to influence a valuable ecclesiastical appointment but also those qualities which he thought most notable in a clergyman and most likely to appeal to others in high places. He was a friend of the Earl of Huntingdon, one of the most notable lay patrons of zealous Protestant ministers, and his concern to secure the services of a learned preacher in the Northumberland dales is reminiscent of the Earl.[45] It was also in the Eure family tradition. In 1575 and 1576 his father had petitioned for two appointments to Crown livings, that of Robert Dixon to Cockfield and of Anthony Garforth to Washington. Both were of sufficient ability to be appointed by Bishop Barnes to undertake preaching tours of the diocese in 1578.[46] Too much should not be made of this coincidence, however. Most of the clergy appointed by the Crown on the initiative of laymen between 1559 and 1578 were at least competent and a number were men of considerable education and ability. In the later period recorded in the Lord Keeper's registers, lay influence was still being exercised in favour of men of a generally high calibre. Seven of the nine clergy recommended to the Crown by laymen between 1596 and 1616 were graduates, a high proportion at a time when less than half of all beneficed parish clergy in the diocese held degrees, and considering that the livings to which they were appointed were of modest value.[47]

There is a contrast between the men so appointed and those presented by other lay patrons either in their own right or by virtue of grants of next presentation. Using academic qualifications as a convenient, if incomplete, measure of clerical sufficiency, the latter were considerably less able than the former. Local connexion, rather than academic attainment, seems to have been the chief influence upon lay patrons. A few clergy presented by laymen are known to have been born within the diocese and a handful were presented to livings by members of their own families; William Carr, for example, nominated Thomas Carr to Ford Rectory in 1582. More commonly laymen presented clergy who were already serving in the diocese. For a few ministers this meant appointment to a second living to be held in plurality. William Duxfield was presented to Bothal Rectory by Ralph Ogle, a devisee under the will of Robert, Lord Ogle, in 1564 and to that of Sheepwash in 1571 by Cuthbert, Lord Ogle. More often, lay patrons chose candidates from the ranks of Durham ordinands or curates. The pattern is hardly surprising. The diocesan clergy were in the best position to hear of vacancies and to make themselves known to those who held advowsons. Except for the very greatest, such as the Earl of Northumberland, the interests of the patrons themselves were circumscribed and any clerical protegés, be they relatives, tutors or domestic chaplains, were by definition men who were serving, or had served, in the area.

The use of episcopal patronage was dictated by a much more evident policy. Its first use was to provide for a favoured group of clergy, often the Bishop's relatives and chaplains, and usually men of good academic standing, on whom he could rely in local administration and politics.[48] The activities of two Bishops, Barnes and Neile, both of whom had good reason to desire a general change among the senior clergy of the diocese and whom fortune favoured in the occurrence of vacancies in livings in episcopal gift, illustrate the point. Bishop Barnes sought through his appointments to counteract the radical tendencies of the zealous Protestants established in Durham by his predecessor. Three prebends only fell vacant during his episcopate, but parochial patronage provided him with greater scope. His first important appointment was of Thomas Burton, his Chancellor in both his previous diocese of Carlisle and, in Durham, to Stanhope Rectory in 1577. In 1578 he collated his brother John Barnes to the Rectory of Haughton-le-Skerne, Robert Bellamy, a prebendary whom he appointed one of his chaplains, to that of Egglescliffe and John Bold, a newcomer to the diocese, to that of Ryton. Bold was transferred to the Archdeaconry of Northumberland in the same year. After 1578 there was less opportunity and perhaps less need to secure the best livings for his henchmen. In 1585, however, Burton added the Vicarage of Kirk Merrington to his holdings and in 1586 the Bishop's son Emmanuel was appointed to Washington Rectory. In a famous denunciation of Richard Neile, Peter Smart claimed that the Bishop's policy was to maintain

> schismatical, heretical, and traiterous Arminians and papists, Cosin, Lindsell, Burgoyne, Duncan etc., to heap livings and church dignities upon his creatures and favourites . . . seven or eight a piece, above all mean and measure.

Smart's objection was to Neile's churchmanship and his use of episcopal patronage, not to its extent. Neile was, however, exceptionally fortunate; all but three of the prebends of Durham fell vacant during his episcopate, some of them two or three times. He was thus able to establish a closeknit group of senior clergy, all of Laudian sympathies, who remained in the diocese to trouble his successors. In addition he used parochial patronage both to buttress the position of the prebendaries and to provide for other members of his circle who could further the cause. Gabriel Clerke, one of his chaplains and a canon of Durham, was collated to the Archdeaconry of Northumberland and its annexed Rectory of Howick in 1619 and to Elwick Rectory in 1620. The Bishop's brother William became Rector of Redmarshall in 1620 and another chaplain, Andrew Perne, Vicar of Norton and Rector of Washington in 1622. Augustine Lindsell was appointed to Houghton-le-Spring in 1623, and in 1624 John Cosin succeeded Clerke at Elwick; both were prebendaries. John Lively, brother of Neile's secretary, received Kelloe Vicarage in 1625 and Yeldard Alvey, who was to make his mark as Vicar of Newcastle-upon-Tyne in the 1630s, that of Eglingham in 1627.[49]

Academic standards among the clergy who received the Bishops' patronage but were outside the immediate episcopal circle were still good. Between half and two-thirds of all those collated by Pilkington and Barnes were graduates, a high proportion at a time when only about a quarter of all incumbents held degrees or had received a University education. In addition, a number of the non-graduates commissioned as preachers by Bishop Barnes in 1578 had received their benefices from him or his predecessor. Those of the two Bishops' nominees who were not distinguished by their education or abilities were for the most part promoted from the ranks of the unbeneficed clergy of the diocese to the poorer livings in episcopal gift. In the seventeenth century the distinctions of education among those collated largely disappear, although higher degrees were generally still the prerogative of the senior clergy. All but two of Neile's appointments were of graduates or University-trained men. Again, standards among the Bishop's nominees contrasted with those of the diocese as a whole, where some 60% of incumbents were graduates in 1634. The importance of local connexion for those collated by Neile is, however, difficult to trace, as records for the early seventeenth century are scarce, and it is not clear whether the Bishop was bringing in fresh talent from the Universities or merely making the best of local men with good qualifications.

The position of the senior clergy was occasionally reinforced by preferments from the Dean and Chapter of Durham. Three prebendaries were presented to livings by the Chapter, in 1585, 1625 and 1629, and others were collated to Chapter livings by lapse. Such appointments were, however, unusual and the moderate value of most livings in the Chapter's gift did not attract many of its members. They made far greater use of their patronage of benefices and curacies to provide livings for the junior clergy of the Cathedral. Some minor canons thus combined curacies within the City of Durham, where the churches of St. Oswald and St. Margaret were in the Chapter's gift, with their Cathedral appointments. Provision for the masters of the schools attached to the Cathedral was particularly good. Francis Kay, Headmaster of the

Grammar School from 1579 to 1593, was appointed to Heighington Vicarage in 1584 and to that of Northallerton in Yorkshire, also in the Chapter's gift, on his retirement in 1593. Mark Leonard, Master of the Song School, received successive appointments to Edmundbyers Rectory and Monk Hesledon Vicarage in 1609 and 1629. Just under half of those whose preferment is noted in the surviving Chapter Act Books of 1578-83 and 1619-39 were presented or appointed by the Chapter to their only cure or to all the livings they are known to have held.[50] Others received preferment from both the Chapter and the Bishop, but it is not clear whether this represents any deliberate congruence of episcopal and capitular patronage or whether it is simply a reflection of the extent of episcopal influence.

University Colleges were also disposed to use their patronage in the interests of their own members. From 1575 Gainford was held by graduates and former fellows of Trinity College, Cambridge. John Lively became Vicar there in 1628 after holding the benefice of Over in the diocese of Ely, also in the College's gift.[51] At Embleton the living was usually held by a former fellow of Merton. At Long Benton and Ponteland, however, the authorities of Merton and Balliol were apparently less concerned to keep the presentation in their own hands or to appoint from their own ranks.

The picture which we have of those who held rights of patronage and the use which they made of those rights, although not complete, is thus a fairly full one. What remains to a great extent uncertain is how each clergyman came to the attention of a particular patron. For the patron with time and interest to devote to the matter there were plenty of candidates from whom to select. For the clergyman seeking a living the problems of finding a patron, preferably one with a cure in his immediate gift, were much greater. Members of a College or Cathedral establishment had a natural advantage. Others, as has been seen, attached themselves to senior clergy who were either patrons in their own right or would act as middlmen, securing appointments from greater patrons. The Archdeacons were particularly well suited to act as intermediaries. They were responsible for the examination of ordinands and as local administrators continued to have close contacts with the serving parish clergy. Ralph Lever's recommendations to Crown livings and John Craddock's suit for the advowson of Long Houghton no doubt arose from such associations. Clergy of less seniority might yet wield some influence in the right quarters. A letter of 1623, unfortunately unsigned, written to a Mr. Marlow, domestic chaplain to Sir Claudius Forster of

Blanchlands, survives in the Hunter MSS. The writer was a clergyman, who entreated his 'reverend and loving brother' to further his cause with Sir Claudius for the Curacy of Bamburgh, a donative in Forster's gift. There was another suitor for the position but Marlow's correspondent had obtained the Bishop's approval and now he needed Sir Claudius's sponsorship and the assurance that Marlow himself did not want the position. He had also obtained letters of recommendation from Sir Claudius's kinsman Sir Matthew Forster, in which Sir Matthew

> passed his word for my fidelity in preaching duty, in carriage towards my superiors and my love and charity towards equals and inferiors, especially to his worship's tenants. As to his worship's stipend, I will according to my place (*oportet unde virorum*) as diligently and reasonably as any in this country or elsewhere without disparagement to any by the grace of God.

He therefore desired Mr. Marlow's good offices on Forster's return to Blanchlands and in the meantime asked that the Bailiff might be instructed that he should serve the vacant cure until a permanent appointment was made.[52]

This approach, with its hope of almost immediate appointment, may have been unusual. Others made preparations well before a vacancy occurred. Grants of the next presentation, obtained while a living was still occupied, were made on this basis; when the clergyman to be presented was named in the grant, as in some of those made by the Chapter, it is clear that both the patron for that turn and his nominee had taken thought in advance. Where a vacancy seemed imminent it was advisable to keep close watch in order to be first in the field. Thomas Oxley, a member of a large clerical family from Northumberland, held the living of Chigwell in Essex. In 1637 he wrote to a Cambridge friend in great indignation, complaining of the close scrutiny to which he had been subjected during a recent illness by certain acquaintances who hoped to influence the disposition of the living.

> I told you I ever thought that Robinson's visit was to no other end, but to see whether I was sick enough and [he] left (as I now perceive) his agent Mr. Everard . . . to see me once or twice a week and to certify how I did frame. [He] hath approved himself a mere spectator and I should not have slept if I had not made him know it. I hope he will see by my letters that there is both life and spirit in me as yet.[53]

Both in seeking presentation from a patron and in any attempt to control the disposition of ecclesiastical livings the clergy must have been drawn towards simony. A study of the court records for a number of years within our period has brought to light only one prosecution for such an offence, that of Edward Calston, Vicar of Chatton, in 1578.[54] The rarity of such cases, however, is no assurance that simoniacal transactions did not take place. Archdeacon Craddock clearly expected to pay the Earl of Northumberland's agent for the advowson of Long Houghton in 1617; it must be presumed that he proposed to recoup the expenditure from the new Vicar. In the 1640s the parishioners of Ponteland petitioned against the many failings of their Vicar, Thomas Gray, including the means by which he had obtained the living. He was alleged to have resigned the Vicarage of Edlingham to Charles Oxley, his predecessor at Ponteland, paying an additional £200 'or some such like sum of ready money, part of his wife's portion' for the exchange.[55] In all these instances, the distance from the diocese of the true patron, the Earl of Northumberland at Chatton and Long Houghton, and Merton College at Ponteland, created opportunities for intermediaries to negotiate for the appointment and so perhaps increased the likelihood of simony. Lack of other evidence of the practice may indicate that it was too widespread even to cause comment and that only flagrant breaches of the law were punished. The strength of ecclesiastical influence may, however, have checked the worst excesses, since elsewhere lay patrons were commonly the most frequent offenders.[56]

The exchange between Gray and Oxley is an example of the way in which clergy might move to suit their own desires rather than waiting upon the wishes of a patron. Exchanges of livings were most common among the senior clergy who held benefices in episcopal gift and presumably obtained the Bishop's willing consent, but they were not unknown among the lower clergy. William Murray and Richard Thursby exchanged Elton and Pittington in 1621 so that each returned to his native parish. They probably settled the matter between them before seeking the permission of the Dean and Chapter of Durham as patrons of Pittington. The subsequent presentation to Elton took place by virtue of a grant of the next presentation, no doubt secured for the purpose. The consent of the patron was, of course, essential; otherwise he might take steps to protect his rights. In 1573 the Bishop of Carlisle instructed his attorney to 'protest of my utter dissenting from any manner of exchange between Talentyre Parson there [Rothbury] and any other.'[57]

A similar arrangement must have been made with the patron when a living was kept within the family; for example when Joseph Wood succeeded his father William as Vicar of Greatham in 1627. An agreement of this kind, however, gave far less control over the disposal of the benefice than the purchase of the next presentation. A few such grants were made to parish clergy in the sixteenth century but no pattern can be traced in their use. In the seventeenth century advowsons were acquired to provide for clerical sons, enabling them to avoid the worst problems of competition for benefices. Although still settled in Essex at the time of his death, Thomas Oxley left to his son Amor the advowson of Whalton in Northumberland and either that Amor or his uncle of the same name was appointed to the Rectory in the 1640s.[58] Similarly Clement Colmore purchased the next presentation to Brancepeth Rectory 'with the purpose to have the same bestowed upon one of my sons, Richard or Matthew Colmore, as themselves shall agree or as myself shall nominate.' The purchase was made in the name of his son-in-law Christopher Fulthorpe and by the terms of Colmore's will Fulthorpe was to present 'whichever of them shall agree betwixt themselves to accept it'.[59]

These glimpses of clerical initiative in obtaining patronage serve as a reminder of how small a part of the process is revealed to the historian. Except where the coincidence of names tells us of the link between patron and clergyman, or some unofficial and exceptional survival reveals the workings behind the stark record of a presentation, it is impossible to gauge the closeness of candidate and patron or the influences, whether those of money, family feeling or religious conviction which determined a patron's choice. It is perhaps dangerous to assume that in every case the motive was well defined. The few incidents related at the end of the foregoing discussion show that the clergy were not hapless pawns, moved at will by those in whom advowsons were vested. Nevertheless, the final decision rested with the patron and in the diocese of Durham the influence of the Bishop of Durham was the most pervasive. Naturally, each Bishop advanced men whose religious outlook was in sympathy with his own and in Neile's appointments the extent and power of episcopal patronage was fully demonstrated. No other patron followed so consistent or so visible a policy. Certainly, there is little evidence of any concerted effort by lay patrons to enforce loyalty to any group or teaching within the Church of England, at least among the beneficed clergy of the diocese; among the lecturers who flourished in the seventeenth century the story is very different, but too long to tell here. Protestant nonconformity was scarcely an issue, at least from the 1560s until Neile's episcopate, in a diocese where the outlying areas had a history of pastoral neglect and where Catholic survivals were strong. What was needed, and what the Bishops, aided by a few laymen such as the Lords Eure, sought to secure, were able Protestant preachers, whatever their churchmanship. Not local conditions, however, but local connexions brought many patrons and clergy together. Both policy, in the reinforcing of interest groups within the two counties, and convenience, in the accessibility of family, friends, and acquaintances, made this the natural order of things.

NOTES

1. *Valor Ecclesiasticus*, ed. J. Caley (1865), V, p. 307.
2. Numbers and types of livings and numbers of clergy in the 1560s have been calculated from B.L., Harleian MS. 594, ff. 186–95.
3. R. Surtees, *History of Durham* (1816–40), II, p. 375; IV, p. 136; D.D.R., I/4, ff. 114–115.
4. B.L., Harl. MS. 594, ff. 186–95; *Ecclesiastical Proceedings of Richard Barnes*, ed. J. Raine, S.S., 22 (1850), pp. 70–79.
5. P.R.O., SP 15/12/108.
6. Jane Freeman, 'The Parish Ministry in the Diocese of Durham *c.* 1570–1640' (unpub. Ph.D. thesis, Durham Univ. 1979), p. 123.
7. *Ibid.*, pp. 72–73, 257–86, 305–15; *Statutes of Durham Cathedral*, ed. Thompson and Faulkner, S.S., 143 (1929), pp. 86–87, 130–33.
8. D.D.R., I/2–4; P.R.O., Indices to E 331, Exchequer, Institution Books. Where no other reference is given, information about patrons and appointments is from these sources.
9. Included in the livings in episcopal gift are Long Newton Rectory, said to have been in the gift of members of the Conyers family before the 1569 Rebellion, but to which the Bishop collated in 1562, and Kirkwhelpington Vicarage, which was granted to the Earl of Northumberland in 1557, but to which the Bishop collated in 1565. E. Mackenzie and M. Ross, *The County Palatine of Durham* (1834), II, p. 66; *Registers of Cuthbert Tunstall and James Pilkington*, ed. G. Hinde, S.S., 161 (1952 for 1946), pp. 144, 148; *C.P.R.*, 1557–58, p. 188.
10. Brancepeth, Easington, Haughton-le-Skerne, Houghton-le-Spring, Sedgefield, Stanhope, Bishop Wearmouth, *Valor Ecclesiasticus*, V, pp. 307, 312–26.
11. e.g. in Coventry and Lichfield diocese: R. O'Day, *The English Clergy* (1979), p. 45.
12. Including Ellingham Vicarage, the advowson of which was granted to the Earl of Northumberland in 1557, but to which the Prior of Durham presented before that date and the Dean and Chapter after it: *C.P.R., 1557–58*, p. 188; *Registers of Tunstall and Pilkington*, pp. 139, 148.
13. D. Marcombe, 'The Dean and Chapter of Durham, 1558–1603' (unpub. Ph.D. thesis, Durham Univ. 1973), pp. 311–48.
14. O'Day, *English Clergy*, p. 113.
15. *C.P.R., 1557–58*, p. 188.
16. Surtees, *Hist. Durham*, III, p. 256; Mackenzie and Ross, *County Palatine*, II, p. 69.
17. A.C., Sion MS. Q II/6/2; D.D.R., I/4, p56.
18. Sources of information about patronage in donative livings are described in Freeman, thesis, pp. 72, 80–81, 101.
19. *N.C.H.*, II, pp. 93–94; D.C.L., Hunter MS. 7/2; *C.P.R., 1566–69*, pp. 250–54.
20. D. M. Barratt, 'The Condition of the Parish Clergy from the Reformation to 1660 with special reference to the Dioceses of Oxford, Gloucester and

Worcester' (unpub. D.Phil. thesis, Oxford Univ. 1949), pp. 354–55; C. Cross, 'The Economic Problems of the See of York', in *Land, Church, and People* (Agricultural History Supplement, 1970), ed. J. Thirsk, pp. 69–73.
21. On Hume's career, see S. Watts and S. J. Watts, *From Border to Middle Shire: Northumberland 1586–1625* (1975), pp. 138–56.
22. *N.C.H.*, XV, pp. 406–07; Surtees, *Hist. Durham*, I, p. 40; II, p. 149.
23. D.D.R., I/3, f. 88.
24. *Ibid.*, f. 15.
25. *Durham Cathedral Statutes*, pp. 132–33.
26. Freeman, thesis, pp. 268–83, 298–305.
27. D.D.R., I/4, f. 72.
28. T. H. Turner, 'Copy of a Commission for Church Livings in Northumberland', *A.A.*, 1st series, 3 (1844), pp. 6–7.
29. D.C.L., Hunter MS 7/2; *C.P.R., 1566–69*, pp. 250–54.
30. D.D.R., I/2–4.
31. Barratt, thesis, p. 366.
32. D.C.L., Hunter MS. 6, pp. 159–63.
33. *The Canons of 1571*, ed. W. E. Collins, Church Historical Society Tracts, XL (1899), p. 29.
34. D.C.R., Chapter Act Book, 1619–38.
35. Freeman, thesis, pp. 275–82, 303, 422–23.
36. A.C., Sion MS. Q III/6/2; *Valor Ecclesiasticus*, V. p. 330.
37. Marcombe, thesis, pp. 217–18.
38. The Strother family allowed the presentation to Kirknewton Vicarage to lapse to the Bishop in 1579 and 1581 while they pressed their claim to treat the living as a donative. D.D.R., I/3, ff. 8–9; P.R.O., Star Chamber, STAC 8/266/11.
39. B. L. Lansdowne MS. 443–44; B.L.O., Tanner MS. 179. The use of the Lord Keeper's patronage is discussed by O'Day, *English Clergy*, pp. 113–24.
40. *Ibid.*, pp. 66–67, 116.
41. *C.B.P., 1560–94*, p. 203; *1595–1603*, pp. 127–28.
42. *Ibid. 1595–1603*, pp. 58, 183, 187, 192.
43. *Ibid.*, pp. 208, 214, 230.
44. *C.S.P., 1594–97*, p. 353; *1598–1601*, p. 217.
45. M. C. Cross, *The Puritan Earl* (1966), pp. 131–42 and *passim.*
46. B. L. Lansd. MS. 443, ff. 225, 235; *Ecclesiastical Proceedings*, pp. 81–91.
47. General standards of clerical education are described in Freeman, thesis, pp. 27–60.
48. D. Marcombe, 'The Durham Dean and Chapter; old abbey writ large?', *Continuity and Change*, ed. R. O'Day and F. Heal (1976), p. 135.
49. P. Smart, 'A Short Treatise of Altars', quoted in *Acts of the Durham High Commission Court*, ed. W. H. D. Longstaffe, S.S., 24 (1858), p. 202; A. Foster, 'The Function of a Bishop: the Career of Richard Neile, 1562–1640', *Continuity and Change*, ed. O'Day and Heal, pp. 45–8; Freeman, thesis, pp. 413–16.
50. D.C.R., Chapter Act Books.
51. M. Spufford, *Contrasting Communities* (1974), p. 295.
52. D.C.L., Hunter MS. 7/2.

53. *Ibid.*, 7/5.
54. Freeman, thesis, pp. 429–30; D.D.R., III/3, f. 105.
55. *The Petition . . . . by the Parishioners of Pont Island against Dr. Gray* (1642).
56. R. Christophers, 'The Social and Educational Background of the Surrey Clergy, 1520–1620' (unpub. Ph.D. thesis, London Univ. 1975), p. 194.
57. *Registers of Tunstall and Pilkington*, p. 173.
58. J. and J. A. Venn, *Alumni Cantabrigiensis . . . to 1751* (1922–27), III, p. 293.
59. B.I., Probate Register 35/435.

The struggle for Parliamentary Representation for Durham, c.1600-1641*

Andrew W. Foster

There is a traditionally accepted account of the struggle for Parliamentary representation for Durham which has stood the test of time. It runs basically as follows: lack of Parliamentary representation is seen as a long-standing grievance in the county and in 1614 thrusting new gentry under the leadership of Sir Henry Anderson, incensed by the rule of Bishop James, tabled a Bill in Parliament to set the matter to rights. The opportunity was ripe because Bishop James had not only alienated the local gentry, but he had also lost favour with that crucial prop to his Palatine authority, the King. Once under way, the campaign was sustained in the Parliaments of 1621 and 1624, when the Bill was only defeated by royal veto, thanks, think some authorities, to the opposition of the new Bishop of Durham, Richard Neile. Complaints were registered in 1627 and a new Bill presented early in 1641, at which stage the Civil War intervened. It was not until 1675 that the county finally gained permanent representation in Parliament.[1]

This story has never really been challenged, primarily because the sources have been considered too meagre to sustain a radically new interpretation.[2] Yet there are several dangers inherent in the above view which should possibly prompt us to question this account. It embodies a tendency to think of the struggle for representation for Durham as an inevitable process, explicable totally in terms of an awareness of the need for the vote – a classic struggle between the forces of the under-privileged, represented in this period somewhat ironically by Northern coalmine owners, and the forces of the establishment, led by the Bishop of Durham. This entails a conflict model of history close to the lines of the now discredited Whig interpretation of the constitutional conflicts of the seventeenth century. Moreover, this story rather presupposes conflict between the centre and the provinces, a view sustained by many county historians, but one which in its turn has perhaps become an all-pervading model.[3]

On a more basic level of questioning, this account is really very hazy about when, how and why this struggle started. Wherever it is found, whether in revered old county histories or in the modified versions of more recent regional studies, this account rarely provides detailed analysis of the chronology of this campaign, of the battles in Parliament or the reasons behind the failure of these early petitions and Bills. It must be confessed that little new information has come to light in either central or local archives, but it is hoped that by conducting a detailed re-examination of the whole episode this paper will offer a challenging re-interpretation of this story.

Many of the assumptions which have too often gone unchallenged concerning this struggle arise from the fact that the Durham Palatinate was a privileged jurisdiction presided over by the Bishop of Durham. Although not nearly as powerful as his Mediaeval predecessors, the Bishop was still king in his own county and it is not unnatural to assume that this power would grate at times on the populace.[4] Yet the Bishop was not an easy figure to challange. As with the Crown Court, many posts and perquisites flowed from his hands; many had a vested interest in the survival of the system.[5] While it is true that relations between the Bishop and his local flock were of crucial importance in this struggle, the key question remains: what upset this delicate balance and prompted some landowners and citizens of Durham to campaign for Parliamentary representation in the early seventeenth century? Why did the struggle not start earlier? When did it start?

To understand the mainspring of this action we need to look not at events in 1614, as most accounts would have us believe, but at those of the preceeding Parliament of 1610. The accession of James I to the throne of England had tremendous ramifications for life in the North. As part of his idealistic unification of England and Scotland, the Borders were officially abolished in 1607 and with them went a whole network of Northern customs involving border service, rents and special rates.[6] The chief justification for the fact that the Northern counties had remained traditionally free from Parliamentary taxation vanished with these changes. When James was so badly in need of money in 1610, it probably seemed only natural that it should be recognised that the four Northern counties of Northumberland, Cumberland, Westmorland and Durham should no longer be exempt from payment of subsidies voted in Parliament. Stories of the poverty of this area, always to hand with references to the Rebellions of 1536 and 1569, were no real protection in a Parliament which was so heavily concerned with debating matters of finance.

It was all settled very quickly. On July 11, without providing reasons, Sir Nicholas Saunders urged that Wales, the Northern counties and the Cinque Ports should no longer be exempt from Parliamentary taxation.[7] In a statement rendered ambiguous by the *Commons Journal*, Sir Edwin Sandys noted that the Northern counties were bound by former statutes, the Cinque Ports were out of the proviso, and moved that these might have burgesses.[8] The suggestion was not pursued, but it became doubly relevant for County Durham when Sir Ralph Gray's attempt to protect the Northern counties failed on July 14 1610.[9] When an exemption was finally negotiated for Berwick, even if not for Newcastle, both significantly represented in the Commons, the proceedings of this Parliament must have provided much food for thought in County Durham.[10]

The Durham gentry may have resented their lack of representation in Parliament before, but the events of 1610 provided a clear need for direct access to the House of Commons.[11] Durham alone of the counties of England and Wales was not represented in the Commons, yet after 1610 it was liable to Parliamentary taxation. When there had been talk of levying taxes in Durham in 1563 a Bill had been swiftly lodged in Parliament explicitly connecting such a change with the demand for two knights for the county.[12] That particular Bill did not get very far possibly because this link was drawn. What is significant about the Parliamentary proceedings of 1610 is that no such scruples about possible related rights were allowed to stand in the way of financial reform. However, the strong argument that those taxed should have a right to representation was not forgotten either in the North or by some stalwarts in Parliament.

Matters might not have come to such a pass if the Bishop, William James, had proved to be an able advocate in the House of Lords and at Court, but his position provides another important ingredient in the timing and later conduct of this campaign. It is not that the Bishop was not assiduous in his attendance in the Lords, nor careless of his duties as spokesman for County Durham, but he found himself in a rather unenviable position in 1610.[13] Unpopular already in the North, where his robust exercise of his rights gave offence to gentry and townspeople alike, Bishop James had few friends at Court and was very reliant upon the support of the Earl of Salisbury, to whom he had actually written to gain the see in 1606.[14] One price for this support was the Bishop's agreement to an exchange of property with Salisbury in the area of Durham House, a transaction which required an Act of Parliament in 1610.[15] It looks as if Salisbury treated James very fairly, providing new stables for Durham House in the deal, but the negotiations must have been delicate at times.[16] As this relatively minor Act passed through Parliament, it cannot have been lost upon the Bishop that his patron had a vested interest in the success of much grander proposals for financial reform. Given this knowledge, it is perhaps hardly surprising that all Bishop James could register in the Lords in July was a feeble plea 'that Durham, after the former manner of that place, may be freed from payment of the subsidy'.[17]

There was probably little more that James could have done, but his failure to take effective action was noted and not forgiven in the North. An ardent Protestant, said to be famous for his hospitality, Bishop James managed to upset Protestants and recusants alike in his diocese. He cut a very different figure from that of his popular predecessor Toby Matthew. It was in his fate and temperament to fight tenants over rents and rights and a classic example of this was his attempt to rescind the charter which Matthew had so recently granted to the City of Durham in 1602. This dispute dragged on throughout his life and is said to have even caused his death when he was scolded over it by King James I in 1617.[18] Verses circulating in Durham on the occasion of the King's visit in that year contained the memorable line: 'William our Bishop hath oppugnant been'.[19] The feelings, however, appear to have been mutual. In a letter to Salisbury in December 1609, Bishop James referred to 'my crabbed neighbours the townsmen of Durham; who in their pride usurp things never granted and challenge things not grantable'.[20] As far as he was concerned these people were only 'fit to be kept under'.[21] This dispute provides yet another reason why James needed Salisbury's support in 1610, something which his contemporaries also noticed.[22]

Salisbury's protection could not last for ever and, in fact, with his demise following so swiftly upon that of the Earl of Dunbar, something of a power vacuum was created in the North. Bishop James found his position threatened by the rise of the royal favourite, the Earl of Somerset. From about 1609, the Bishop had served the office, even if not held the title, of Lord Lieutenant of County Durham.[23] Deprived of a protector at Court, he discovered in 1615 that this post was to be given to Somerset. In an anxious letter to King James the Bishop begged:

> that if Your Majesty do appoint a Lieutenant, that the country may understand your royal pleasure, that it is not for any neglect, or omission

> of mine, in the execution thereof, for that would much grieve me, for so much pains taken, to receive in the end disgrace.[24]

Bishop James could ill afford this blow to his prestige. It looks as if he was the victim of a campaign by Somerset to build a power base in the North, but this does not seem to have made him alter his ways. Although word had reached him that the Earl was only looking for an opportunity 'that (I know not for what) my liberties might be seized and all things turned upside down', the Bishop still had the temerity to rebuke Somerset for associating with recusants on St George's Day 1615.[25]

Another source of friction within the diocese lay with the large and prosperous corporate town of Newcastle-upon-Tyne. The Bishop's control of Gateshead and with it his claims to a share in the lucrative rights from the Tyne was a matter of constant irritation to the corporation.[26] They sought every opportunity to embarrass the Bishop and frequently elected Durham gentry to represent them in Parliament. When James felt that the Durham citizens were encouraged 'by some, who ought not so to do', such encouragement was as likely to have come from Newcastle as from the Somerset faction.[27] Moreover, an increasing number of Newcastle merchants and gentry, like Sir Thomas Riddell at Gateshead, Sir Francis Brandling at Felling and Thomas Liddell at Ravensworth, were choosing to live within County Durham during this period and thus came to identify more closely than ever with the frustrations of the local gentry.[28] These were expressed quite vividly by William Morton, Vicar of Newcastle, in a letter to Secretary Winwood in September 1616. As far as Morton was concerned the Bishop was 'clean perverted' and should be stripped of his power.[29] He ingeniously claimed that this was for the Bishop's own good for:

> He that is made Bishop of Durham is made an absolute king in his country nay, more than a king. God forbid any king should so rule over any as he rules over them in the Bishopric which though it may seem beneficial to him for a time, yet it is exceeding hurtful to him for his soul's health.[30]

The combined effect of these miscellaneous feuds was to split the Bishop from the gentry and ensure that when the opportunity came to voice grievances in Parliament, he too would be a subject of complaint.

It is one thing to clarify why Bishop James was unpopular and to provide reasons why a Franchise Bill was soon to be laid before Parliament, it is quite another to analyse accurately the combination of social groups who gave their support to this campaign. Northern society was extremely complex and it is possible to distinguish many factions during this period; the problem lies in not being trapped by labels. On a superficial reading of the situation it is tempting to see the campaign as part of a conflict between an alliance of coal-owners and ancient families on the one side and, given the opposition of the Bishop, a church faction on the other.[31] Also behind the campaign are to be found the major citizens of Newcastle, Durham and various towns within the county. This view accords well with some of the facts for the Newcastle coal-owners, newly establishing themselves on Durham estates, were indeed in the forefront of this campaign, as were representatives of ancient families like Sir Talbot Bowes who had strong interests in Barnard Castle. Problems occur with the other side, for although families closely connected with the church like the Blakistons, the Calverleys and the Fetherstonhaughs may have held aloof under Bishop James, they were certainly to the forefront of the campaign in the North in the 1620s.[32] If the conflict model is to hold good one would surely not expect to find Sir William Bellasis, a Deputy Lieutenant and High Sheriff of the county after 1625, amongst those petitioning Parliament for the franchise in 1620?[33]

The closer one looks into support for this campaign the more complicated the matter becomes. Neat divisions break down. By a simple switch of labels, many of the coal-owners could become 'new' gentry. The rhetoric used in Parliament, particularly by Sir Henry Anderson in 1614, may give the impression that this was a 'Protestant cause', but many recusants, chiefly amongst the ancient families, of course, were also actively involved like the Conyers and the Lawsons.[34] One big problem with the label 'coal-owners' is that it conceals the fact that William Jennison, Sir Thomas Riddell and Sir George Selby all had recusant connections.[35] According to Morton, Selby was 'in these parts he that hath done most for recusants whose he is underhand both body and soul'.[36] It is hard not to escape the conclusion that support for these Bills cut across all interest groups in the county, particularly when one finds relatively minor officials in the Palatine administration like Timothy Comyn and Hugh Wright also named on the petition of 1620.[37] That the leadership came from Newcastle-centred gentry may partly be due to the fact that they possessed relatively easy access to seats in the Commons through that town or county Northumberland. Another important factor is the almost universal hostility which Bishop James seems to have aroused in his diocese. There is no evidence that his successors, Bishops Neile, Howson and Morton, aroused such feeling.

Personal feuds, fired possibly by the impetuosity of youth, probably ensured that Sir Henry Anderson, still anxious to prove himself in Newcastle, emerged as the dominant leader of this campaign.[38]

Study of events in Parliament, when these grievances were all revealed in 1614, makes it hardly surprising that previous accounts of this story have possibly dwelt more upon the personalities involved, rather than the issues, and have seen 1614 as the starting point of this campaign. This remained the memorable Parliament for John Cosin, writing in 1669 at the height of his own struggle to defend his episcopal rights:

> Never did any attempt this matter (i.e. the presentation of a Bill in Parliament) without the consent of the Bishop, but only Sir (Henry) Anderson, who hated Bishop James, about 57 years ago.[39]

Sir Henry Anderson was one of the local coalmine owners, one of the rising gentry of merchant origins who had moved out of Newcastle in favour of a country house in County Durham, Haswell Grange. A staunch Protestant, he was thought by William Morton to be 'a man of an active stirring spirit' which he soon demonstrated in debates over the Durham Bill presented in Parliament in 1614.[40] When somebody made the fairly innocuous suggestion that perhaps the Bishop should be consulted before a Bill was drawn up, Anderson expostulated:

> That this moved the last Parliament, when they pressed to grant subsidies. The motion then thought reasonable. That all the country groaneth under the burden of the government there. That he charged by some great ones, to have been the only occasion of this innovation. That my Lord sent down special messages. That his officers bestirred themselves, as if his *jura regalia* had been in question.[41]

During the course of this rambling tirade, from which it seems that some held the Bishop directly responsible for the changes of the last Parliament, Anderson drew the remarkable analogy: 'To sit in Rome, and strive with the Pope – to strive with the Bishop in Durham'.[42]

This personal feud, which went so far that Anderson threatened to bring in a petition of grievances against Bishop James, has dominated our view of events in 1614. It is worth a moment to consider from whence other support for the Bill in the Commons came, and also the way in which the arguments, when finally heard, were couched. It is interesting that in 1614, the chief Northern spokesman for the Bill, the man who actually presented it for its first reading on May 21 1614, was William Jennison, the other member of Parliament for Newcastle.[43]

Here is a perfect example of how hostility towards Bishop James cut across barriers, for although Jennison was also of a fairly recently established family, he was apparently 'inwardly inclined towards popery'.[44]

Anderson and Jennison proved notable supporters once a Bill was moving in the Commons, but attention should also be paid to the role of that wily Parliamentarian, Sir Edwin Sandys, who had first noted problems of principle in the passage of the Subsidy Act in 1610. Only a couple of days after Parliament commenced work, when discussion was drawn to the North, thanks to election irregularities surrounding Sir George Selby's election as member for Northumberland, it was Sandys who moved that since Durham was now subject to Parliamentary taxation, they should petition the King that the county might have knights and burgesses, for they were 'said to be dumb men, because no voices.'[45] An objection raised by one Mr. Ashley that 'they of Durham hold it a privilege, not to be bound to the attendance of the Parliament' was brushed aside.[46]

Although recent work on Parliament has cast doubts about the existence of 'parties' in the Commons during this period and attacked the idea of conflict over major constitutional issues, it is important to remember by what piecemeal means Parliament was clarifying its own procedures and powers throughout this period. In this very Parliament of 1614, the case of Sir George Selby's election for Northumberland was added to those test cases concerning the inability of sheriffs to stand for Parliament, in this case, even when they had been appointed Sheriff of County Durham by the Bishop.[47] Likewise, Sir Edwin Sandys was keen to make the Durham representation issue a test of principle, revolving here on the question of taxation. When the matter was next debated in the Commons on May 14, it was Sandys who reported from the Committee of Petitions and the issue of the subsidy was to the forefront of his argument:

> that county now stands in a worse plight than any other part of the kingdom; and that much touches the kingdom. That every man has a propriety in his goods, which will not suffer that to be transferred to another without his own consent; and not to be governed by laws whereunto they no parties.[48]

Sandys scornfully dismissed worries that this represented needless innovation, that it was not desired and that the charges for such a poor area still impoverished by the Northern Rebellion of 1569 would be too great.

The case might have been clearcut to the likes of Sandys, but it was also clear to many that they were flying in the face of the Bishop. Even Sandys noted that Bishop James claimed to be able to prove 'that all the principle men, noble gentlemen and grand jury, were against it.'[49] He was forced to concede that 'this would disgrace the Bishop; and that the Bishop before further proceedings, might be heard . . .'.[50] It was this remark which drew forth vitriol from Sir Henry Anderson. Although he blustered that he could not counter the Bishop's claims, it is not that evident from the *Commons Journal* that support was at this stage forthcoming from many other Northerners. Mr. Ashley was not afraid to speak up for the Bishop, but despite his objections a Bill was eventually permitted by the Speaker, if only to provide a fitter context for the debate.[51]

When the Bill was finally presented to the Commons on May 21 1614 it was couched in fairly simple terms. It called for two knights for County Durham, two citizens for the City of Durham and two burgesses for the borough of Barnard Castle.[52] The latter request would appeal to the older gentry in the county, particularly the Bowes family who were said to control that small town.[53] The preamble was brief and to the point; rights were requested because:

> the County Palatine of Durham has been always excluded and separate from having any knights or burgesses in Parliament and yet not withstanding are bound by the Acts there made and are contributors to the subsidies there granted by the temporality as far forth as other places are that have knights and burgesses to speak for them as occasion serves.[54]

Parliament was assured that 'the said County Palatine is of large circuit and peopled with gentlemen and others of quality and estate' and thus able 'to send to the Parliament men of sufficiency for the service of his Majesty and the kingdom.'[55]

The taxation/representation issue was clearly central to this debate, but the question of whether or not the county could bear the cost of maintaining members of Parliament was to prove a constant anxiety to some in this and later Parliaments. The Bill was given a second reading on May 31.[56] It was when the indomitable Mr. Ashley moved that since such harsh words had been spoken about the Bishop, he should at least be allowed to clear himself, that Sir Henry Anderson threatened that worse might follow in the form of a petition of grievance 'which will bite nearer than any of those aspersions'.[57] Sir William Walter assured the House that 'all the gentlemen and the commons, that have not dependence upon the Bishop, willing with the proceedings of this'.[58] It was accordingly passed to the committee stage with the diplomatic rider that 'my Lord of Durham may have his counsel heard at the said committee' and any gentlemen of County Durham present were allowed to attend.[59]

This Bill foundered like everything else, without ever reaching the Lords, on the dissolution of what rapidly came to be known as the 'Addled Parliament'. We have no knowledge of its committee stage, but it is clear from what has already been said that the opposition of Bishop James to the Bill can be taken for granted; whether it would have been sufficient to stop the Bill if Parliament had continued is less easy to judge. The 1614 Parliament left the issue in the air and with it a number of problems for historians. Evidence of grievances, hostility towards the Bishop and a good cause for representation exists, but it is not necessarily so clear from this Parliament who was promoting the Bill, the cross-currents of opinions in the Commons, or how widespread support for it really was in the North.

Study of events in 1621 clarifies a number of these points. It is not clear when the Bill was given its first reading in the Commons, it probably came up under the order to the clerk to look up Bills from the last Parliament, but a Bill which was evidently much more ambitious than that of 1614 was given its second reading on March 6 1621.[60] We know it was more ambitious because now a possible fourteen Members of Parliament for Durham towns and county were under discussion. As before, six related to Durham City, county and Barnard Castle, but with hopes aroused, several other towns were now in on the act. There is possibly a hint of urban unrest in the appearance of these towns on the list and, as has already been pointed out, it was probably no accident that the most outspoken supporters of this Bill represented that noteworthy centre of sedition, Newcastle. These new towns included Hartlepool, Darlington, Stockton and either Gateshead or possibly even Bishop Auckland.[61] There is an element of mystery here because by the debate on March 6 and the following report stage it was clear that the Durham campaigners had over-reached themselves; the Commons was prepared to consider six new members at most.

A possible reason why they may have over-reached themselves in 1621 is that they felt more confident of gaining the Bishop's support for this Bill. This would accord with one plausible reading of Cosin's words already noted that Anderson was the only man to petition without the support of the Bishop. Certainly there is more evidence that support for such legislation was widespread in the North, including many gentry close to the new Bishop. In 1617 Bishop James had been succeeded by

Richard Neile, news of whose appointment was said to have actually quietened mobs rioting in the streets![62] Unlike his predecessor, Bishop Neile was a firm favourite with King James I, a fact attested by his almost automatic appointment as Lord Lieutenant of County Durham in November 1617, the post much coveted by Bishop James.[63] Although Neile presided over liturgical changes which had far-reaching effects for the see and which led to uproar in the Commons when finally reported in 1629, he does not seem to have alienated the local gentry to anywhere near the same degree as his predecessor.[64]

Thanks to the stand taken by Bishop James, and later by John Cosin, the position of the Bishop has tended to be taken for granted.[65] It is tempting to think that conflict was inevitable between a Bishop striving to retain his authority and new gentry and town corporations anxious to exercise power. Hence, although the evidence is very thin, it has generally been assumed that Bishop Neile had some hand in the failure of the Bills presented during his time as Bishop of Durham.[66] This view is doubly tempting given what is known of the man: he was never happy to see towns gain charters, he increased clerical control of the bench while at Durham and when at York fought for greater clerical say in the running of that city.[67] Allegations of excessive clerical representation on the bench in County Durham were made in this very Parliament of 1621.[68] Yet there is still no clear evidence that Neile saw fit to oppose these Bills.

In fact, what slim evidence does exist points to the idea that Neile may have been quite happy to countenance such Bills; Parliamentary representation could be used to enhance as well as detract from his power. The election of his close friend and family solicitor, Edward Liveley, to represent Berwick-upon-Tweed in the Parliaments of 1624 and 1628, plus the election of his son Sir Paul Neile to represent Ripon in the Short Parliament of 1640, suggests that Neile was not naive come Parliamentary elections.[69] A petition drawn up by Durham gentry and townspeople in November 1620 carries a fair cross-section of names including virtually all of Neile's Deputy Lieutenants, the captains of the trained bands and representatives of both established and new gentry, including what have been termed by one authority, 'church families' of the region.[70] The list included the names of other less well known people close to Neile, such as the townsmen George Martyn, Hugh Wright and Timothy Comyn, who all fulfilled minor offices in the Palatine administration, and a key figure who was to become his Attorney General, William Smith.[71]

A letter from George Martyn to Neile dated January 10 1621 goes so far as to take Neile's support for granted and also to acknowledge that it could bring Neile more power and influence:

> As the passage of this business is not only likely by your Lordship's favourable consent to be much facilitated, but wholly effected, so I pray God that that respect may be given to your Lordship in the choosing of our knights and burgesses, (when there shall be occasion), that you may receive as good content therein, as always you have given in this to all the country.[72]

The gentry who gathered at the January Sessions appear to have been so confident of success that they squabbled amongst themselves over who should have the honour of presenting the petition. This apparently fell to Sir Henry Anderson, Sir Timothy Whittingham, Sir Thomas Liddell and Sir Talbot Bowes, but this choice was not much liked by Sir Bertram Bulmer and Ralph Fetherstonhaugh, who promptly set off to join them.[73]

Whatever the real attitude of Bishop Neile, there was certainly a different atmosphere surrounding discussion of this matter in 1621 than that which had prevailed in 1614. Other factors also emerged which may help explain the failure of this Bill in other than the simplistic terms than that it was opposed by the Bishop and hence by the King. For example, the claim for fourteen members upset many in the Commons at the very outset of proceedings. Pressure for new seats may have revealed the healthy state of political life in Early Modern England, but it also put pressure on practical facilities. One Mr. Ravenscroft only felt able to allow four members for Durham and even then he called for an enlargement of the House to cope with new members.[74]

When the matter was next discussed at the report stage of the Bill on March 14 1621, the case for a large number of members seems to have been lost already in committee. Knights for the county and citizens for Durham were quickly agreed upon, but the discussion was really taken up with whether Barnard Castle or Hartlepool deserved representation. It was urged for Barnard Castle because that was Prince Charles's town, a factor of some significance in the next Parliament, but also for Hartlepool because that was a port.[75] Sir Thomas Hoby urged that the rest be rejected, interestingly enough, 'because of pestering the House; and because these incorporated by the Bishop, not by the King'.[76] At this juncture inter-county rivalries appeared as a factor in the debate. Sir Walter Earle pointed out that the number of burgesses requested was too great and they ought to rest content with two knights and two burgesses as possessed by Chester. Much the same was said on behalf of Gloucestershire.[77]

Such was the confidence of the men of Durham, that later on in the proceedings Sir Talbot Bowes took up Earle's point and asserted that they in Durham were as heavily charged as counties which possessed eight burgesses and paid more for purveyance and arms than the East Riding of Yorkshire. Yet, even he, sensing the way the debate was going, drew a distinction between Barnard Castle and Hartlepool and ditched the latter by saying they had no 'sufficient' men to serve.[78] This echoed talk of 1614 and raised some concern which led to Hartlepool being struck out with the rest when the matter was put to the question. What saved Barnard Castle more than anything was the frequent reminder that this was the Prince's town. County jealousies were well aired, but much of this discussion seems to have been a foregone conclusion. The Bill went forward and gained a successful third reading in the Commons on April 26 1621.[79]

There was another fear, very real in the North and expressed by George Martyn in his letter to Neile, but barely touched upon in this Parliament. This concerned the power of Catholics. It has been noted that prominent supporters like Sir George Selby, Sir Thomas Riddell and the Conyers family had recusant backgrounds. In his letter of January 1621, Martyn revealed just how optimistic the gentry of Durham were when he commented:

> if it be not timely prevented, it is generally thought that the popish faction will make a very strong party for choice of one at least, if not of both, the knights of the shire, having so far already proceeded, upon hope to have had knights this Parliament, that the most of the freeholders of this county have been already by them, and those of their party, intreated and earnestly solicited for their voices.[80]

This fear lay dormant in the Parliament of 1621, given voice by only one member who feared that the people of Hartlepool were much given to popery.[81]

The point about the 'Prince's town' adds an interesting new dimension to the story. It is commonly accepted that Prince Charles was becoming a force at Court about this time and indeed the next Parliament of 1624 has been given the soubriquet of the 'Prince's Parliament'.[82] There is evidence that he was attempting to build up his own power base in Parliament, based primarily on the Duchy of Cornwall, but also his Earldom of Chester.[83] In 1624 he is known to have promised to support Hertford's attempt to regain borough representation.[84] What more natural than that he might have made similar promises elsewhere? The mutual needs of the Prince and campaigners for new seats go some way towards explaining the repeated Bills of 1621 and 1624. Implicit in the same argument is an explanation for why such Bills ceased in 1625, when Charles became King and presumably no longer felt the need for an independent power base from the Crown. It might be no small coincidence that the Crown was happy to sell off its interest in Barnard Castle to the Vane family in 1626.

To return to the fate of the much altered 1621 Bill; it gained its first reading in the Lords on May 25.[85] The second and third readings followed soon after on the same day, May 31, and there is no evidence from the *Lords Journal* of any dispute.[86] There is no indication that Bishop Neile spoke on the matter or ever attempted to influence debates in the Commons, but records of debates in the Lords between May 18 and the June adjournment seem to have been lost.[87] In many ways it looks from the speed of this process as if the Lords was simply 'rubberstamping' the conclusions of the lower house. Yet after this, the Bill, passed by both houses, appears to have been lost. Parliament was adjourned soon after and the best explanation is that the King was in no mood to increase the size of the House of Commons after the stormy session at the end of the year.

It has been argued that because charges were made about excessive clerical representation on the Durham bench in this Parliament and Chancellor Craddock arraigned for corruption, the gentry were attempting a two-pronged attack on Neile through these allegations and the Durham Franchise Bill.[88] It is possible that by bringing such charges some people thought to put pressure on Neile, but it is also possible to exaggerate personal antipathies in a Parliament which evinced a genuine concern for matters of principle and the issue of corruption. Several clergymen and lawyers, from the Bishop of Llandaff and Sir John Bennett to more lowly Chancellors like John Lambe and John Craddock were called to account for themselves and the activities of their ecclesiastical courts during this Parliament. Members of the Commons were always careful to declare that their enquiries related to individuals as examples of the need for reforms in the system. The suggestion that the Durham commission was dominated by clergymen was clearly an exaggeration and was made in a fit of pique when it was thought that Neile had influenced the King to over-react to a Bill in preparation clarifying the status of clergy thought eligible to serve on such commissions.[89] Likewise, the charges against Craddock have to be taken with a pinch of salt because they emanated from John Richardson, a Durham barrister recently sacked by Neile, and really involve the internal politics of the Dean and Chapter, where big changes were now being experienced, rather than the wider community in the North.[90] Several aspersions about the Bishop's leniency towards Catholic recusants may also be taken as a comment by strong Protestants about the new direction of Arminian policies within the Cathedral and the diocese.[91] It has already been noted that gentry concern for their Franchise Bill seems to have cut across such disputes.

Despite what had been said in 1621 about 'pestering the House', a new Durham Franchise Bill was entered in Parliament in 1624. The feeling that this was 'the Prince's Parliament' may have affected this decision as has already been indicated. The Bill was given its first reading in the Commons on March 23; its second two days later.[92] It was sent to a committee consisting, as was customary, of interested members from the region concerned and we know Neile's views would have been represented because Edward Liveley was one such member.[93] The Bill emerged for the report stage on April 14 1624, when Sir John Saville challenged the appearance once again of Barnard Castle in the Bill.[94] Not all members of the Commons were happy about the wisdom of setting up new seats already known to be subject to the 'influence of great men'.[95] A new committee was constituted to consider the objections to Barnard Castle.[96] That town was still the bone of contention when the Bill re-emerged on May 4. Sir John Saville was proving adamant, but Sir Thomas Trevor and the redoubtable Henry Anderson eventually carried the day in urging compliance with the original Bill. They were quite open in arguing that this would please the Prince. On the other hand, those great Parliamentarians, Sir Edwin Sandys and Sir Edward Coke, were also notable speakers on behalf of the Bill.[97] It was engrossed on May 4 and eventually passed its third reading four days later.[98] There is little indication of real controversy surrounding this Bill, rather a genuine concern to allocate the correct number of members to the Palatinate, distributed to the right towns. The house was reassured over Barnard Castle by talk of Sir Talbot Bowes's influence there as well as that of the Prince.[99] At no stage does the general principle of the Bill appear to have been challenged.

Unlike 1621, there is some evidence that Neile must have been involved in the formal discussions of this Bill when it reached the Lords. On its second reading on May 22, Bishop Neile was appointed to the committee to cover the legislation in detail.[100] If he did have reservations, he does not appear to have made them public effectively, for the Bill subsequently passed its third reading without incident on May 25 1624.[101] Just as in 1621, the Bill had now passed all due Parliamentary process and only awaited royal assent to become law. All it received from James I was the royal veto. We do not have to leap to conspiracy theories to explain this, however, for a fairly convincing reason was provided at the time by Sir Francis Nethersole in a letter to Dudley Carleton written in June 1624:

> Of private Bills, the King refused to ratify one for the County Palatine of Durham to send knights to Parliament, on the ground that the House of Commons was already too large and that some decayed towns, as Old Salisbury, must be deprived of their members before this desire could be granted.[102]

The same letter noted that the King was greatly displeased with those who had opposed the York House Exchange Act. As Neile had raised some minor objections to that Act, he may hardly have been in a good position to influence the King over Durham.[103] Nethersole's explanation fits the logical James to a tee and there is no reason why we should not take it at face value as the best explanation for the failure of these Bills before the 1640s.[104]

With the accession of a new King the whole issue seems to have been dropped. No doubt it was expensive to petition Parliament and keep people in London should they be needed as witnesses. A royal veto was pretty final and it is probable that earlier warnings about pestering the House were at last taken to heart. Moreover, there is every indication that Bishop Neile was a more effective spokesman for County Durham in the Lords than Bishop James had ever been. He spoke with authority on matters of defence in 1624, 1625 and 1626 and was instrumental in gaining a complete review of the defences of Newcastle.[105] His record as a working Bishop in Parliament was second to none. It could also be useful to some that Neile had the ear of the King. In 1621 Robert Henryson petitioned Neile on behalf of poor Scottish miners who were being taxed as aliens in Newcastle, contrary to the spirit of the new laws and the legal opinion of William Smith, Neile's legal adviser. Neile passed the petition directly to the King and the appeal was upheld thanks probably to his personal interest in the case.[106]

More important, Neile was effective on an issue dear to the hearts of a more substantial section of the community. When asked to draw up a list of gentry from whom loans could be extracted in September 1625, Neile spared many of the notable families in the area, such as the Eures,

Conyers, Bowes and Blakistons: 'which I humbly beseech your good lordships to understand to proceed, not of partiality, or omission; but upon due consideration of their decayed estates.'[107] He suggested Sir William Bellasis as a 'faithful and careful man' to act as a local receiver.[108] When the loan was being collected in April 1626, Bellasis and John Calverley complained to Neile that the list had been altered and 'that some other hath had a hand in it, that hath had little consideration and less knowledge of the state of the country'.[109] It could be that Neile was being Machiavellian, but on petition from Sir Henry Anderson, the Privy Council did reduce the loan assessment.[110]

What was probably also telling in killing further attempts to gain the franchise in the new reign was the war effort against Spain and France. This had a pronounced effect upon the Commons in particular, which became obsessed with a witch-hunt for all those in public office with Catholic connections. Lists were drawn up as early as 1624 and it cannot have helped the Durham cause that prominent men like Sir William Eure, William Jennison, Sir Ralph Conyers, Sir Thomas Riddell and Sir William Selby appeared on the sheet.[111]

The matter did continue to surface from time to time, especially when money was being demanded, emphasising once again the centrality of the issue of taxation and representation to this campaign. When Durham commissioners were collecting yet another 'loan' in April 1627 they assured the Council:

> There did not appear before them any to oppose or contradict the loan, but one thing grieved the minds of many that, albeit they have of late submitted to many new and unaccustomed charges, never known to their ancestors and whereto they were not liable by law, yet they have not been held worthy to be called to Parliament, but alone, of all the counties of the kingdom, are excluded therefrom as aliens and remain as a tribe cut off from Israel.[112]

They recalled that before 1610 they had never been charged with subsidies 'because their county being a County Palatine, in which the King's writ did not run'; they requested that they should either be allowed to send members to Parliament or enjoy their ancient exemptions.[113]

This line of argument had become a veiled threat by March 1640. The City of Durham petitioned for Bishop Morton's support for another Bill, which notably enough they were promised, meanwhile Sir William Bellasis, High Sheriff of the county and responsible for collecting Ship Money, wrote to Windebanke.[114] He too noted that:

> Our gentlemen and freeholders are still very desirous to have knights and burgesses like their neighbouring counties and they have with general consent entreated my brother Darcy and myself to solicit the business.[115]

Bellasis was anxious to know what the King might think and added somewhat ominously:

> I have made it one of my arguments to them to pay the Ship Money more cheerfully or else they cannot expect it from his Majesty. The truth is, if they find me still an instrument to press payments and can do nothing else, I shall not have that credit amongst them that may be so useful for his Majesty's service as were needful.[116]

There is no evidence that a Bill was presented in the Short Parliament of 1640. One was given two readings early on in the proceedings of the Long Parliament, but was then lost amidst a welter of more notable business.[117]

The Civil War closes this episode in the story of Durham's fight to gain Parliamentary representation in the seventeenth century. The Bills failed during this period primarily because of a concern on the part of James I to maintain the *status quo* when faced with demands for Parliamentary reform. Or to put it more kindly to James, his vision of such reform was more logical and radical than Parliament was inclined to accept. It is possible that genuine fears about Catholicism and a lack of substantial citizens in some areas also played a part in the decision; they certainly did for the most ambitious proposals of 1621. It cannot have impressed James that at times during the debates the Commons stood revealed as a cockpit of jealous factions, anxious that Durham should not gain at their expense. Whatever the reasons for the failure of these early Bills, it is not as clear as was once thought that the Bishop was always to blame; while it is true that Bishop James opposed the Bill, the case is unproven against Neile and Morton and if anything the evidence suggests they were happy to countenance reform.

It is perhaps in keeping with the current trend in writing about Parliament during this period that much of this paper, partly by its very deliberately detailed approach, confuses issues once held simple. When theories have become entrenched one way of breaking new ground is to pay close attention to the details of cases. It is a service which local historians frequently perform when they challenge general theories with precise local case studies. In this instance, close attention to the springs of action in the provinces, so natural with local historians, is modified by a glimpse of how important 'Parliamentarians' of the likes of Sandys and Coke were in ensuring that these Bills ever got beyond a first or second reading. It is also deemed possible that a Bill might not even have appeared in 1624 had it not been for Prince Charles and politics of a very different order from those of County Durham. Moreover, the appearance of Bills is not seen as clear evidence of conflict and strife in the North; if that was really the case, why did good Protestants hold back from talking of altars and candles in Durham Cathedral until 1628? Yet all is not confusion, for the vague grievances against Bishop James and the general situation in the North have been clarified to a large extent by an appreciation of the major issue which greatly affected the timing of this campaign, namely that of taxation and representation. It is fashionable to decry the idea of constitutional conflicts, but the constant recurrence of this theme is evidence that people were groping towards this principle, just as they were clarifying the more well known freedoms of speech, elections and freedom from arrest. That the case was not won completely for County Durham until after the Restoration does not detract from the significance of this fight in the early seventeenth century.

NOTES

*I am most grateful to John Fines, Chris Kitching, David Marcombe, Mike Tillbrook and my wife Liz for valuable discussions during the preparation of this paper.

1. This account can be traced, with some minor modifications, through the following standard works: R. Surtees, *The History and Antiquities of the County Palatine of Durham*, 4 Vols. (1816), I, Appendix II, pp. cxlvii-cxlviii; *The Victoria History of the County of Durham*, ed. W. Page, 3 Vols., II (1907), pp. 167–8, 171–2, III (1928), p. 37; M. James, *Family, Lineage, and Civil Society* (1974), pp. 3, 165–7. Details of members of Parliament who represented the County and City, briefly during the Interregnum and regularly after 1675 (1678 for the City), can be found in W. Bean, *The Parliamentary Representation of the Six Northern Counties of England* (1890), pp. 97–178.
2. We are basically dependent upon the printed Journals of both Houses of Parliament, odd letters in the Public Record Office and items printed in Surtees, *History of Durham*. I am grateful to Roger Norris in Durham and to the archivists of the House of Lords for attempting to find more material for me without much success.
3. C. Russell, *Parliaments and English Politics 1621–1629* (1979), has placed the most recent nails in the coffin of the Whig view of these Parliaments; C. Holmes, *Seventeenth Century Lincolnshire* (1980), and 'The County Community in Stuart Historiography', *Journal of British Studies*, XIX (1980), pp. 54–73 has caused a stir amongst county historians by re-emphasising the connections between London and the provinces, playing down the isolation and distinctiveness of county communities.
4. See the papers by Chris Kitching and David Loades for fuller discussion of the fluctuating fortunes of the Bishops.
5. G. Lapsley, *The County Palatine of Durham* (1900), is the standard work on this subject.
6. S. & S. Watts, *From Border to Middle Shire: Northumberland 1586–1625* (1975), chpt. 7.
7. *C.J.*, I, p. 448.
8. *Ibid.*
9. *Ibid.*, p. 449.
10. *Ibid.*, pp. 449–50.
11. The Durham gentry did have access to the House of Commons if they cared to stand for constituencies outside their own county. Sir George Selby represented Newcastle in the Parliamentary sessions of 1610; Bean, *op.cit.*, p. 564.
12. *C.J.*, I, p. 63; T. Oldfield, *The Representative History of Great Britain and Ireland*, 6 Vols. (1816), III, p. 423.
13. If one judges by his attendance record of 79 out of a possible 88 days during the first session of the 1610 Parliament held between February and July, Bishop James was at least regularly present in the Lords. Sickness seems to have prevented him from attending on more than 10 out of a

possible 21 days in the final session held between October and December. *L.J.*, II, pp. 548–685.

14. P.R.O., SP/14/18/72, Dean James to Salisbury, Feb. 8 1606.
15. *LCC Survey of London*, Vol. XVIII, The Strand, Part II (1937), pp. 91–2; For some of the debate on this *Act for the assurance of certain lands and rents to the Bishop of Durham and his successors, and of certain other lands to Robert, Earl of Salisbury, and his heirs*, (7 Jac. I, c.6. private Acts), see: *Proceedings in Parliament 1610*, ed. E. Foster, 2 Vols., (1966), I, pp. 107–8, 110, 240–2; P.R.O., SP/14/55/27 is a copy of the Bill dated June 16 1610.
16. P.R.O., SP/14/48/52, Bishop James offers profuse thanks for the stables in a letter to Thomas Wilson, Sept. 25 1609; SP/14/68/63, James was still showering Salisbury with gratitude for his conduct over the Durham House purchase in a letter of Feb. 16 1612.
17. *Parliament 1610*, ed. Foster, I, p. 149.
18. *V.C.H. Durham*, III, pp. 33–8 provides a full account of this dispute, including the ingenious reason given for the Bishop's death.
19. *Ibid.*, p. 36 n78.
20. P.R.O., SP/14/50/72.
21. *Ibid.*
22. In a long report to Secretary Winwood dated Sept. 24 1616, William Morton, using the alias 'Zeth Beridge', commented that Bishop James had gained Salisbury's support in the dispute over the charter in return for compliance over the Durham House purchase. P.R.O., SP/14/88/94.
23. This information is given by Bishop James in his letter cited below, P.R.O., SP/14/80/8; for information on official holders of the post see: J. Sainty, *Lieutenants of Counties, 1585–1642*, Bulletin of the Institute of Historical Research, Special Supplement 8, May 1970, p. 19.
24. P.R.O., SP/14/80/8, Jan. 24 1615.
25. P.R.O., SP/14/80/128, Bishop James to John Packer, attendant to the Lord Chamberlain, c. June 1615; Mike Tillbrook has pointed out to me that it is highly indicative of the Bishop's loss of prestige in the North that this letter was not addressed personally to Somerset; James, *Family, Lineage and Civil Society*, pp. 151–3 talks of a campaign to revive the power of the Neville connection in the North, basically recusant gentry, in favour of Somerset; Watts, *Border to Middle Shire*, chpt. 9 reveals how faction fighting at Court between the Howards and their political opponents was played out in the North and illustrates the fragility of this Northern Somerset faction.
26. R. Howell, *Newcastle-upon-Tyne and the Puritan Revolution* (1967), pp. 23–32.
27. P.R.O., SP/14/50/72, James to Salisbury, Dec. 18 1609.
28. James, *Family, Lineage and Civil Society*, pp. 69–70.
29. P.R.O., SP/14/88/94, Morton (alias Beridge) to Winwood, Sept. 24 1616.
30. *Ibid.*
31. James, *Family, Lineage and Civil Society*, pp. 164–67 provides a clear exposition of this case; it is thanks to James that we have the notion of 'church families' as a force in Durham society, pp. 72, 116, 150–1, 164. Use of this label is fraught with difficulties because it need not follow that just

because an ancestor made his fortune serving the church several generations before, so his descendants should remain loyal to later Bishops.
32. See p. 186.
33. *Durham Civic Memorials*, ed. C. Whiting, S.S., 160 (1952) p. 25.
34. On May 12 1614 Anderson claimed that County Durham had 'more recusants than in any part of England', something which he blamed on the lack of a preaching ministry in the diocese. *C.J.*, I, p. 482; in a later tirade against the Bishop personally on May 14, he spoke of 'one speaking against a penal law, checked; because that against the Bishop's profit . . .'. *C.J.*, I, p. 484. For the involvement of the Conyers and the Lawsons in the campaign see the petition cited above, *Durham Civic Memorials*, Whiting, pp. 25–26.
35. James, *Family, Lineage and Civil Society*, pp. 138–141.
36. P.R.O., SP/14/88/94.
37. *Durham Civil Memorials*, Whiting, p. 26.
38. Anderson's dislike of Bishop James seems to have originated when the latter was Dean of Durham for on hearing that James was soon to become Bishop in 1606, Anderson wrote to Salisbury complaining of the Dean's poor treatment of his tenants, of whom Anderson was one. *H.M.C., Salisbury (Cecil) MS., at Hatfield*, XVIII, p. 141, letter dated May 21 1606. I am grateful to Mike Tillbrook for this reference and also for reminding me of Anderson's comparative youth; he was only 23 in 1606, 31 when he entered Parliament in 1614. He was obviously something of a controversial figure in Newcastle politics because there was trouble over his election as Alderman in 1613, hence my suggestion that he may have had something to prove in his native town. Howell, *Newcastle and the Puritan Revolution*, p. 52.
39. *Cosin's Correspondence*, II, ed. G. Ornsby, S.S., 55 (1872), p. 212.
40. P.R.O., SP/14/88/94.
41. *C.J.*, I, p. 484, May 14 1614.
42. *Ibid.*
43. *Ibid.*, p. 492, May 21 1614.
44. P.R.O., SP/14/88/94.
45. *C.J.*, I, p. 457, April 9 1614.
46. *Ibid.*, p. 458; David Marcombe has reminded me that the Bishops of Durham traditionally tried to retain some friends in the Commons, Pilkington going so far as to pay Fleetwood a retainer for services rendered. I draw attention to Neile's use of his secretary, Edward Liveley, as an MP later, but I have been unable to find evidence of such a connection between Bishop James and Ashley, who was presumably Francis Ashley, MP for Dorchester. Ashley claimed to have spoken on the matter 'by accident', but it is noticeable that he was sent for by the Bishop and instructed to inform the Commons that the County did not desire representation. *C.J.*, I, p. 484, May 14 1614.
47. *C.J.*, I, p. 458, April 9 1614, 'Resolved, upon the Question, that Sir George Selby, Sheriff of Durham, cannot be chosen Knight for the shire for Northumberland'.
48. *C.J.*, I, p. 484. The importance of the taxation issue in this story has been

picked up in general works even if it has been neglected by historians of the region: D. Hirst, *The Representative of the People? Voters and Voting in England under the early Stuarts (1975)*, pp. 176, 236.
49. *C.J.*, I, p. 484.
50. *Ibid.*
51. *Ibid.*
52. *Ibid.*, p. 492.
53. The inclusion of Barnard Castle is interesting for not only does it illustrate the alliance of gentry interests involved in this campaign, but it was one of the few towns in the area where the Bishop's influence could be said to have been minimal.
54. H(ouse (of) L(ords) R(ecord) O(ffice), Main Papers, April 8 1614 to May 24 1614, f. 93.
55. *Ibid.*
56. *C.J.*, I, p. 502.
57. *Ibid.*
58. *Ibid.*
59. *Ibid.*
60. *Ibid.*, p. 539.
61. Darlington, Stockton, Bishop Auckland and Gateshead had all been incorporated by past Bishops of Durham and would thus have proved likely pocket boroughs. Mike Tillbrook informs me that in terms of wealth and population, Darlington and Gateshead had the best claims for representation and that Sir Thomas Riddell would probably have stood more to gain in the latter case than the Bishop. Everything is relative, however, and it does not inspire confidence that Darlington was apparently described by James I as 'Darnton i' the dirt', J. Patten, *English Towns 1500–1700* (1978), p. 204. For background information on these boroughs see: M. H. Dodds, 'The Bishops' Boroughs', *A.A.*, 3rd Series, 12, 1915, pp. 81–185. Hartlepool's claims stemmed from being a port town, something which had been picked up in the 1614 Parliament, *C.J.*, I, p. 502. Surtees, *History of Durham*, I, App. II, p. cxlvii and R. Welford, *History of Newcastle and Gateshead*, 3 Vols. (1887), III, p. 236, assumed that Bishop Auckland had the weakest claims to be placed on the list.
62. P.R.O., SP/14/92/33, Robert Cooper to Thomas Lake, May 19 1617.
63. P.R.O., S(ignet) O(ffice), 3/6, Commission of Lieutenancy, Nov. 14 1617.
64. For Neile see: A. Foster, 'A Biography of Archbishop Richard Neile, 1562–1640', (unpub. D.Phil. thesis, Oxford Univ. 1978), and 'The function of a bishop: the career of Richard Neile, 1562–1640', *Continuity and Change*, ed. R. O'Day and F. Heal, 1976, pp. 33–54.
65. *Cosin's Correspondence II*, p. 212.
66. See, for example, the interpretations provided by: Surtees, *History of Durham*, I, App. II, p. cxlviii; IV, p. 68; James, *Family, Lineage and Civil Society*, pp. 166–7, which has been accepted by Russell, *Parliaments 1621–1629*, p. 44 n2.
67. When moving from Winchester to York in 1632, Neile took the trouble to warn Laud that Farnham was seeking incorporation, which he felt would 'become very prejudicial to the inheritance of the Bishopric'; *H.M.C.*

Cowper MS., 3 Vols (1888), I, p. 466. The increased clerical representation on the bench at Durham is picked up by James, *Family, Lineage and Civil Society*, p. 163. For information on York see Foster, thesis, pp. 269–70.

68. *Commons Debates 1621*, ed. W. Notestein, F. Relf, and H. Simpson, 7 Vols. (1935), II, p. 334; VI, p. 396.
69. For the election of Liveley see: Bean, *Parliamentary Representation of the Six Northern Counties*, p. 503 and C. Hunter Blair, 'Members of Parliament for Berwick-upon-Tweed and Morpeth, 1558–1831', *A.A.*, 4th Series, 24, 1946, pp. 77–8; for details of his relationship with Neile see: Foster, thesis, pp. 92, 155, 242. For the context to Sir Paul Neile's election for Ripon in 1640 see: J. Gruenfelder 'The Election to the Short Parliament', *Early Stuart Studies*, ed. H. Reinmuth Jnr., 1970, pp. 180–230. It may have been thanks to the Bishop that Meredith Morgan, a minor Treasury official, represented Berwick in Parliament in 1614; T. Moir, *The Addled Parliament of 1614* (1958), p. 193. Neile took a close interest in Berwick where he supervised the building of a bridge for which he apparently laid the last stones personally in 1624, making himself ill in the process. *A.P.C., 1619–21*, p. 254. A letter from Robert Jennison to Samuel Ward in 1624 reveals that Neile was closely interested in the outcome of the Newcastle election and apparently blamed Jennison for the fact that Sir Peter rather than Sir Thomas Riddell was elected for the town; B.L.O., Tanner MS. 73, f. 437.
70. *Durham Civic Memorials*, Whiting, pp. 25–6; the petition carried forty-nine names including those of J.P.s Anderson, Calverley, Fetherstonhaugh, Lawson, Place, Smith, Bellasis and Tonge. Sir Bertram Bulmer and Sir George Selby, High Sheriff for the county in 1620, and Sir George Conyers, one of Neile's Deputy Lieutenants, all had Catholic connections. I am grateful to Mike Tillbrook for help in analysing this list.
71. *Ibid.*; Timothy Comyn was Neile's Receiver General, Hugh Wright was Clerk of the Halmote courts and George Martyn was connected with the Chancery court. William Smith was of Yorkshire stock and became Attorney General in May 1623.
72. Surtees, *History of Durham*, IV p. 158.
73. *Ibid.*, pp. 157–8; Mike Tillbrook assures me that for Liddell one should read Riddell. This selection seems highly likely as Anderson, Riddell, Fetherstonhaugh and Bowes had all just been elected to Parliament. Mike Tillbrook feels the turnout at the January session was unusually high in 1621, which suggests that the petition had been well canvassed amongst the county gentry.
74. *C.J.*, I, p. 539.
75. *Ibid.*, p. 553.
76. *Ibid.*
77. *Ibid.*
78. *Ibid.*
79. *Ibid.*, p. 592; Barnard Castle had become vested in the Crown by the attainder of the Earl of Westmorland after the Northern Rebellion. The Bowes family gained favourable leases to large amounts of this property because of their loyalty during the Rebellion. The manor was later granted

to the Earl of Somerset, but on his fall from favour, again reverted to the Crown. With Brancepeth and other forfeited estates it was settled for the maintenance of the Prince's household. The property was sold off to Sir Henry Vane in 1626. Surtees, *History of Durham*, IV, pp. 67–8.
80. *Ibid.*, p. 158.
81. *C.J.*, I, p. 553.
82. Russell, *Parliaments 1621–1629*, chpt. 3.
83. R. Ruigh, *The Parliament of 1624. Politics and Foreign Policy (1971), chpt. 2.*
84. *Ibid.*, p. 119.
85. *L.J.*, III, p. 132.
86. *Ibid.*, p. 146.
87. *Notes of the Debates in the House of Lords officially taken by Henry Elsing, Clerk of the Parliaments 1621*, ed. S. Gardiner, Camden Society Old Series, 103 (1870), p. vi.
88. James, *Family, Lineage and Civil Society*, p. 166.
89. This exaggeration is noted by James above, p. 163; there were 19 gentry on the commission in 1620 and only 9 clerical justices. The remarks about clerical domination in County Durham were made on May 1 1621. *Commons Debates*, III, pp. 111–12 & n.
90. John Richardson seems to have had a chequered career in County Durham. A close ally of Bishop James, he was for a time Solicitor General, but he fell from power soon after Neile's arrival in 1617. It is possible that he was sacrificed because he was so closely identified with the Bishop's position over Durham's charter. *V.C.H. Durham*, III, pp. 37–8.
91. Foster, thesis, pp. 131–2, 213–20, 78–9 provides details of Neile's work in Durham. When Neile deigned to distinguish between secular priests and Jesuits in a debate in February 1621, Locke wrote to Carleton 'The Bishop of Durham was their friend in the Upper House, for which he had as much thanks as for that he did the last Parliament. Their fingers did itch at him in the Lower House'. P.R.O., SP/14/119/106.
92. *C.J.*, I, pp. 747, 749–50.
93. *Ibid.*, pp. 749–50.
94. *Ibid.*, p. 766.
95. Russell, *Parliaments 1621–1629*, p. 197 draws out this general point and interestingly enough pinpoints the discussions of the Durham Bill as an example. See likewise Hirst, *Rep. of the People*, pp. 232–4.
96. *C.J.*, I, p. 766: this simply consisted of adding eight people to the original committee.
97. *Ibid.*, pp. 697, 782.
98. *Ibid.*, p. 786.
99. *Ibid.*, p. 697; it was Sir Henry Anderson who made this point.
100. *L.J.*, III, p. 402.
101. *Ibid.*, p. 404.
102. P.R.O., SP/14/167/10.
103. *Notes of the Debates in the House of Lords, 1624 and 1626*, ed. S. Gardiner, Camden Society New Series, 24 (1879), pp. 93–5 gives details of the York House exchange when Neile seems to have aligned himself with

Archbishop Abbot in expressing doubts about the Bill.

104. This explanation is accepted by J. Cannon, *Parliamentary Reform 1640–1832* (1973), p. 3.
105. Foster, thesis, chpt. 5 – A Bishop in the House of Lords.
106. D.U.L., Mickleton and Spearman MS. 2, f. 336.
107. P.R.O., SP/16/7/65.
108. *Ibid.*
109. D.U.L., Mickleton and Spearman MS. 2, f. 387.
110. *A.P.C., 1625–26*, p. 445.
111. *C.J.*, I, p. 776.
112. P.R.O., SP/16/59/6.
113. *Ibid.*
114. *Durham Civic Memorials*, Whiting, pp. 35–6.
115. P.R.O., SP/16/449/23.
116. *Ibid.*
117. *C.J.*, II, pp. 38, 40, 61, Jan. 1 1641 when a committee was appointed after the second reading of the Bill.

Arminianism and Society in County Durham, 1617–1642

Michael Tillbrook

Durham was perhaps the first English county to witness the disintegration of the 'Calvinist concensus' and its replacement as the dominant creed within the Church of England by the anti-predestinarian beliefs associated with the English followers of the Dutch theologian Jacobus Arminius. Such views did not emerge, in English terms, from a theological vacuum. At Cambridge in 1595/6 the French divine, Peter Baro, had argued, in opposition to the dominant view within the Church of England, that free will had a role to play in the obtaining of salvation.[1] Archbishop Bancroft dissociated himself from predestinarianism, yet remained an isolated figure. Nevertheless, after his death an Arminian group within the Church of England began to emerge.[2]

The key early figures in this group were two bishops, Richard Neile and Lancelot Andrewes, who both enjoyed a cordial relationship with James I despite the fact that the King did not share their doctrinal tendencies.[3] The initial influence of this group, whose significance lay, as Dr. Tyacke has argued, in the redefinition of that formerly vague term 'puritanism' so that it came to embrace all forms of Calvinism which had hitherto linked nonconformists to the leaders of the established church, came when its members were able to seize the ear of the youthful Prince Charles. Once he succeeded his father, the group was able to set about capturing the Church of England in the second half of the 1620s.[4] I shall argue here that this national phenomenon had been foreshadowed in Durham where the emergence of Arminianism was early and rapid, but that by the 1630s Arminianism in Durham had passed its peak and assumed, for the most part, a more defensive outlook conditioned by divines whose influence, though not necessarily their background, proved to be latitudinarian, and whose influence proved more pervading than that of the few remaining Arminian zealots.

The rapid establishment of Arminianism in Durham can be attributed largely to the ease and success with which Bishop Neile exploited his often fortuitous opportunities for patronage following his translation from Lincoln in 1617. Over the years both Neile as an individual and his role in Durham have been misunderstood by historians.[5] However, recent research has led to the emergence of a more balanced picture of the Bishop's activities. Dr. Foster has stressed Neile's abilities as an organiser and administrator, while Dr. Tyacke has emphasised his fundamental role in building a system of patronage and protection which facilitated the promotion of a group of younger Arminian divines when their beliefs were still considered heterodox by the bulk of church leaders.[6]

Aided by his enjoyment of the King's favour and by the diocese's traditional freedom from archiepiscopal visitation from York, Neile was able to exploit for the benefit of his adherents the fruits of an unusually concentrated degree of available patronage. This had particular liturgical significance in the first three years of Neile's episcopate because the Bishop was able to appoint to three major canonries in Durham Cathedral while the prebendaries themselves were in control there as a result of the Deanery being in absentee and lay hands. Neile handled these appointments with characteristic aplomb. Not only did he appoint two members of his own circle: Augustine Lindsell, later described by Peter Smart as 'a profest disciple of that arch-heretic and enemy of God, Arminius, and a ringleader of that cursed sect in England', and Daniel Birkhead; but he also smoothed relationships with the existing diocesan hierarchy by granting a major canonry to the Archdeacon of Northumberland, John Cradock, whose diocesan position was shortly afterwards consolidated by his appointment to the diocesan Chancellorship.[7]

Neile's subsequent pattern of prebendal patronage showed a similar judicious blend of doctrinal considerations, family loyalty and readiness to reward local clerics. His half-brother, Robert Newell, received a canonry in October 1620, as did three of his chaplains, Gabriel Clarke, who was to marry Neile's neice, John Cosin and Eleazar Duncon who were members of the Durham House group of promising Arminian academics who had gathered under the Bishop's protection at his London residence, while he also appointed John Robson, Rector of Morpeth, whose precise doctrinal position is not easy to determine.[8]

Furthermore, Neile benefited from the apparent haste with which some of the existing prebendaries sought to accommodate themselves to the new order. Thus, Marmaduke Blakiston, who enjoyed local significance as a link between the clerical establishment and the county gentry, appears cheerfully to have acquiesced in the changes and he was able to reinforce his connection with the Arminian group through his daughter's marriage to John Cosin. Francis Burgoyne, the long-serving Rector of Bishopwearmouth who received a major canonry during the vacancy which followed the death of Bishop James, played an active role in the Arminian changes both in the Cathedral and in his parish church. Ferdinand Morecroft, who had served Bishop James as a chaplain, attached himself to the Arminians and served as the Dean and Chapter's Treasurer at a time when expensive changes in the setting of Cathedral worship were taking place, though he may never have completely reconciled his new attachments with his former beliefs. Neile was thus able to control the Chapter through the appointment of his protégés who were ably assisted by the temporising of the local clerical careerists.

He was able to effect a similar transformation in the major diocesan offices. The death of the eccentric Archdeacon of Durham, William Morton, in 1620 enabled the Bishop to fill this vital disciplinary office with Gabriel Clarke, thus adding to the control which the Arminians could already exert through the Officialty jurisdiction of the Dean and Chapter. The Chancellorship of the diocese was granted to the local temporiser, John Cradock, who used the office as a convenient means of enrichment and was thus unlikely to be too bothered by the changes in attitude and practice within the diocese.

To a more limited extent, such changes were mirrored at parochial level. The Bishop and the Dean and Chapter controlled a high proportion of the county's more substantial livings which passed to members of Neile's circle when they became available. Thus Lindsell received the rich Rectory of Houghton-le-Spring in 1623 and Cosin was appointed to Elwick in the following year. However, the availability of such livings was limited by the grip of the careerists like Blakiston, Morecroft and William James on parishes such as Sedgefield, Stanhope and Ryton.[9] In this context, therefore, the scope of Neile's patronage was more limited and while he had ample opportunity to reward his closest followers, the extent of his success in Durham was determined largely by the closeness of his relationship with the local careerists and, given the extremes of clerical incomes in Durham, there was little incentive for ambitious young men to leave Cambridge or Oxford for the more onerous existence of parochial life in the county's more poorly endowed livings.[10]

There remained, however, a potential threat to Arminian predominance in the person of the Dean of Durham. Before 1620 the Deanery had been held by an absentee layman. This had enabled the prebendaries to elect a Sub-Dean from among their number to exercise some of the Dean's functions. This changed following the possibly simoniacal appointment of Richard Hunt to the Deanery.[11] Hunt was a rather shadowy figure and it should not be assumed automatically that he invariably favoured Arminian innovation, a supposition which is strengthened when it is remembered that Cosin sought to make his point about the Cathedral's rearrangements by manhandling one of the Dean's servants.[12] Furthermore, Hunt in 1632 permitted the anti-Arminian prebendary, Peter Smart, to sit in his stall wearing his surplice and hood, though Smart, having been excommunicated and degraded, was not entitled to do so.[13]

Hunt, however, despite his long tenure of the Deanery, never exercised much influence on capitular matters in either direction, partly because of poor health and partly, so Smart thought, because of the mildness of his temperament.[14] Hunt's impotence, the dominance within the Chapter of Neile's devotees and the influence of the Bishop at Court combined to give the Durham Arminians an ideal opportunity to introduce into the setting of Cathedral worship the liturgical innovations necessary for the underpinning of their doctrinal preoccupations.

When faced with such innovatory threats, the hitherto dominant Calvinist episcopalians had three possible courses of action. In the manner of some of the Durham prebendaries, they could accept or even enthusiastically propound Arminian innovations. Those of a radical or restless disposition could assert their doctrinal distinctiveness by drifting into nonconformity. Some, however, chose to fight Arminian innovation from within. Thus Robert Hutton, a veteran Calvinist Prebendary and Rector of Houghton-le-Spring, was alleged to have preached a sermon which reflected 'on the King, the Bishop, the Church and its ceremonies', though this eighteenth-century description, followed by subsequent writers, may well misrepresent and exaggerate what actually happened, for while an attack from a conservative Calvinist standpoint on the Bishop and the newly-introduced ceremonies is understandable, it is difficult to envisage how it might have incorporated criticism of a King, James I, who shared the preacher's fundamental assumptions.[15]

A clearer example of clerical opposition to Arminian practices occured at Darlington in 1626 when the Curate there was compelled by the High Commission to apologise for claiming that the use of the sign of the cross in baptisms was papistical and that standing during Gospel readings and bowing at the name of Jesus was superstitious.[16]

However, the most significant denunciation from within the Church of Arminian practices in Durham came in a sermon preached in the Cathedral on July 27 1628 by Peter Smart, a Durham Prebendary and Rector of Boldon. Smart, like his colleague Ferdinand Morecroft, had been associated with Bishop James since the latter's time as Dean of Christ Church. However, whereas Morecroft had been quick to accommodate himself to the new régime, Smart's attitude initially seems to have been more circumspect, for it seems reasonable to assume that at this stage the Arminians would have been as anxious to attract Smart as his other active colleagues. Smart did undertake some minor tasks in capitular administration during the 1620s and he was in fact the Chapter's Receiver in 1620.[17]

Perusal of the Chapter Act Book suggests that he acceded in some of the innovations but was absent from Chapter meetings when some of the crucial decisions were taken.[18] Unfortunately, this source does not reveal any clues about Smart's motives in preaching his undeniably vituperative sermon at the time he chose. Both the indications of his character and the rambling and inconsistent nature of the sermon suggest that the matter was spontaneous rather than planned, although the translation of Neile to Winchester earlier in the year may have prompted Smart to try his luck during the vacancy. Furthermore, he seems to have been pushed beyond endurance by his younger opponents, Cosin and Lindsell, who not only failed to accord Smart the respect he thought merited by his age and seniority but also demonstrated an indifference to their inferior social origins which Smart, among others, found intensely irritating.[19]

Interpreting Smart's sermon merely in view of his anger, ill-temper and alleged fanaticism is futile for, while this may explain the general vituperativeness of the attack, it does not explain the circumstances or chronology of the controversy.[20] It is essential, on the other hand, to interpret Smart's sermon in the context of the circumstances of the Church of England at that time, for to judge Smart as a fanatical puritan whose sentiments adumbrated the changes in religion which took place under the Long Parliament is to confuse his manner of expression with the matter expressed. Smart's language was certainly colourful and intemperate, although in that sense his sermon was typical of a style of exposition which had been characteristic of English proselytising. However, an examination of his sermon and other works does not reveal a puritan proto-revolutionary. Rather, it demonstrates that Smart was nothing more than an orthodox and old-fashioned Calvinist episcopalian of the type which had flourished during the reign of Queen Elizabeth. His attitudes were fundamentally conservative, even reactionary. He consistently stressed the length of his association with the Durham foundation and was always keen to point the contrast between the good ordering of services during the time of Bishop James and the malpractices of more recent times. He himself had 'taught the people to observe the old, confirmed and established' forms.[21]

The fundamentally conservative Erastianism of his attitudes was emphasised in his attitude to the Royal Supremacy, not only in his criticism of Cosin's alleged questioning of the Supremacy, but also in his argument that acceptance of the Supremacy permitted the monarch to practise innovations in his private worship which were not allowed elsewhere.[22] This notion of the Royal Supremacy was vital to Smart's argument. He considered himself the upholder of a church polity which embraced the Royal Supremacy, the ceremonies and the vestments which the Church of England had adopted and evolved over more than sixty years, episcopal government and doctrinal Calvinism. Conservative Calvinists like Smart held that Arminian ceremonial necessarily possessed popish connotations. It was understandable therefore that Smart should exploit the allegation that Cosin had termed the Reformation a deformation.[23]

Smart did not emphasise doctrinal differences in his castigation of Arminian practice. This does not, however, invalidate Dr. Tyacke's emphasis on the doctrinal distinctions between Arminianism and English Calvinism.[24] Smart may have been reluctant to tackle his sophisticated opponents on doctrinal grounds. He did contend that Cosin's recently published *Collection of Devotions* contained 'speculative and theoretical popery', but he did not analyse what he doubtless considered self-evident.[25]

His criticism of Arminian administration of the Eucharist was stimulated partly by its style, 'turned well near into a theatrical stage play' as well as by the sacrificial connotation of the Eucharist administered at the altar rather than at the communion table.[26] Furthermore, by his emphasis upon visual imagery Smart was undoubtedly hoping to elicit a response from his hearers, most of whom would have lacked the sophistication to comprehend the intricacies of doctrinal debate. This was especially important in view of the doctrinally ambiguous content of the Book of Common Prayer.[27] Such ambiguity had hitherto been resolved by differing emphases on forms and ritual and Smart's sermon can be placed within this context, for the stress on the changes in ritual was the most immediate way in which Smart could impress upon his audience the nature of the gulf which existed between the Arminians and their opponents.

Nevertheless, many of Smart's criticisms of Arminian practices had deeper implications. The removal of the communion table and its replacement by an altar had resulted in 'an inundation of ceremonies' with popish connotations.[28] The greater emphasis upon and changes in the style of Cathedral music, a particular interest of Cosin, incurred Smart's ire because of the reduced intelligibility of the liturgy, 'that though it be not Latin, yet by reason of the confusedness of voices of so many singers, with a multitude of melodious instruments, directly contrary to the Injunctions and Homilies, the greatest part of the service is no better understood, than if it were in Hebrew or Irish', while he found the continued playing of music during the administration of the sacraments of baptism and communion offensive.[29]

Copes were worn at morning service and at prayers following sermons 'contrary to the express words of the canons' while one of the copes so used had been a Roman Catholic cast-off.[30] Smart also objected to the introduction of images with their intimations of idolatry which were exacerbated by the Dean and Chapter's employment of a Roman Catholic painter to advise on coloration.[31] The excessive use of candles was considered akin to Mariolatry.[32] The new font was elaborately and expensively debased by alleged Roman Catholic imagery.[33]

Smart's sermon provoked an immediate response from the Durham Arminians and their fellow-travellers. He was forced to appear immediately before the Durham High Commission, of which he himself was a current member. The case, however, dragged on interminably, though its conduct does shed light on both Arminian strength and the nature of the opposition to Arminianism in the diocese.[34] The conduct of the case in Durham suggests that Arminian strength there was less monolithic than might have been supposed. Two of the four commissioners present at the initial hearing seem to have been equivocal in their opposition.[35] Robson, one of the two prebendaries to whom Smart's prebend was entrusted after sequestration, seems also not to have wholly identified with Arminianism.[36] Most significantly of all, Bishop Howson, a moderate Arminian much criticised by Smart, lost sympathy with the extreme conduct of Lindsell and Cosin and, alienated by their habit of appealing behind his back to Laud and Neile, attempted to ease Smart's position.[37]

Nevertheless, the Arminians were strong enough in the area and possessed close enough links with the Crown to ensure that expressions of support for Smart remained muted. He received no overt support from anyone in the upper reaches of the diocesan hierarchy and only very limited support from its lower ranks.[38] Overt lay support was similarly limited. He was vigorously though incompetently supported by a prominent Durham lawyer, Edward Wright.[39] There are hints that other members of the county's legal establishment might have been prepared to help. Thomas Tempest, an associate of Attorney General Noy, came into this category.[40] Nevertheless, it is significant that there seems to have been no identification of support for Smart from the county's most influential opponent of Bishop Neile, John Richardson, who might have been expected additionally to support Smart because of their former mutual links with Bishop James. However, Richardson, although assumed to have been a supporter of Smart by the House of Commons, was more concerned with reingratiating himself with the local clerical establishment in order to exploit its legal and related patronage, to involve himself too deeply in the case.[41]

There is little evidence of substantial support for Smart among members of the county's political establishment. This was partly a reflection of the dependence of a substantial proportion of the lay establishment upon the local patronage distributed by the church.[42] It also reflected the success enjoyed by Bishop Neile in his relations with the county's political élite, a key feature of Durham society which may have eluded those anxious to fit the Bishop's role more neatly into a predetermined pattern.[43]

In some respects Neile had enjoyed a notably successful episcopate. He had managed to secure the co-operation of the county's leading gentlemen, including the prickly alleged oppositionist Sir Henry Anderson, in the furtherance of the county's lieutenancy service.[44] He had shown commendable managerial skills in coaxing reluctant gentlemen to take on burdensome local offices.[45] Through his encouragement of some of its leading citizens, he ended the damaging dispute which had bedevilled relations between the civic authorities in Durham and Bishop James and in the process prevented the development of tensions in Arminian Durham which were later to characterise York, Norwich and Chichester.[46] He sided also with the bulk of the county's gentry who wished to secure Parliamentary representation for Durham, sensibly realising the potential danger of opposing the political will of the county on such a sensitive issue.[47] In an important sense, therefore, Neile created a community of interest between the Arminians and the leading local gentry which helps to explain the subsequent contrast between Durham and some other shires in which much of the opposition to Arminianism was undertaken by those of secure and established status.[48]

Smart, starting from a position of local political weakness, exacerbated his problems because of his characteristic insensitivity and tactical ineptitude.[49] Having lost, through dissolution, the assistance of a House of Commons in which some influential members saw the growth of Arminianism and the survival of Parliament as incompatible, Smart failed crucially to exploit the tension which existed between Bishop Howson and the Arminian militants, Cosin and Lindsell, and he seems to have spurned the assistance of Howson whose commitment to ceremonial innovations he seems not to have questioned.[50] He spurned offers of compromise, including one involving financial compensation devised by Howson's successor, Thomas Morton, and Sir Richard Hutton, the Chancellor of the County Palatine.[51] His conduct of affairs was vehemently criticised by his wife who saw his relentless pursuit of trivialities as a significant contribution towards his enemies' triumph.[52]

On account both of his character and the conservatism of his views, Smart was to find himself increasingly isolated. His opponents deliberately misrepresented his standpoint in 1638 by accusing him of stirring up the Scots against episcopacy.[53] Most significantly of all, perhaps, Parliament soon lost interest in its 'proto-martyr' after he had served his purpose by providing the grounds for the destruction of High Commission and his brand of episcopalian Calvinism looked increasingly anachronistic, for by the early 1640s most of those who approved Smart's strictures against Arminianism could no longer stomach a Royal Supremacy which since 1625 had actively succoured its exponents, whereas most upholders of the Supremacy came almost naturally to associate Smart's brand of Calvinism with schismatical puritanism.[54]

The proceedings against Smart marked the peak of Arminian influence in Durham. With Neile's translation to Winchester the local Arminians no longer possessed effective episcopal leadership, although they enjoyed the approbation of Neile and Laud from afar.[55] The numerical influence of the Arminians was reduced. Lindsell was promoted to the Bishopric of Peterborough. Cosin reduced his Durham commitments following his election to the Mastership of Peterhouse in 1635. Among Smart's other principle opponents, Burgoyne died in 1633 and Blakiston resigned his preferments in favour of his son.[56] The successors of these clerics at both prebendal and parochial level exerted what amounted to a moderating influence. Anthony Maxton, a Scottish episcopalian and Chaplain to Charles when he was Prince of Wales, seems to have been more concerned with estate management than ecclesiastical politics.[57] John Wemyss, another Scotsman and like Maxton a royal appointee, tended to be lumped by his Presbyterian critics with Montague and Cosin, though his Erastianism had more in common with the attitude of Smart than with the exalted conception of the clerical state associated with Laudianism.[58]

Some of Bishop Morton's appointees, such as Isaac Basire, the Huguenot Prebendary and Rector of Egglescliffe, and John Johnson, who succeeded Burgoyne at Bishopwearmouth, seem to have been genuinely latitudinarian, cultivating links with both Arminians and Calvinists.[59] Given the appointment of such men and the declining influence within the Dean and Chapter of the Arminian militants, Morton was able to improve relationships which had become poisoned during the episcopate of his predecessor, although, ironically, he was helped in this because of the high personal regard in which he was held by Cosin who had long enjoyed a link with Morton through his friendship with the Bishop's long-serving Secretary, Richard Baddeley.[60]

Morton, of course, did face a dilemma in his administration of the diocese. He sympathised with the local Calvinists and he was not slow to give practical effect to that sympathy.[61] On the other hand, he was obliged to reach a *modus vivendi* with Arminians, the more militant of whom interpreted concessions to the Calvinists as signs of weakness. The two chief representatives of militant Arminianism still active regularly in Durham in the later 1630s were Eleazar Dunçon and Thomas Triplet. The former, a Chaplain to Neile and intimate member of the Durham House circle, had helped to secure the silencing of two preachers imported into the diocese by Morton.[62] The latter, who was not a member of Neile's circle and whose other associations might have indicated a more open minded approach to ecclesiastical matters,[63] sought to set himself up as a spy on behalf of Archbishop Laud to report on the activities of the Sunderland Presbyterians, of whom the most prominent was George Lilburne.[64] In the process, of course, Triplet was by-passing the ordinary jurisdiction of Bishop Morton, an ironic commentary on the usual Laudian emphasis on *iure divino* episcopacy.[65]

Despite the difficulties involved in dealing with zealots who, on the one hand, like Triplet, equated opposition to their point of view with covenanting sympathies and, on the other hand, like John Fenwick, saw

Morton as a nepotist, persecutor of true religion and encourager of Roman Catholicism and Arminianism, the Bishop sought to establish a *via media* which foreshadowed future developments in the Church of England. However, his compromise probably leaned more towards Arminianism than he himself would have wished, for he was not in a position to withstand the Arminian pressures which, by the time of Morton's episcopate, were mainly exogenous, the Bishop being faced by circumstances in which most fundamental Arminian assumptions were shared equally by the Crown and the two Archbishops. Laud, through his centralising activities, was attempting to impose a uniform Arminian practice on the whole country.[66] Furthermore, the Archbishop enjoyed the crucial support in Durham of the Archdeacon, Gabriel Clarke, formerly a member of Neile's Durham House set though not considered by Smart to be as culpable in the matter of ritualistic innovation as Cosin and Lindsell.[67] Under such pressures Durham began to experience at a parochial level the type of changes in the setting of worship from which, with the exception of Bishopwearmouth, it would seem to have been ironically exempt during the period of local Arminian predominance.[68]

The changes of the 1630s had three fundamental objectives: to emphasise the distinctiveness of the role of the priest and his separation from the congregation, to reaffirm the ritualistic elements of divine service at the expense of the sermon which under Arminianism had lost the soteriological significance which it may once have possessed and to improve the physical setting of worship. The most important change concerned seating arrangements within parish churches, because some reform was necessary, given Arminian preoccupations, as the traditional system of stall possession, which had faithfully reflected social gradations within the parish, could, through their irregularity and the right of occupiers to embellish stalls, restrict the ability of the congregation to witness the ritual effectively and even offend Arminian notions of sanctity and decorum by encroaching upon the choir.[69] This placed the Arminian clerics in something of a quandary. On the one hand, they were dedicated to reforming a system which nevertheless reflected the structure of parochial society. On the other hand, any proposed reforms required the approbation of precisely that segment of local society whose role and status were most strongly emphasised under the existing system, the Select Vestry of twelve or twenty four leading residents of the parish. Therefore a compromise was necessary in many parishes between Arminian decorousness and secular concerns with status and cost. The new stalls were ordered and seemly. They also, however, retained seating arrangements based on social precedence. Thus, in 1634 the Chancellor of the diocese, Thomas Burwell, issued a commission according to a standard form authorising the churchwardens of Gateshead

> to settle and place in the seats newly erected in the parish church all and each parishioner and inhabitants according to your discretions and their several qualities.

They were to be paid for in proportion to the usual parochial rating obligations.

The assigned stalls seem fairly to have reflected the distribution of local influence, for the most prominent and therefore most expensive stalls were allocated to the leading local landowners, merchants and coal-owners, Sir Thomas Riddell and Ralph Cole. Except in the case of Riddell, no places were assigned to families in general and many wives received special places separate from their husbands. Most of the stalls were shared at fees per stall ranging from two shillings to ten shillings. In addition there were cheap seats in the gallery. The occupational descriptions given to some of the individuals assigned places suggest that the churchwardens did not altogether overlook the allocation of stalls to those of comparatively humble status. However, both the limited provision which the churchwardens could make in terms of the increasing population of the parish and their apparent inability to assign all of their stalls testify to the failure of the established church to appeal, despite the compulsions at its disposal, to many in the poorer sections of society.[70]

The example of Gateshead is better documented than that of many other Durham parishes. In the absence of alternative evidence it was assumed that the principle proponent of this reform in the parishes was John Cosin, to the extent that it has become convenient and conventional to describe the incipient Gothic revivalism in Durham church furnishings as the 'Cosin style'.[71] This is partly a reflection of the role which Cosin played as Bishop of Durham after the Restoration when he was responsible directly for the rebuilding of the chapel at Auckland Castle in which he used newly commissioned and splendidly elaborate communion plate, partly a reflection of the parochial developments which took place during his episcopate and partly a reflection of the developments in his parish church at Brancepeth before the Civil War.

However, it would be misleading to ascribe the pre-War developments solely to Cosin's inspiration. Some of the developments usually attributed to the post-Restoration period may, in fact, date from the 1630s and owe much more to the enthusiasm of Archdeacon Clarke than to Cosin himself.[72] Many of the earliest developments took place in parishes with which Cosin had no direct connection, although it would be misleading to assume that he was unable to exert an indirect influence. Furthermore, Cosin's own enthusiasms were selective. He seems to have been largely unconcerned with his first Durham incumbency, Elwick, and even at Brancepeth matters were not perfect, for in 1636 presentments laid against the churchwardens there alleged a variety of neglects.[73] Studies of the evidence of Cosin's role have tended to lead to two contradictory inferences. On the one hand, it was felt that because Cosin inspired the elaborate furnishings at Brancepeth, he must also have been primarily responsible for the work which preceded it in other parishes. On the other hand, it has also been suggested that because Cosin had no official position in such parishes, he could have had no influence on furnishings there.[74] What such explanations fail to take into account is the complexity of circumstances involving the interaction of national policy, regional policy, as exemplified by the relationship between the diocesan and his officers and other clerics, and local circumstances, characterised by the willingness or unwillingness of individuals to acquiesce in and pay for the charges imposed upon them.[75]

The national policy by which Archbishop Laud attempted to impose an Arminian uniformity was reflected in the Visitation Articles issued by Bishop Morton in 1637. These provided a means of emphasising to the churchwardens in particular and through them to parishioners in general the broadly Arminian stress on order, ritual and seemliness in services and on sacerdotalism and the more narrowly Laudian concern with exalting the role of church and cleric within society. In response to these Articles, churchwardens reported on a wide variety of deficiencies which exercised the Arminian mind. There were occasional presentments against parishioners who had failed to pay parochial assessments levied for the repair of churches.[76] Funds collected for repairs were allegedly misappropriated.[77] There was a crop of complaints against impropriators who had failed to maintain their chancels properly.[78]

What is especially apparent among these presentments is the contrast between the inadequate provision of basic facilities at some impropriate parish churches and the expenditure lavished on beautification in some of the wealthier churches, especially when it is remembered that the diocese's first centre of Arminianism, the Dean and Chapter, was itself responsible in its capacity as impropriator for some of the decays.[79]

The more general condition of some churches was unsatisfactory. In some cases this stemmed from an unwillingness or inability to provide barely adequate facilities.[80] In others it suggests a reluctance to acquiesce in expensive Arminian plans for reforming the setting of worship.[81] The comparative absence of such cases from the admittedly fragmentary records suggests that churchwardens were reluctant to present, partly, perhaps, out of a lack of sympathy for changes which necessarily involved rejection of previously acceptable standards, partly because of inconvenience and partly out of fear of the costs involved, for in the absence of financial help from the incumbent or local landowners they found themselves responsible for the setting and collection of parochial rates to pay for the necessary craftsmanship and materials.[82]

Arminian concerns also extended to the churchyards. Many of these were reported to be in decay, an indication of how minor a consideration this had been hitherto. A change can be detected in Neile's 1624 Articles which, by emphasing the consecrated nature of the churchyard, effectively gave it equal status with the church itself in terms of possible profanation.[83] This may not have been properly acted upon, for it took direct intervention in 1633 by King Charles himself, though presumably prompted by Laud, to ensure that the condition of the Cathedral's churchyard conformed to Arminian aesthetic standards by criticising the existence of mean tenements 'upon the churchyard adjoining the walls of the church' and by complaining that the annexing of the churchyard to one of the tenements by lease was 'a thing by no means to be endured'. The leases were not to be renewed and no dwelling was allowed to be built upon the churchyard or against the Cathedral.[84]

There is little suggestion that this concern for Cathedral churchyards filtered down to parochial level. At Barnard Castle and Gateshead, for example, the inhabitants were accustomed to urinating in the churchyard. The churchyard at Barnard Castle also suffered from a conduit which came out of a neighbouring yard across the corner of the churchyard.[85] Complaints were made about unfenced churchyards, which in one case enabled it to be soiled by pigs, while some parishioners were presented for the failure to mend the churchyard wall.[86] At Houghton-le-Spring there was an attempt in 1633 to overcome this problem of the upkeep of the churchyard wall by dividing its entire length among the parish's townships, each of which became responsible for an allotted length.[87] What all of these impositions had in common, whatever their aesthetic justification, was their costliness which became more difficult to bear because it coincided with a period during which the incidence of secular taxation was rising. At Pittington, for example, the flagging of the church in 1635 cost £4 16s. 8d. out of a total expenditure of £11 16s. 6d., and to pay for this the churchwardens and Select Vestry had to levy no fewer than six separate cesses of sixpence in the pound as well as subscribing to additional taxation imposed by the Crown.[88]

A few of the presentments dealt with matters arising from an attempt to revive pre-Reformation practices, presumably as part of the attempt to present the Arminian form of Anglicanism in the context of a continuous national tradition which was distinct from Roman Catholicism. The most important of these was the beating of the bounds of the parish at Rogationtide, a practice ill-suited, as the Arminian fellow-traveller Ferdinand Morecroft found, to such vast upland parishes as his own at Stanhope. His churchwardens doubtless enjoyed presenting him for this understandable neglect.[89]

Apart from such presentments, which can be closely associated with one particular form of Anglican churchmanship, much of the material revealed in the presentments was of common concern to clerics of all persuasions. In particular, however, there was official keenness to detect cases of misbehaviour during divine service.[90] Such misbehaviour was more likely to indicate indifference to organised religion in general than considered opposition to recent innovations. In this context, therefore, it is misleading to impute 'puritan sympathies' to one of Cosin's parishioners at Brancepeth who was presented 'for speaking disorderly words against the minister and saying further he cared not for any priest in England'. The author does not here define 'puritan sympathies' and there seems to be little to distinguish this outburst from all of the other contemporary examples of anticlerical abuse in the county.[91] At Sedgefield the Curate was described as a 'rascal and renegade fellow', while the parish clerk there also abused him. An Escomb man was presented 'for a fearful swearer and taker of God's name in vain and for his irreverent carriage to his pastor'. A Hartlepool Roman Catholic uttered slanderous words against his minister, an offence which brought him before the High Commissioners.[92]

However, there was one example of anti-social behaviour in church which was quite clearly related to the tensions created by the Arminian innovations upon a hostile or indifferent populace. It was no coincidence that this incident should have taken place at Barnard Castle, a market town whose church was a mere dependent chapelry of the parish of Gainford and the centre of an area, Teesdale, where the roots of the established church had never been strong. Religious tensions exacerbated a dispute between two women of the parish. One of the women, Damaris Sayer, was presented 'for saying in scolding manner . . . to Janet Wharton that she was an idolater in bowing at the name of Jesus' and further remarked that Mrs. Wharton would not have dared to do so if their old preacher had still been there. Furthermore, Mrs. Sayer took to

> kicking and treading upon Gabriel Wharton's legs as also rushing upon Janet Wharton his wife violently in the church when they were at their devotions, thereby disturbing them, whereupon the said Janet received such hurt that she went out of the church.[93]

The case had much wider connotations, for George Sayer, husband of the presented woman, had been ordered to appear before the High Commission on behalf of the preacher Anthony Lapthorne, the success of whose peripatetic preaching in Teesdale and Derwentdale, both areas bereft of satisfactory clergy, had perturbed the local Arminians. He had been ordered to appear along with Matthew Stoddart who 'went under the name of a puritan, an invidious name by which the Papists prejudiced many against Protestant Christianity' and who kept his own private fastings, humiliations and conventicles attended by, among others, Sir Henry Vane the younger.[94]

The relationship between Calvinism and Arminianism was not always so fraught, and by the late 1630s there may have been some measure of agreement over the occasionally controversial issue of profanation of the Sabbath. Although Sabbatarianism was predominantly a puritan concern, the Arminian monarch, Charles I, gave his royal assent to a Bill in 1628 which prohibited various kinds of work and travel on Sundays and members of his hierarchy like Montague and Duppa continued to give practical support to attempts to restrict the Sabbath's profanation. In this sense, therefore, the Calvinist Bishop Morton and his Arminian subordinates were likely to agree.

The attitude of churchwardens may have been different, and presumably they failed to present on occasions when offences against the Sabbath had been committed. As Mr. Fletcher has pointed out, the churchwardens were likely to look sympathetically upon a farmer forced to labour on the Sabbath lest his crops be damaged or lost.[95] In Durham only the churchwardens of Bishopwearmouth, a parish regarded with increasing disfavour by some of the more zealous Arminians in the diocese, seem to have interpreted this article rigorously. Three men were presented for grinding corn on a Sunday while a fourth was presented 'for shearing on the Sunday being a very poor man'.[96] Less obviously essential labour was treated with marginally less sympathy.[97] However, absence from divine service and combining that absence with such obviously nefarious anti-Sabbatarian activities as drinking and gambling were far more likely to attract the disapproval of churchwardens.

Apart from a Stanhope purge against bowlers who played during evening prayers but who may perhaps have attended morning service, drinkers were the main offenders and it may perhaps be more than coincidental that the parishes of Gateshead and Whickham should apparently have experienced a disproportionate number of presentments from drinking and card-playing in time of divine service, possibly indicating that the miners who formed an increasing proportion of the population there were indifferent or antagonistic towards the established church.[98] There were also indications of apparently widespread indifference in parishes and chapelries which were badly endowed and in which the quality of observation of the Anglican liturgy was unlikely to be high. At Esh, for example, a small chapelry dominated by the Roman Catholic Smith family, the Curate was presented for his failure to read prayers on Sundays as well as Holy Days, Wednesdays and Fridays, a shortcoming which he attempted to justify by claiming to be

> ready and willing to perform the said duty in case he could get a auditory, for want whereof he hath been negligent therein.[99]

At St. Helen Auckland the eccentric Curate John Vaux was presented for failure to read the litany on Wednesdays and Fridays, having 'neglected the premises for want of a congregation'.[100] At Billingham three out of the five persons presented for non-attendance were paupers.[101] Such evidence of indifference to the established church must be considered lest it be thought that the fundamentalist Presbyterianism of George Lilburne and his associates or the proto-Independency of parts of Teesdale represent the predominant reaction of the inhabitants of Durham to the enforcement of Arminianism.

In this sense Arminianism in Durham may have differed from Arminianism in Sussex. There, 'probably more than any other single issue', Arminianism had hardened the gentry against the Crown.[102] Perhaps if the attitudes of Triplet and Duncon, who considered that 'if we who are in the right way of church obedience were as zealous in our course as puritans are, I believe by this day a puritan had not been a weed in our garden', had been more representative of the Durham hierarchy and its attitudes in the late 1630s, then circumstances in the two counties might have been more alike.[103] However, the inchoate latitudinarianism of Morton and his associates appears to have curbed much religious, if not more purely political, passions. Indeed, the extent of the introduction during the 1630s of church furnishings of the type associated with Arminian emphases suggests that many of the county's gentry, represented by the more important members of Select Vestries and by lay impropriators, found something reassuring in the visual and aural experience of services with an Arminian emphasis. This should not be regarded with too great surprise. The earliest defence of Durham Arminian practices came from the grandson of a Marian exile, while even Sir William Brereton, the formidable Cheshire puritan, was seduced by the quality of services in Durham Cathedral.[104] Unlike their alienated counterparts in East Sussex, the Durham gentry may have found the stress on order and deference reassuring, especially when the alternative appeared to be Scottish Presbyterianism.

NOTES

1. A. G. Dickens, *The English Reformation*, (1967), pp. 426–7; P. Lake, 'Matthew Hutton: a Puritan Bishop?' *History*, 64, (1979), pp. 200–1.
2. N. R. N. Tyacke, 'Puritanism, Arminianism and Counter-Revolution', in *The Origins of the English Civil War*, ed. C. S. R. Russell (1973), pp. 126, 130.
3. On Andrewes see P. A. Welsby, *Lancelot Andrewes, 1555–1626* (1958). On Neile see A. Foster, 'The Function of a Bishop: the Career of Richard Neile, 1562–1642', in *Continuity and Change: Personnel and Administration in the Church of England, 1500–1642* (1976), pp. 33–54.
4. Tyacke, 'Puritanism, Arminianism and Counter-Revolution', p. 121.
5. These misunderstandings have been discussed in M. J. Tillbrook, 'Some Aspects of the Government and Society of County Durham, 1558–1642' (unpub. Ph.D thesis, Liverpool Univ., 1981), pp. 480–1.
6. Foster, 'Function of a Bishop', pp. 42–3, 51; N. R. N. Tyacke, 'Arminianism in England in Religion and Politics, 1603–1640' (unpub. D.Phil. thesis, Oxford Univ., 1968), pp. 212–36.
7. Tillbrook, thesis, pp. 481–3; *The Correspondence of John Cosin I*, ed. G. Ornsby, S.S., 52 (1869), p. 165. For Cradock's activities as an orthodox Archdeacon of Northumberland see S. J. Watts, *From Border to Middle Shire; Northumberland, 1586–1625* (Leicester, 1975) pp. 185–7.
8. Tillbrook, thesis, p. 483; Tyacke, thesis, pp. 228–9; P. Mussett, *Deans and Canons of Durham, 1541–1900* (1974) passim.
9. Tillbrook, thesis, pp. 484–90.
10. An almost complete list dating from the 1630s of the value of Durham livings can be found in D.C.L., Hunter MS. 22 No. 19. This list may well have been compiled originally in response to the need to impose Ship Money on the clergy as well as the laity.
11. *Correspondence of John Cosin, I*, p. 208. Hunt, 'a man well respected there', was defended by Bishop Howson who claimed that Cosin and Lindsell had spread the rumour about simony out of 'a factious humour'. But cf. D.C.R., Chapter Act Book, 1619–38, f. 17.
12. Cf. Tyacke, thesis, pp. 227–8; D.C.R.O., QS/I/12.
13. *H.M.C., Twelfth Report, Coke MS.*, I, p. 446.
14. B.L., Harleian MS. 176, f. 276.
15. The quotation was taken from W. Hutchinson, *History and Antiquities of the County Palatine of Durham* (1785–94) II, p. 180. Hutchinson's ecclesiastical comments are often banal and unreliable and should be treated with great caution. A clue to the nature of Hutton's sermon may be gleaned from the diary of Sir Simonds D'Ewes who recorded that the committee of the House of Commons which was investigating one of Peter Smart's petitions reported that one of the prebendaries had preached that 'it was dangerous lest ornaments be turned into idolatry'. B.L., Harleian MS. 176, f. 276.
16. D.C.L., Raine MS. 41 No. 29.
17. D.C.R., Dean and Chapter Register 9 f. 614.

18. *Ibid.*, Chapter Act Book, 1619–38 passim.
19. See, for example, *Correspondence of John Cosin, I*, p. 198.
20. For descriptions of Smart's character from sources which on religious grounds were likely to be sympathetic see P.R.O., SP 14/88/94, SP 16/147/35. This evidence is discussed in Tillbrook, thesis, pp. 498–9.
21. B.L.O., Rawlinson MS. A441, f. 2v.
22. *Correspondence of John Cosin I*, p. 189.
23. P. Smart, *A Briefe but True Historicall Narration of Some Notorious Acts and Speeches of Mr. John Cosens and Some Other of his Companions Contracted into Articles* (no pagination); P. Smart, *The Vanitie & Downe-fall of Superstitious Popish Ceremonies, or a Sermon Preached in the Cathedrall Church of Durham by one Mr. Peter Smart, a Prebend There* (1628), p. 20; *Correspondence of John Cosin, I*, pp. 164, 172, 178, 184. Smart attempted to exploit the subsequent Parliamentary proceedings against Cosin through his son-in-law, Thomas Ogle, who presented a petition which wrongly claimed that Cosin had spoken the offending words in a sermon at Durham. Ironically, Ogle's next reported allegation was that Cosin had 'wished there were not a sermon in 7 years in England'. *Commons' Debates, 1629*, ed. W. Notestein and F. H. Relf (1921), p. 124.
24. Tyacke, 'Puritanism, Arminianism and Counter-Revolution', pp. 119, 128.
25. Smart, *Historicall Narration of Some Notorious Acts and Speeches of Mr John Cosens.*
26. Smart, *Vanitie & Downe-fall of Superstitious Popish Ceremonies*, p. 24.
27. The Book of Common Prayer had been modified in 1559 in accordance with what was perceived as Queen Elizabeth's doctrinal conservatism. Dickens, *The English Reformation* pp. 413–4. From his point of view, Cosin was dissatisfied with the Book of Common Prayer and desired a return to the first Edwardian Prayer Book of 1549. G. J. Cuming, *The Anglicanism of John Cosin* (Durham Cathedral Lecture, 1975), p. 3.
28. *Correspondence of John Cosin I*, pp. 164, 169, 177; Smart *Vanitie & Downe-fall of Superstitious Popish Ceremonies*, p. 11.
29. *Correspondence of John Cosin, I*, pp. 165–7, 174n, 182, 193. Cathedral music seems to have been a particular enthusiasm of Cosin. The need to maintain standards by employing skilled musicians and by copying additional music manuscripts meant that extra expenditure was incurred by the Dean and Chapter. Furthermore, the conduct of some of the musicians was rather at variance with Arminian standards of seemliness. For a fuller discussion of the role of music as part of the Arminian scheme at Durham see Tillbrook, thesis, pp. 505–10; G. B. Crosby, 'Durham Cathedral's Liturgical Music Manuscripts, c. 1620–c. 1640', *Durham University Journal*, 66 (1973–4) pp. 40–51.
30. *Correspondence of John Cosin, I*, pp. 171, 183. The first cope had been taken from a Roman Catholic priest and hawked round the city's alehouses until bought by Ferdinand Morecroft. Another cope had been allegedly used by children for over forty years in their May games. The Chapter, however, was keen to ensure that the meanings were altered into copes in accordance with the Church's canons.
    D.C.R. Chapter Act Book, 1619–38, f. 47.

31. *Correspondence of John Cosin, I*, pp. 169. In one of his more vituperative passages Smart claimed that this image had actually become an object of Roman Catholic reverence. The image 'betokens in the Pope's school some deity in the head which it covereth, if it might be known to be an extraordinary idol to be worshipped, as this image hath been, by some popish people which came to see it'. Smart, *Historicall Narration of Some Notorious Acts and Speeches of Mr John Cosens.*
32. *Ibid.; Correspondence of John Cosin, I*, pp. 162, 187.
33. *Ibid.*, p. 168 and n.
34. For a full discussion of the legal proceedings see Tillbrook, thesis, pp. 515–35.
35. Two of the four commissioners at the original hearing, convened unprecedentedly on a Sunday, were Cosin and Marmaduke Blakiston, the latter significantly making his first appearance as a commissioner. The other two commissioners present were Dean Hunt and William James. *The Acts of the High Commission Court within the Diocese of Durham*, ed. W. H. D. Longstaffe, S.S., 34 (1858), p. 270. On Hunt's attitude to Smart, see above. According to Smart's wife, James thought 'that your matter was good, "but that your bitter words before the Commission and other great men did undo you"'. *Acts of the High Commission*, p. 208.
36. Robson, along with Ferdinand Morecroft, had sought to effect a compromise between Smart and his enemies. Ibid., p. 238.
37. P.R.O., SP 16/173/73; /174/64; /186/97; /187/107; /187/108. For Smart's inaccurate perception of Howson's position see P. Smart, *A Short Treatise of Altars, Altar-Furniture, Altar-Cringing and Musick of all the Quire, Singing-Men and Choristers, when the Holy Communion Was Administered in the Cathedrall Church of Durham, by Prebendaries and Petty-Canons in Glorious Copes Embroidered with Images* (1629), Introduction (no pagination). Howson's sympathy towards Smart has led Professor Lamont to see in him an examplar of 'Low Church Arminianism'. However, he does not specify any Low Church Arminians other than Howson and his interpretation may be slightly misleading in that it does not take into account the personal and political pressures which Howson was facing in Durham, W. M. Lamont, *Godly Rule: Politics and Religion, 1603–60* (1969), p. 64.
38. He was publicly supported by two veteran members of the Cathedral establishment, Christopher Boucke, a minor canon and Vicar of Billingham, and Nicholas Hobson, a lay clerk. Tillbrook, thesis, pp. 532–3.
39. *Acts of the High Commission*, pp. 206–10.
40. *Ibid.*, p. 207.
41. Richardson had been dropped from the commission shortly after the start of Neile's episcopacy and lost other offices as well. He came to the notice of the House of Commons by passing on an information against John Cradock's exercise of the Chancellorship of the diocese. *Commons' Debates, 1621*, ed. W. Notestein, F. H. Relf and H. Simpson (1935) III, pp. 261–2. He was publicly associated with the opposition to Bishop Neile. In 1626 his information led to the commencement of an Exchequer suit against the Bishop and some of his officers for allegedly detaining some of the temporalities of the see gathered during the previous vacancy. D.D.R., C(hurch) C(ommission

Deposit), 220750. He managed to regain his place on the Bench thanks probably to the good offices of Sir John Coke. He was requested to testify against Cosin by the House of Commons during the abortive impeachment proceedings of 1629. *Commons' Debates, 1629* ed. Notestein and Relf, p. 140. This seems to have been Richardson's only involvement in the case and the House may simply have been recalling his earlier record of antagonism towards Neile's establishment in Durham. The dissolution resolved Richardson's dilemma, for once Neile was out of the way he was more keen to regain episcopal favour and local influence.

42. The dependence of a substantial proportion of the lay establishment upon patronage distributed by the church should not be taken as an indication of the existence within the County of an immutable 'church interest'. Cf. M. E. James. *Family, Lineage and Civil Society: a Study of Society, Politics and Mentality in the Durham Region, 1500–1640* (1974) p. 72. For a fuller discussion of the notion of a 'church interest' see Tillbrook, thesis, pp. 638–40.
43. Cf. James, *Family, Lineage and Civil Society*, pp. 113–8.
44. Tillbrook, thesis, pp. 206–23. Cf. James, *Family, Lineage and Civil Society*, p. 164.
45. See, for example, Tillbrook, thesis, pp. 238–9, 284–5, 290.
46. Civil-episcopal relations had become poisoned during the episcopate of Bishop James. Relations were quickly restored by Bishop Neile who dropped the City's chief opponent, John Richardson, from his administration and instead gave Palatine office to some of Durham's prominent citizens like Hugh Wright and Timothy Comyn. For a summary of church-civic relations in other cities see A. J. Fletcher, 'Factionalism in Town and Countryside: the Significance of Puritanism and Arminianism', *Studies in Church History*, ed. D. Baker, Vol. 16 (1979), pp. 297–8.
47. See above pp. 185–94.
48. On the different circumstances of, for example, Sussex see A. J. Fletcher, *A County Community in Peace and War: Sussex, 1600–1660* (1975), pp. 76–93.
49. On the insensitivity and ineptitude of Smart see, for example, Tillbrook, thesis, pp. 525–8.
50. C. S. R. Russell, *Parliaments and English Politics, 1621–9* (1979), pp. 404–5; P.R.O., SP 16/186/97; /187/107; /187/108; Smart, *Treatise of Altars*, Introduction (no pagination).
51. P.R.O., Palatinate of Durham, Entry Book of Decrees and Orders of Court of Chancery, DURH 4/1 pp. 72–3.
52. *Acts of the High Commission*, pp. 206–8.
53. *Ibid.*, p. 211.
54. Tillbrook, thesis, pp. 538–40.
55. Cosin and Lindsell deliberately sought the interference on their behalf of Neile and Laud when they objected, without having legitimate grounds for doing so, to Howson's attempt to exercise his ordinary jurisdiction over the Cathedral. *Correspondence of John Cosin, I*, pp. 204–7.
56. Tillbrook, thesis, pp. 546–7.
57. *Ibid.*, pp. 547–8.
58. Lamont, *Godly Rule*, pp. 63–4.

59. Tillbrook, thesis, pp. 549–50. Johnson's abilities as a preacher were especially stressed by Bishop Morton's biographers. R. Baddeley and J. Naylor, *Life of Dr. Thomas Morton, late Bishop of Duresme* (1669), pp. 83–4.
60. *Correspondence of John Cosin, I*, p. 8; D.C.L., Hunter MS. 132, f. 63; *H.M.C., Twelfth Report, Coke MS.* II, p. 156. Despite their respective roles in the York House Conference, it would be misleading to over-emphasise the adversarial nature of the relationship between Cosin and Morton.
61. Tillbrook, thesis, pp. 552–3.
62. *C.S.P., 1639–40*, p. 542.
63. Triplet was a peripheral member of the circle of divines associated with Lucius Cary, Viscount Falkland. In 1660 Triplet wrote a preface of Falkland's *Discourse of Infallibility* in which he claimed that 'Great Tew (was) so valued a mansion to us, for as when we went from Oxford thither, we found ourselves never out of the University'. Quoted by R. R. Orr, *Reason and Authority: the Thought of William Chillingworth* (1967), p. 36. Triplet's link with the 'Great Tew circle' was ironic in view of Laud's disapproval of the group. I. M. Green, *The Re-Establishment of the Church of England, 1660–1663 (1978), p. 93.*
64. *C.S.P., 1639–40*, p. 519. Through this approach to Laud, Triplet may have been aiming primarily to offset his relative lack of diocesan preferment by attempting to gain favour with a potentially influential patron.
65. For the Laudian emphasis on *iure divino* episcopacy see Lamont, *Godly Rule*, pp. 56–77. There was nothing, of course, peculiar to Laudianism in this emphasis.
66. Tillbrook, thesis, pp. 557, 567; Fletcher, *Sussex*, p. 81.
67. Clarke was not specifically named as an offender in the fullest recital of Smart's grievances. *Correspondence of John Cosin, I*, pp. 161–99.
68. At Bishopwearmouth Burgoyne had been quick to replace the communion table with an altar set up at the East end of the chancel before which he bowed so extravagantly that he hit his nose on the ground, causing it to bleed. *Ibid.*, p. 175.
69. This matter is discussed in detail in James, *Family, Lineage and Civil Society*, pp. 122–5. However, this discussion contains one very misleading assertion, that the poor and those who could not afford pew rents were excluded from church. The only evidence cited includes nothing about exclusion. Admittedly it does reveal that in the parish of Pittington such accommodation was very restricted, although this is not a synonym for exclusion. *Churchwardens' Accounts of Pittington and other Parishes in the Diocese of Durham, 1580–1700*, ed. J. Barmby, S.S., 84 (1888), pp. 2–4. Specific arrangements were made for accommodating the poor in St. Oswald's parish in Durham. *Ibid.*, p. 185.
70. G(ateshead) P(ublic) L(ibrary), St. Mary's Vestry, Gateshead: Minute Book, 1625–78, ff. 50–7.
71. See, especially, N. Pevsner, *The Buildings of England: County Durham* (1953), passim.
72. Tillbrook, thesis, pp. 560–2.
73. On the condition of Elwick see D.C.R., Correction Book, 1635–6, f. 16v.

For the Brancepeth defects see Correction Book, c. 1634–7 (fragments).
74. Pevsner, *Durham*, pp. 31–4; cf. H. L. Robson, 'The Cosin Furniture in Durham Churches', *The Antiquities of Sunderland*, 24 (1969), pp. 1–12.
75. The dating of the Brancepeth alterations suggests that what was exemplified there was primarily a response to the national drive for Laudian uniformity rather than a reflection of local Arminian vitality. In this sense Cosin may have had to defer to the reluctance of the parishioners of Brancepeth voluntarily to pay for the work undertaken there in 1638, a reluctance stimulated, no doubt, by the remembrance that the parishioners had had to make a substantial contribution to repairs in the years before Cosin became Rector. *Correspondence of John Cosin, I*, p. 222; D.D.R., DR/V/11 (Churchwardens of Brancepeth v William Baxter, 1625).
76. Such presentments were made, for example, at Whickham and Sedgefield. D.C.R., Correction Book, c. 1634–7 (fragments).
77. *Ibid.*, Correction Book, 1637 (Whickham).
78. See, for example, *Ibid.*, (Dalton-le-Dale, Jarrow, Kelloe, Middleton St. George, Seaham).
79. There were defects in the chancels at Dalton-le-Dale and at St. Oswald's in Durham. *Ibid.*, (Dalton-le-Dale, Durham St. Oswald's).
80. At Medomsley the church lacked proper seating and a paved floor, at Croxdale the choir was unflagged, at Sockburn the floor was unflagged and the walls were inadequate, at Sadberge the church was unpainted, unwashed, unrepaired, unflagged and unplastered and the roof was faulty, while at Barnard Castle the seats in the church were decayed and broken and much of the church was unflagged. D.C.R., Correction Book, c. 1634–7 (fragments); Correction Book, 1637 (Croxdale, Barnard Castle); Correction Book, 1635–6, ff. 5v, 6v.
81. At Monkwearmouth the stalls had not been repaired in a uniform manner. Even Elwick, one of Cosin's two parishes, lacked adequate seating and flagging. *Ibid.*, ff. 10r, 16v.
82. At Brancepeth, however, there was an attempt to raise the money voluntarily. *Correspondence of John Cosin, I*, p. 222.
83. Neile's second article in 1624 asked whether 'the church or churchyard (had) been abused and prophaned by any fighting, chiding, brawling or quarrelling, any plays, lords of misrule, summer-lords, morris-dancers, pedlers, bowlers, bearwards, butchers, feasts, schools, temporal courts or leets, lay juries, musters or other prophane usage'. D.C.L., Hunter MS. 67 No. 7. The main significance of this is twofold. Not only does it demonstrate an Arminian readiness to destroy the traditional social role of the parish church within the local community, it also suggests that it would be misleading to associate too exclusively a narrowly moralistic conception of social mores with their religious opponents.
84. *C.S.P., 1633–4*, p. 83.
85. D.C.R., Correction Book, 1635–6, f. 6v; Correction Book, 1637 (Gateshead).
86. *Ibid.*, Correction Book, 1635–6, f. 19r; Correction Book, c. 1634–7 (fragments); Correction Book, 1637 (Elwick).
87. *Churchwardens' Accounts*, pp. 299–300.

88. *Ibid.*, pp. 97–8.
89. D.C.R., Correction Book, 1635–6, f. 3r.
90. Among the cases noted there was one at South Shields where the presentment was 'for going up and down drunk in time of divine service', one at St. Mary-le-Bow in Durham for 'blaspheming God's holy name in the Church', and one at St. Oswald's for 'being drunk upon a Sabbath day and abusing himself before the minister and churchwardens', while at Barnard Castle and Witton-le-Wear respectively there were cases of talking during prayers and sleeping through the sermon. D.C.R., Correction Book, c. 1634–7 (fragments); Correction Book, 1635–6, f. 21v; Correction Book, 1637 (Durham St. Oswald's, Barnard Castle, Witton-le-Wear).
91. D.C.R., Correction Book, c1634–7 (fragments). Cf. J. G. Hoffman, 'John Cosin's Cure of Souls', *Durham University Journal*, 81 (1978), p. 76.
92. D.C.R., Correction Book, 1637 (Sedgefield); Correction Book, 1635–6, f. 5r; Correction Book, c. 1634–7 (fragments); *Acts of the High Commission*, p. 146.
93. D.C.R., Correction Book, 1637 (Barnard Castle).
94. *Acts of the High Commission*, p. 193; *Memoirs of the Life of Mr Ambrose Barnes*, ed. W. H. D. Longstaffe, S.S., 50 (1867), pp. 31–2; V. A. Rowe, *Sir Henry Vane the Younger: a Study in Political and Administrative History* (1970), p. 7.
95. J. E. C. Hill, *Society and Puritanism in Pre-Revolutionary England* (1964), p. 156; Fletcher, *Sussex*, pp. 87–8.
96. D.C.R., Correction Book, 1637 (Bishopwearmouth).
97. See, for example, D.C.R., Correction Book, c. 1634–7 (fragments); Correction Book, 1635–6, ff. 4r. 6r; Correction Book, 1637 (Denton, Cockfield).
98. *Ibid.*, Correction Book, 1635–6, f. 3v; Correction Book c. 1634–7 (fragments); Correction Book, 1637 (Whickham, Gateshead).
99. *Ibid.*, (Esh). In addition, 36 recusants were also presented there and George Smith was presented for keeping a schoolmaster in his house.
100. *Ibid.*, (Auckland St. Helen). On Vaux's other activities see *Acts of the High Commission*, pp. 34–42; K. V. Thomas, *Religion and the Decline of Magic* (1971), p. 356.
101. D.C.R., Correction Book, 1635–6, f. 15v.
102. Fletcher, *Sussex*, p. 93.
103. *C.S.P., 1640,* p.542.
104. R. Hegg, *The Legend of St. Cuthbert, or the Historie of his Churches at Lindisfarne, Cynecascestre and Dunholm,* (1663), p. 92; W. Brereton, *Travels in Holland, the United Provinces, England, Scotland and Ireland*, ed. E. Hawkins, Chetham Society (1844), pp. 83–4.

The Durham Lilburnes and the English Revolution

William Dumble

Early in 1640 Thomas Triplet, the Arminian Rector of Whitburn, wrote to Archbishop Laud and reported the appearance of a mendicant puritan preacher in the pulpit of Monkwearmouth church. 'To him amayn', he wrote bitterly, 'came the Sunderland puritans like rats over the water'.[1] It had been Triplet's unhappy lot through the 1630s to observe from nearby Whitburn the growth of puritan spirit in Monkwearmouth and Bishopwearmouth parishes, nor had he any doubt as to who was its moving force: that was George Lilburne 'the great factotum that rules both the religion and wealth of the town.'[2]

George was a second son; his elder brother, Richard, held the family's original seat in the county at Thickley Punchardon near Bishop Auckland, and was the father of the celebrated John and the significant Robert, and a youngest son, Henry. George, who was twice married, had produced a substantial progeny of sons and daughters many of whom had put down roots in London, augmenting the family connection there. Only George's eldest son, Thomas, could properly be regarded as a Durham Lilburne in these years. Freeborn John also, despite his education in Bishop Auckland and Newcastle and his strong family links with Durham, was born in Greenwich and in truth a Londoner.[3] Those Durham Lilburnes who were so much to personify twenty years of puritan revolution in the North were represented by Richard and George, Robert, Thomas and Henry.

Around the turn of the century George Lilburne had established himself in Sunderland to try his fortunes there, untrammelled by the commercial exclusivity with which Newcastle Hostmen and Merchant Adventurers guarded themselves on the Tyne. His ascendant prosperity was coincident with that of the town itself. By the 1630s he was one of the first Mayors of the newly-created borough, a Durham Justice and the business associate of local gentry families – Lambtons, Hiltons Boweses and Bellasises – as well as a variety of other county figures who shared his interest in coal, shipping and the general commercial expansion of the lower Wear. George's success brought him wealth and influence in which his elder brother shared to an extent, although the family's status was not entirely certain. The Durham Lilburnes probably came to the county as middling gentry, a minor branch of the Northumberland family,[4] and despite George's affluence his detractors bridled at his pretensions. In 1650 Thomas Saunders sneered at him as an erstwhile coal-filler who was now a coal-owner and '. . . stiling himself Esquire, though it would puzzle a Herald to make it appear.'[5]

The pugnacious, defiant spirit which made Freeborn John famous was an inherited trait, possessed by his father and uncle. The latter in particular combined his oppositionist nature with the desire for unhindered scope to exploit new opportunities. In doing so he created the need to question and resist, almost as a matter of course, those institutions – secular, clerical, royal – which seemed to stand in his way. George's religious stance also accorded well with his inclinations as an oppositionist and in which his puritanism was polarized and made intransigent by the attitudes of the prelatical party it opposed.[6] With much satisfaction Thomas Triplet informed Laud in one of his reports of how Lilburne, in a religious altercation with the Rector of Bishop Wearmouth, had had the Magnificat quoted to him, to which Lilburne had countered: 'Prove it out of scripture or you say noth(ing)'.[7] His reply revealed him as a Biblicist and yet an astonishingly illiterate and ignorant one; his religious stance as much conditioned as considered, a predilection as much as a presuasion, and very much enmeshed with his secular radicalism.

George, and the family generally, was Presbyterian in outlook, a fact which was to prove fatal to Henry Lilburne and which sustained George Lilburne in the tolerationist mood of the 1650s in his bitter hostility towards sectaries such as Baptists and Quakers.[8] Robert Lilburne went furthest in his religious as well as his political radicalism. During the Interregnum years, when he was influential in Durham and the North generally, he was identified with the Baptist movement and as a patron of that faith in the region.

In the later 1630s, as tension and resentment grew nationally in the face of the King's personal rule and Laudian pretensions, it was George Lilburne's name which was the inspiration of local opposition. In 1635 over Ship Money he resisted the demands of the Crown and the encroachments of Newcastle.[9] He prevaricated over later writs and urged against the payment of coat and conduct money in 1640.[10] His verbal opposition to Arminian innovations and criticism of Laudian clerics brought him before the Durham High Commission.[11] In 1640, as the crisis between the King and his Scottish subjects grew once more, Thomas Triplet was urging the danger that lay in a man like Lilburne and tried to involve him in a charge of treasonable activity which took Lilburne and others to the Quarter Sessions, the Durham High Commission and finally before the King himself in Council in London where they 'are come off with a great deal of credit,' Triplet was finally forced to note.[12] Triplet's disgust was understandable; he was left sensing the animosity of the county's gentlemen over his part in the affair,[13] and yet he had shrewdly recognised the dilemma personified by a 'Covenanter' like Lilburne for King and Bishop in the growth of commercial and maritime centres like Sunderland under the drive of such entrepreneurs. 'I confess it an honour to the Kingdom to have such towns as Sunderland was, to come up and flourish from small beginnings,' he observed, but went on '. . . I think . . . that the King's Majesty had better for a while despise that honour and profit that accrues to him that way . . . than to suffer little towns to grow big and anti-monarchy to boot.'[14]

By the year's end Durham and Northumberland were under a Scottish occupation and a petition of George Lilburne was one of those which inundated the Long Parliament when it met in November 1640. In this he championed the puritan parishes of Derwentdale in the upland North West of the county, reciting their struggle with the ecclesiastical establishment over the previous few years,[15] and the Commons heard another of Lilburne's petitions, against Dr. Isaac Basire and other Durham Arminians, in February 1641.[16] In the fierce agitations now released by the appearance of the Long Parliament Durham's resentments and tensions of other kinds also reappeared, directed and organised by close radical associates of Lilburne like George Grey of Southwick and Anthony Smith of Durham City. These two fanned into flames once more the century-old grievance of the Durham Dean and Chapter tenantry over leases and fines which, when the affair reached the King's Council, Laud denounced as a stratagem against the Durham church.[17] By March 1642 the Durham Justices reported themselves helpless to the Commons after a series of riotous assaults upon episcopal enclosures in the county. Parliament called for the organisers to be named, but none was.[18] Yet it is difficult to believe that such genuine feelings of socio-economic grievance were not given direction as well as

which Vanes and other gentry appear to have largely withdrawn.[31] The opportunist acquisitiveness which was to be alleged against George Lilburne from 1644 began when he and other well-affected coal owners on Tyne and Wear repossessed not only their own property but were urged to lease and work the collieries of delinquents and papists by Scots and English commissioners anxious to realise coal and coal revenues out of the North East.[32] The irregular, or at least uncertain, possession by Lilburne and his associates of Lambton, and later Harraton, collieries, made possible by the confused circumstances of the time, subsequently became a bitter cause of dispute, an eventuality not unforeseen by some who looked askance at it.[33] Between 1644 and 1648 Lilburne's activities, ostensibly on behalf of the state as a County Sequestrator and, from 1646 as a Surveyor for the Sale of Episcopal Lands, brought him complaint and conflict with a variety of figures, not least the Vanes, John Blakiston and Thomas Shadforth. The quarrel with these two last degenerated into mutual accusations between Shadforth and Lilburne of deliquent activities and Lilburne's manner of possessing Lambton colliery and Ford manor on the lower Wear.[34]

In late December 1647 Parliament appointed Sir Arthur Haslerig Governor of Newcastle.[35] He was blunt and efficient, an Independent and a republican, with a reputation for acquisitiveness.[36] He remained a grandee figure, like Vane, and although he had no quarrel with the Durham Lilburnes – indeed he had aided George in the presentation of his 1641 petitions[37] – he was soon in conflict with them. There were several factors. Colonel Robert Lilburne, Richard's eldest son, was acting Governor of Newcastle and had expected to have the position confirmed.[38] Animosity arose with George Lilburne the State Surveyor over Haslerig's purchase of Bishop Auckland manor and, in the crisis of the Second Civil War in the summer of 1648, Lilburne refused to allow the increase in the impost upon coals leaving the Wear which Haslerig had ordered upon the Tyne.[39] In August the death of Colonel Henry Lilburne could not have helped matters, but ultimately most significant of all was Haslerig's position as a leading member of the Parliamentary Committee investigating the activities of John Lilburne.[40] The personalised clash of the two eventually spilled over messily in the North.

By early 1649 Haslerig was throwing his considerable influence against the Lilburnes and their friends. George had to answer the delinquency charges against him before a Parliamentary Committee upon which both Haslerig and John Blakiston sat,[41] and although cleared found the charges renewed, together with the new ones as to his behaviour as a Sequestrator, in the Northern Sequestration Committees.[42] One of these concerned Harraton colliery, a lower-Wear pit of huge potential which had become operational once more in 1647, under a state lease to Lilburne and George Grey, who claimed to have leased it earlier from a London speculator, Josiah Primate. Thomas Wray, a sequestered papist and delinquent, also claimed an interest in it which had been suppressed by the Lilburne faction at the time when they 'were uncontrolable,'[43] and it was this claim which Haslerig chose to champion. In October 1649 Haslerig's closest associate, the Northumberland man Colonel George Fenwick, initiated the violent dispossession of the Lilburne faction at Harraton and the colliery was subsequently leased to Colonel Francis Hacker, Major Tolhurst and Captain Shepperdson, all close military associates of Haslerig.[44] Despite a long-drawn-out and bitter wrangle over the next two years there was no redress for the Lilburne side,[45] but it had drawn in on its behalf George's nephew, John Lilburne. His involvement proved disastrous.

In July 1651 John Lilburne published an accusation of collusion and dishonesty among Haslerig and the London Sequestration Commissioners[46] which was echoed by Josiah Primate's petition to Parliament in December. Parliament rounded savagely on both men with fines; Lilburne was ordered to quit the country on pain of death. It has been observed that Freeborn John was permitted no defence, indeed, had no specific charge laid against him. 'By this arbitrary procedure the Rump was defending the privileges of an influential member.'[47] Faced with Haslerig's powerful influence in the North and in London also, the Durham Lilburnes and their Harraton associates had little option but to continue their case in the Committee halls and the Parliament house of the capital and to welcome the help of a figure like John Lilburne. But in the personalised duel between such antipathetic figures as Lilburne and Haslerig the Durham faction and its friends inevitably sank or swam with their advocate and were lost, as it were incidentally, in the fierce currents which at last overwhelmed Freeborn John.

It would be bold to say where right truly lay in the Harraton affair, although fair to assert that it lay with neither side exclusively. Haslerig appeared as the uncompromising, impersonal administrator, bringing order and justice to the disrupted region: the Lilburnes as loyal but aggrieved Parliament men, attacked by an alien and unscrupulous interloper who overawed local opposition by resort to soldiery and other intimidation – a view also heard from other voices in the North.[48] Yet despite the real commitment of both Haslerig and the Lilburnes to the

Parliamantary cause since 1642 both parties showed an acquisitive interest in the valuable properties within the county and especially along the middle and lower reaches of the Wear, for the gain of themselves or their associates. Behind their admirable efforts as Parliament's agents of government their personal activities revealed the triumphant puritan radicals in power as at best distasteful, and often a good deal worse, and gave force to the ironic comment of the Northumberland Royalist Daniel Collingwood:

> Your only smooth skin to make vellum is your puritan's skin, they must be the smoothest and sleekest knaves in a county.[49]

In the course of these protracted wrangles the Second Civil War took place and threw two other Lilburnes into prominence in its events in the North. The seizure of Carlisle and Berwick in April 1648 saw Northern cavaliers flocking to Sir Marmaduke Langdale's banner near Alnwick, so that by May a real threat was posed. Northumberland was worst affected but in Durham too George Lilburne could not venture abroad upon the state's business.[50] During May and June Royalist forces gathered and manoeuvred across the four Northern counties awaiting the advent of Scottish support, but on the night of June 30/July 1 the field force of some one thousand two hundred Durham and Northumberland cavaliers which was posing a substantial threat to Newcastle and other Parliamentary garrisons in the North East was dealt a severe blow by a force of some nine hundred horse led by Colonel Robert Lilburne. The Parliamentarians carried out, during the hours of darkness, a bold and telling move in which they fell upon the scattered Royalist horse dispersed in billets along the valley of the Coquet to the West of Alnwick and by morning had taken three hundred and fifty-nine prisoners including Sir Richard Tempest leader of the Durham cavaliers and some six hundred horses.[51]

This reverse and the entry of Hamilton's Scottish army soon after by a Western route, eased the pressure and raised the confidence of the Parliamentary interest in the North East. It was the best of the cavaliers of Durham and Northumberland which had been attacked along the Coquet,[52] but faced by the soldierly competence of officers like Robert Lilburne, George Fenwick and Francis Wren the leadership of the North Eastern Royalists was made to look distinctly amateurish. It was noteworthy, too, that despite the animosity that was rife between the Lilburne family and Haslerig, with his close confidant George Fenwick, at this time, it was not apparent that it in any way hindered the concerted efforts all made on the Parliament's behalf.

The Royalists in the North East were not defeated, however, and the region remained tense and unsettled. While one Lilburne had helped to ease an early crisis another was the creator of a further one. On the afternoon of August 9 Colonel Henry Lilburne, younger brother of Robert and John and Governor of Tynemouth Castle, declared that the place was now held for the King.[53] From Newcastle Sir Arthur Haslerig despatched a force which retook the castle that same night, Henry Lilburne being killed in the assault. His sudden and totally unexpected defection was acutely embarrassing, not least to his immediate superior Haslerig, who reported to the Commons that Lilburne was

> known to be a valiant man: he did not give the least suspicion of being a traitor . . . till the day of his revolt: it was not for me to have put out such a man from his place.[54]

Another account of Lilburne's action published in Scotland asserted that he 'rather chose honourably to fall in that loyal action, than live longer under the tyranny and oppression of sectaries.'[55] Henry Lilburne exemplified, in fact, the dilemma growing for more and more Presbyterian supporters of the Revolution in the face of the widening religious rift which, by the middle of 1647, had left a Presbyterian Parliament looking to Scotland for support against an English army bitterly resentful of the proposed Presbyterian establishment, albeit for three years only. In November, Lilburne's regiment was one of those which sent a remonstrance to Sir Thomas Fairfax, perhaps the most influential and moderate of the army's Presbyterian element, declaring its intention to stand or fall with him in his endeavours to achieve a settlement which ended intolerable oppressions and brought disbandment.[56]

From the outset of the Second Civil War Royalist propagandists sought, not without success, to sway the susceptibilities of wavering Presbyterians of his kind. By August 1648 Henry Lilburne had watched the struggle on behalf of the Crown, constitutional government and peace and order under a Presbyterian church structure, and found himself the custodian at Tynemouth of those captured Northumberland and Durham Royalists who had rallied to Langdale, brought in the Scots and raised the new war in the North.[57] It seems that contact with these men brought Henry Lilburne to his final, fatal decision. Ironically, both his brothers were of those hated sectarian soldiers. Robert it was who had acted decisively for the Parliament in July, John it was who later spoke in the most bitter terms of his brother Henry, accusing him of involvement in the Presbyterian plot to remove the King from the army's custody and asserting that his brother had 'suffered the deserved reward of a perfidious traitor.'[58]

In the aftermath of the Second War moderate opinion nationally still sought an accommodation with the King, but among the soldiers and radicals feelings now ran strongly against him and the remaining majority of the Lilburne family clearly identified itself with this mood. From September 1648 a series of petitions to Parliament from county Grand Juries began to demand justice upon the monarch. The town of Newcastle sent up a petition in October,[59] while in Durham George Lilburne and his son Thomas took up the task of gathering subscriptions to the county's petition for the trial of Charles.[60] Beyond those few radicals of the Lilburnes' ilk feelings about such a step were mixed and unhappy; other local figures such as Haslerig and the Vanes avoided involvement. It was left to the Durham prebendary's son John Blakiston and the modest Durham gentleman's son Robert Lilburne to provide Northern complicity by supplying their signatures to the monarch's death warrant.

While the Lilburnes thus placed themselves forthrightly in the van of the onward surge of the national Revolution, their fortunes and influence locally in the two or three years from 1649 fell to a low ebb. This was seen chiefly in the figure of George and was the consequence of his dissentions with powerful local interests like the Vanes, Blakiston and Haslerig and culminated in the disastrous outcome of the Harraton affair. By August 1649 George had been forced out of the Commission of the Peace and about the same time lost his position as a Militia Commissioner and a Commissioner for Religion.[61] In March 1650 the positions of both George and Richard as Sequestrators disappeared in a Parliamentary reform of all county sequestration bodies[62] and the new Committee set up was closely identified with Haslerig's regime.[63] A county petition, protesting about George Lilburne's treatment, revealed the paucity of his support; among its one hundred and five signatures were the names of three Presbyterian ministers and but half a dozen middling gentlemen.[64] In 1651 the appointment of Thomas Shadforth as High Sheriff was a further blow to the Lilburnes who were still embroiled in delinquency charges through Shadforth's person.

That Shadforth could occupy such an office with serious charges of delinquency hanging unresolved over him was a measure of the control possessed by those personalities the Lilburne interest had quarrelled with. Together with Haslerig, the Vanes controlled, by Parliament's nomination, the Parliamentary Committees of Sequestration and Religion, as well as the appointment of the county's Justices.[65] The elder Vane headed the new militia body established in 1650 and he and four of his sons served on the Durham Bench. As Governor of Newcastle Haslerig gathered adherents – old associates like George Fenwick, gentlemen like James Clavering and Francis Wren, sectarian soldiers such as Colonel Paul Hobson, his deputy at Newcastle, and possible erstwhile Royalists like Henry Draper and Thomas Delaval. Those county names which had been associated with the Parliamentary cause since 1642 – Timothy Whittingham, Anthony Smith, Gilbert Marshall, John Middleton, Robert Hutton, the Greys, Fulthorpes and Lilburnes – also acceded to the shibboleth of the Engagement and, it seems, the reality of the situation and became Commonwealth men. While Richard Lilburne was apparently never disturbed as a Justice, George remained some time in seclusion,[66] although as '. . . a zealous Parliamentarian (which is something rare in that county)'[67] the denial of a role to him could not be indefinite. By June 1652 the names of George, Richard and Thomas Lilburne all appeared in the commission together.[68]

It was the period of the Protectorate, from December 1653, which brought the Lilburnes to their high point of influence, however. The elder Vane died early in 1654 and both Henry the younger and Haslerig, while still Governor of Newcastle, were among those adamant republican grandees alienated from Cromwell by commercial and foreign policies and conciliatory moves at home. Vane at the family seat of Raby and Haslerig at his recently purchased episcopal estate of Bishop Auckland were watched suspiciously by the Protectorate authorities.[69] With but one or two exceptions however, the county's Commonwealth men moved with the Lilburnes into the Protectorate regime and it was the figure of Colonel Robert Lilburne whose presence was to be constantly felt in the region's affairs until the Restoration. The Civil Wars had established him as an able soldier and administrator. He had defeated the Earl of Derby at Wigan in 1651 and had served as Commander-in-Chief in Scotland in 1653/4 during the absence of Monk.[70] He was a significant, if secondary rank, figure nationally – a Baptist,[71] republican and regicide. Cromwell's Protectorate regime hinged upon the adherance of soldiers like Lilburne, and Robert himself enjoyed a close association with John Lambert in the ordering of the Protectorate's affairs in the North generally.

The meeting, on September 3 1654, of the first Protectorate Parliament made manifest the fact that the Lilburnes now constituted a substantial nub of the county's Cromwellians. Colonel Robert Lilburne of Thickley Punchardon and George Lilburne of Sunderland were returned as Knights for the County and Anthony Smith the Durham City mercer and long-standing associate of the Lilburnes was returned for the City.[72] The Lilburnes and those with them were willing to project the Protectorate's aura of relative moderation and appeasement for all who would be reconciled.

In 1654 the last Commonwealth Sheriff, Francis Wren, was succeeded by Roland Place of Dinsdale, a delinquent, formerly a Lieutenant Colonel under the Earl of Newcastle.[73] But there is little to suggest that the majority of the county's gentry could be reconciled or brought to participate in the county's government; indeed, the adamant nature of a Royalist county kept it alive with the rumour of plots and risings.[74] In December 1655 Robert Lilburne's own exasperation was expressed in a letter to Thurloe:

> I am wondering sometimes that your instructions concerning the cavaliers are not put in execution in these parts, as in other counties . . . I could wish you would think of disposing of these persons that we might be free of the trouble of them.[75]

Lilburne by then was speaking as a Major General. Although Penruddock's Rising in early 1655 created only feeble tremors in the North[76] it brought the military to the fore once more to bolster civil government. With the Major Generals came a new militia, paid for by a decimation tax which took a tenth of the annual value of all Royalists' estates, and collected by Decimators, special commissioners appointed by the Major Generals. John Lambert assumed supreme responsibility as Major General for all Northern England and created Robert Lilburne as one of his two deputies, with responsibility for Yorkshire and Durham. To aid him in his task Lilburne named as his special commissioners his father Richard and cousin Thomas, together with the Anabaptist soldiers Paul Hobson and Thomas Gower and two county gentlemen, Francis Wren and Robert Hutton, who in February 1656 were writing to the Protector of the difficulties of securing the peace in the county.[77]

The short rule of the Major Generals from October 1655 until early 1657 meant that Robert Lilburne's despotic authority in Durham matched almost exactly the term of office as High Sheriff of his uncle, George Lilburne. It was the high point of the family's prestige and influence in the county, but the circumstances were unfortunate. The observation: 'It was the fact of the Major Generals and the Special

Commissioners, more than what they did, which became a folk memory, an English upper-class bogey,'[78] was well borne out in Durham where the son of a middling gentleman and his relatives – in particular his uncle, the erstwhile coal-filler who now styled himself Esquire – drew the bitter resentment of the traditional, ousted, cavalier gentry. In Durham it was perhaps Thomas Lilburne who in fact incurred the greatest odium in the direct execution of his cousin's wishes. Bishop Cosin was to write bitterly of him at the Restoration as '. . . acting violently upon the power given to the Major Generals which the said Thomas did much more than any man.'[79]

Reaction in the county to rule by Major General was manifest in the elections held for members of the Parliament which met in September 1656, the second and final occasion that Durham enjoyed true Parliamentary representation during the Interregnum. By the summer of 1656 feelings in Durham were apparent in the agitation preceding the election. On August 9 Robert Lilburne wrote to Secretary Thurloe of the plans afoot in Yorkshire to keep supporters of the government out of the Parliament and observed that the same spirit was abroad in Durham and Northumberland

> where the people (whether by Sir Ar. H.[80] mean (who is at Auckland) I know not) are perfect in their lesson, saying they will have no swordsman, no decimator, or any that receives salary from the state to serve in Parliament.[81]

In Durham neither George nor Robert Lilburne sat again for the County although Robert was elected for the North Riding and Thomas Lilburne took his father's place along with James Clavering, while Anthony Smith again sat for the City.[82]

Despite the endeavours of the Major Generals there were a good many opponents of the government in the new assembly and Haslerig, no longer a member for Newcastle but returned for Leicester, was among the hundred or so members excluded. Along with him went a number of other Northern men – the Durham Royalists Thomas Bowes and Henry Tempest, George Fenwick and the Durham member who had stood with Thomas Lilburne, James Clavering. Prominent in a wide range of offices in Durham and the North since 1644 Clavering made a clear break with the Protectorate regime in 1656. Robert Lilburne suspected him of plotting with Royalists and of having loaned £4,000 to Charles Stuart.[83]

When the Parliament went on to seek a new and acceptable constitutional base for Cromwell's government by offering him the Crown,

Captain Thomas Lilburne was one of the Parliamentary Committee appointed to confer with the Protector over his doubts and scruples and both Lilburne and Anthony Smith were among those who ultimately voted for the proposal.[84] There was an irony of fate for the county's Royalists in the measure of representation gained during the Protectorate, for the incessant demand for members since the early years of the century had not been confined to any sectional group or stratum but had been a comprehensive desire of the county's knights, gentlemen and freeholders as it was to become again after 1660. Yet in 1653 and again in 1656 an overwhelming proportion of the county's Royalists chose to take no part, or else became an intractable opposition, refusing to be represented by men like the Lilburnes and what they stood for. Their loyalty was used against them when they renewed their agitation for members in 1660 and they were told that no precedent could be drawn from the Protectorate representation, when the members had been

> chosen by a disaffected and disloyal party of the country, the rest (far more considerable than that party was) not consenting to them.[85]

Behind these agitations the years 1656–7 saw the realisation of a long-desired event in Durham. The foundation, out of former episcopal and capitular resources, of a centre of learning at Durham was the wish of many across the Northern counties, but the scheme was driven forward by the impetus supplied by that stratum of Durham's modest gentry which was prominent in the ordering of the county in the Interregnum years. From 1650, when the scheme seems first to have been voiced,[86] the involvement of Anthony Smith in particular, Gilbert Marshall, John Middleton, the Lilburnes and Durham townsmen like John Ayreson, Richard Lee and Henry Rowell can be discerned in the venture.[87]

By May 1657 Letters Patent in the Protector's name were granted and a Provost, fellows and visitors were being named. Seven of the eleven figures nominated as constant visitors were Durham men and were the virtual nucleus of the Protectorate's supporters in the county. These were Robert and Richard Lilburne, Sir Thomas Liddell, Timothy Whittingham, Anthony Smith, John Middleton and Gilbert Marshall. Among the occasional visitors were Henry and George Vane, Thomas Lilburne, Robert Hutton, Rowland Place, Sir Arthur Haslerig and Paul Hobson.[88] Although the new institution was soon in difficulties and foundered upon the death of Cromwell, the efforts of the county's Interregnum personalities to establish a centre of learning at Durham was a manifestation of that desire for educational experiment which was one feature of the English Revolution and revealed one of the best faces of puritan radical intent.

Although Cromwell finally refused the Crown in May 1657 the growing unhappiness and uncertainty of republican, sectarian soldiers persisted. In Durham an episode, slight in itself, revealed how uncomfortably the Protectorate's supporters often stood with regard to one another. On a Sunday in August the wife of Colonel Paul Hobson, while riding to a Baptist meeting-place in Sunderland, was stopped by George Lilburne in his capacity of Justice and told she had contravened the Parliament's Acts for Sabbath observance by riding a horse. The animal was seized until twenty shillings had been paid. The Hobsons made complaint to the Council of State who referred the issue to Major General Robert Lilburne and the High Sheriff, Timothy Whittingham. The latter recommended to the Council that George be put out of the commission.[89]

On the surface it was an unpleasant little clash of religious sensitivities, but Paul Hobson was a lowly-born, Anabaptist republican, risen up as soldier, the epitome of that increasingly dissatisfied support upon which Cromwell's regime relied. The Presbyterian Lilburne embodied the outlook of those appeasers and compromisers who looked earnestly to the Protectorate to produce an enduring constitutional settlement which precluded the return of the Stuarts. Robert Lilburne, insofar as he concurred in Whittingham's recommendation, revealed, perhaps, the first open signs of estrangement from his family – and in truth his status and outlook were those of Hobson rather than his uncle. Timothy Whittingham's response was also significant. His family had impeccable puritan credentials and he had supported all phases of the Revolution since 1642 and earlier. He could not be identified with any group or interest – Vane, Haslerig, Lilburnes – but he almost certainly represented grass-roots puritan radicalism in the county equally as well as a Lilburne or anyone else. In this Hobson-Lilburne incident, whatever his precise motivation, he felt strong enough to declare unequivocally against a principle county representative of the Protectorate government.

On April 21 1658 at the first Durham Sessions after the dissolution of Cromwell's third Parliament the Sheriff, Justices and Grand Jury sent up an address of loyalty to the Protector. The names of only seven Justices appeared, however, all of them predictable – Francis Wren, Thomas Delaval, George Lilburne, not put out of the commission, and his son Thomas, Anthony Smith, Henry Eden and Richard Rowe.[90] Whittingham, serving a second year as Sheriff, signed too, but there was still rancour between him and the Lilburnes. On October 11, little more than a month after Cromwell's death, Thomas Lilburne complained of Whittingham's demeanour to Thurloe:

> since the Parliament was dissolved good men, was afflicted at the cause thereof, others too ready to hold forth what single persons would do with Parliaments and in such a time the Sheriff came not to the Sessions, nor kept that correspondence with the Justices in their Sessions as formerly.[91]

His negligence, added Lilburne, had caused him to be fined by the Judges at the last Assize. It is not clear whether Lilburne was accusing Whittingham of disaffection or incompetence, but the Sheriff's tardiness in seeing Richard Cromwell proclaimed in Durham brought other complaint from him.[92]

In the heightening national crisis of 1658–9 it was Thomas Lilburne who firmly identified himself in the maintenance of Richard Cromwell's cause in Durham. He communicated frequently with Thurloe and on October 12 1658 wrote: 'I am so settled upon this government, that I am ready to part with anything for the maintaining of it.' At the same time he expressed misgivings over the proposed increases in the army's control over its own affairs,[93] the issue which was one of the reasons for Richard Cromwell's first and only Parliament, in January 1659. Because it reverted to the electoral system prior to 1642 there was, once again, no representative for the County or City of Durham. Thomas Lilburne, however, as one of the reeling government's supporters, was one of the two members elected for Newcastle.[94]

By April 22 Cromwell had abdicated and his Parliament had disappeared. The Rump was restored and expelled again by Lambert and by autumn a Committee of Safety had appeared in its stead. In Durham, as elsewhere, it was the radical republican soldiers who answered to it – Paul Hobson as Deputy Governor of Newcastle, Thomas Gower as commander of the Durham militia, John Jobling the keeper of Durham gaol and Lambert's principal deputy in the North East, Robert Lilburne.[95] The announcement by Monk, after the Rump's expulsion, of his intention to intervene in English affairs, had an immediate effect upon Durham Royalists. 'They rant high with Monk's declaration and this last week there was a declaration abroad from Charles Stuart, which much heightens them,' Hobson and Jobling reported to the Committee of Safety on October 31.[96]

The influence in the North, in November and December, of Haslerig, who had parted company with the army irreconcilables of the Committee of Safety earlier in the year, was considered crucial by Monk, although it is doubtful whether Haslerig could still control those Northern forces nominally still under his control in the welter of contradictory orders flying about from Gower, Hobson and Robert Lilburne. In Durham it was Thomas Lilburne who was attempting to realise the wishes of Haslerig in London to preserve the county for Monk and the Parliament. Thomas had spent some time in Scotland in 1658/9 and had accepted a commission from Monk there.[97] In the last few weeks of 1659, under Monk's orders, he was attempting to counter the supporters of the Committee of Safety and to rally support in the county by announcing that the moderate and politically unsullied Fairfax would soon show himself and act for Monk in Yorkshire. When, in mid-December, Lambert moved Northwards with his forces to Newcastle accompanied by Robert Lilburne as Governor of York, Thomas Lilburne, not without difficulty, purged his own troop of horse and marched to York to join Fairfax. From there he reported to Haslerig in London on January 3 1660 and of his cousin Robert asserted that he 'is known to be altogether his (i.e. Lambert's) creature,' and had expressed as his sentiments of the Parliament, 'he hoped never a true Englishman would name the Parliament again and that he would have the house pulled down where they sat for fear it should prove infectious.'[98]

In the event, there was no conflict, and Monk entered London on February 3, rightly greeted as the harbinger of a restored monarchy. In the City of Durham three weeks later, Monk's garrison of soldiers were being invited to drink the King's health by a crowd gathered at a market-place tavern. Bonfires were lit and the cry went up for King and free Parliament before the soldiers at last roughly dispersed the crowd.[99]

The open opposition of Robert and Thomas Lilburne revealed the split which the crisis had wrought in the family. George, Richard and Thomas – and until his defection, Henry – had endured as committed servants of the Revolution since its earliest days. They were Presbyterian in religion, however, and the fierce, covenanting spirit exemplified by George Lilburne in 1640 became, like virtually all English Presbyterian sentiments, muted and took on a reactionary aspect beside the currents of Independency from 1647 onwards, and which brought Henry Lilburne to a fatal shift. All remained loyal to the subsequent regimes; radicals in calling for the King's trial, reliable Commonwealth men despite local grievances and wielders of high authority as servants of the Protector. At the same time their political radicalism had become moderate and relatively respectable in its support of Cromwell and his son.

Robert Lilburne, however, like his brother John, was imbued with a more uncompromising spirit in religion and politics which carried him through the roles of republican soldier, sectary and regicide and had caused him to serve Cromwell with the mounting unhappiness of many in the army and which brought him into the General Council of Officers in October 1659 with Lambert, Fleetwood, Vane, Desborough and others.[100] The rift in the family caused by the final progression of events was indicative of the gulf which had grown between that minority of republican soldiers and that swelling majority of all other shades and degrees of conviction which had trodden the gradual road of moderation and stability which ended in the return of the King.

The Restoration in Durham was an unmistakeable restitution of the past. From the old Laudian John Cosin, who returned as Bishop, downwards, the faces and names which had filled the temporal and spiritual government of the county before 1644 reappeared in force. Those unequivocal and long-serving supporters of the Interregnum regimes were at pains to make what peace they could. Most, if not all, quickly disappeared from their offices, some were faced with retribution, suspicion and dislike – not least among these the Lilburnes, albeit their fortunes were varied and not overwhelmingly disastrous.

Robert Lilburne was one of those twenty-six regicides still living who were expected out of the Act of Amnesty which had been promised by Charles II from Breda. He was committed into the charge of the Sergeant of the House by the Convention Parliament and tried and condemned as a regicide although he had submitted himself and accepted the King's pardon early in June.[101] In October his forfeited property at Thickley Punchardon was being petitioned for by the widow of a Royalist sufferer as restitution for her late husband's losses.[102] On October 31 1661 Lilburne was sent to St. Nicholas Island near Plymouth and died there in 1665 at the age of fifty-two.[103] He could count himself fortunate, perhaps, to escape execution – certainly in comparison to the treatment meted out to his near neighbour in Durham, Henry Vane. Under house arrest at Raby Castle since January 1660, Vane was, of course, of much greater political significance and although he had taken no part in the King's trial he was denounced as one of the King's Judges.[104] His execution was justified as an expedient against a man too dangerous to let live.[105]

On July 6 1660, soon after his return to England, John Cosin was writing to the Court to make a particular attack on two other Durham Lilburnes, George and Thomas. He recalled their roles as instigators of the county's petition for the trial of the King and identified them as the principle agents of the Protectorate regime in Durham. 'They are now looked upon . . . as men below all public employment,' asserted Cosin, 'they have too exceedingly served the designs of the tyrant Oliver beyond any men in the County.' He was especially harsh upon Thomas Lilburne for his role as a commissioner under the Major Generals and as a Protectorate M.P. 'Yet he saith,' ended Cosin bitterly, 'he hath of late got into the General's (i.e. Monk's) favour and hopes by some means he hath used to him, to be freed from his deserved punishment.'[106] Despite Cosin's chagrin Thomas seems to have done just this. There is nothing to suggest that he did not live quietly, without harrassment, at his father's estate of Offerton near Sunderland, helping his father found the hospital at Houghton-le-Spring before his death in 1665. His monument in Houghton church bore a reference to his part in the King's restoration.[107]

His father did not fare so well. Now entering advanced age, George Lilburne had been, since the 1630s at least, the personification of puritan radicalism in the county, both as the opponent of conciliar absolutism and Laudian innovation, and had not figured greatly in the county's affairs in the Interregnum's last few years. For several more years, however, his name continued to be linked with the body of resistance to the Restoration which threatened – or was believed to threaten – it in Durham as elsewhere. Typical of this was a warrant issued by Cosin as Lord Lieutenant for Lilburne's arrest as a dangerous and disaffected person who had failed to appear before him when summoned and had left his usual dwelling. Cosin ordered his house to be searched for arms and Lilburne committed to Durham gaol when found.[108] When, in 1664, the Derwentdale Plot was uncovered in the county almost inevitably the informer Ellerington listed George among his plotters as 'Oliver's captain.'[109] Nothing was ever pressed against him in what was at best an insubstantial intrigue. Things improved however. In January and February 1666 he was still exercising influence and authority on his own stamping-ground of Sunderland when he was responsible for the distribution of £50 from a county fund for plague relief in the town[110] and in 1669 he spent £2,750 on the purchase of the manor of Barmston on the lower Wear.[111] Nothing if not a survivor, he died in wealth and comfort in 1676 at an extreme age.

George's elder brother Richard seems not to have been harried at all. Father of the most celebrated and notorious of the Lilburnes and continuously active in the county's affairs throughout the years of Revolution, he appears, nevertheless, in his own person never to have been the force that his brother George was and his role was always essentially a subordinate one and apparently recognised as such. He lived out the initial Restoration years quietly and was one of only two former prominent Cromwellians who were invited, or permitted, to sign a Loyal Declaration of Association for the King's Safety made by the county's gentlemen in January 1664.[112] With the Lilburnes there disappeared into obscurity those other personalities who had served the Revolution in the county for twenty years – Anthony Smith, Timothy Whittingham, John Middleton, Robert Hutton, Francis Wren and others. Like the Lilburnes they were tainted men and the re-establishment, almost in its entirety, of the old Palatine structure brought with it those families, patiently Royalist, who emerged once more to renew their traditional roles within it. The Cromwellians at least appear to have sunk into obscurity by and large in a spirit intended by the Act of Indemnity, without serious molestation.

There was loss also for all those who had attempted to benefit from the purchase of crown or church lands since 1646. The Lilburnes contested their right to the Dean and Chapter land they had bought up at Bearpark near Durham,[113] and their old associate Thomas Midford threatened to defend his prebendal purchases near Pittington.[114] It was soon clear that resistance was unavailing, however, and other local purchasers had their speculation set at nought too. Yet county men like the Lilburnes were not large-scale losers: these were the families of Haslerig and his confederate the late George Fenwick with their huge episcopal and capitular purchases in Durham, and Thomas Andrew and Walter Boothby, representative figures of London capital who lost substantially in this falling-out of events.

About 1650 Thomas Shadforth, at that time in dispute with the Lilburnes, charged George:

> Truth is, your play was always to save stakes and now you have run through Cavalier, rigid Presbyterian, Independent and arrived at . . . and doubt will never prove martyr if there should be a further gradation or change.[115]

Indeed, Shadforth, himself by no means constant in his loyalties, was to see the Lilburnes shift their ground again, becoming Commonwealth men, Cromwellians and ultimately agents of the Restoration – albeit with the family politically rent, at least, by that time. Since the 1630s the brothers George and Richard had been recognised as political and religious oppositionists and their overall sincerity of conviction can scarcely be doubted. Yet despite this commitment there always remained in their actions an element of pragmatism and opportunism in the changing stream of events. There is evidence, for instance, which shows that George had indeed committed a delinquent offence in co-operating with Royalist authorities in September 1642 as his enemies later pressed against him.[116] Lilburne was forced to an admission but claimed he acted under duress: he was indeed no martyr – but in this too he was unexceptional.

The family generally was marked by Presbyterian beliefs which proved the undoing of Henry Lilburne in 1648, yet George, Richard and Thomas were able to make the transition into supporters of a Commonwealth of Republicans and Independents while carrying their own narrow tenets with them. Thomas Lilburne, particularly in his influential years towards the conclusion of the Interregnum, also showed the same accommodating latitude for his convictions in the final sequence of events. Against the stances of George, Richard and Thomas, Robert Lilburne's steady, adamant adherence to his beliefs is more admirable and attractive. As a Baptist his religious thinking went beyond the pale set by his father and uncle and if his social and political radicalism did not extend as far as his celebrated brother's he was yet without Freeborn John's exasperating truculence and defiance. He produced military and administrative qualities of a high order in the service of his own view of the Revolution and more than any other member of the Durham Lilburnes he succeeded in holding to something like a straight and constant identity.

Of the years of the English Revolution it has been remarked:

> To very few men active in public affairs can a single political or religious label be attached which remains valid from, say, 1638–1662.[117]

The observation is to a certain extent a statement of the obvious insofar as any revolutionary pattern is marked by spontaneity and uncontrolled changes of direction which demand new responses and attitudes from participants. Yet the changing stances of the Lilburnes in altering circumstances serve out the truth of it well. The family penchant for vigorous involvement and confrontation was indulged in these years and in so doing the Lilburnes secured for themselves the odium of being the

Great Rebellion's ogres in Durham and the North East – a reputation which still clings to them. Yet that was a possibility which they forthrightly or foolishly – and from the viewpoint of the Lilburne disposition it is not easy to decide which – chose to ignore. It was, then, undoubtedly out of an admixture of personal conviction, convenience and advantage that the Lilburnes, together with that not over-large nucleus of men who served the governments of the Revolution in Durham, accommodated themselves to its changing phases and its demise.

NOTES

1. P.R.O., SP 16/447/27.
2. *C.S.P., 1639–40*, pp. 515–6.
3. H. L. Robson, 'George Lilburne, Mayor of Sunderland'. *The Antiquities of Sunderland*, 22 (1960), pp. 86–132.
4. W. Fordyce, *History and Antiquities of the County Palatine of Durham* (1857), Vol. I, p. 400.
5. Thomas Saunders, *An additionall Answer to a Pamphlet called A Remonstrance written by Mr George Lilburne* (n.d.) Huntingdon Library, San Marino, California.
6. M. James, *Family, Lineage and Civil Society* (1974), p. 195.
7. P.R.O., SP 16/447/27.
8. *C.S.P., 1657–8*, pp. 78, 101; *Ibid., 1658–9*, pp. 148–9; J. W. Steel, *Early Friends in the North* (1905) p. 18.
9. *C.S.P., (Additional), 1625–49*, p. 521.
10. *C.S.P., 1640*, pp. 346–7.
11. *Records of the Committees for Compounding with Delinquent Royalists in Durham and Northumberland* ed. R. Welford, S.S., 111 (1905), p. 276.
12. *C.S.P., 1639–40*, pp. 427, 546–7, 566–7.
13. *Ibid.*, pp. 566–7.
14. *Ibid.*, p. 516.
15. George Lilburne, *A Most Lamentable Information of part of the Grievances of Mugleswick*, B.L., Thomason Tracts, 669 f. 4(62).
16. *C.J.*, II, p. 77.
17. *Allen Tracts*, ed. G. Allen (1777) 28; *Historical Collections of John Rushworth*, ed. J. Rushworth, 8 Vols. (1721), Vol. III, p. 1052.
18. Rushworth, *Historical Collections*, Vol. IV, p. 375; *C.J.*, II, pp. 469, 471; B.L., Thomason, E 141 (5).
19. His last appearance at the Durham sessions was on April 20 1642. D.C.R.O., Durham Quarter Session Order Books, Q/S/OB/ 3/23.
20. P.R.O., SP 23/103/153.
21. *C.J.*, II, p. 802.
22. They were George and Richard Lilburne, Francis Wren, Thomas Shadforth, Ralph Grey, Clement Fulthorpe, Thomas Midford, Robert Clavering and Robert Hutton, *C.J.*, II, pp. 853–4.
23. P.R.O., SP 23/247/291.
24. *H.M.C., Portland*, I, p. 75.
25. D.N.B.; G. E. Aylmer, *The King's Servants* (1961) pp. 85, 350–1.
26. *C.J.*, II, p. 424.
27. J. Lilburne, *The Resolved Man's Resolution* (1647), p. 17.
28. P.R.O., Commonwealth Exchequer, 28/227.
29. *C.S.P., 1644–5*, p. 275.
30. For contemporary sentiments see S. Shepard, *The Committee Man Curried* (1647).
31. The original committee was Sir Henry Vane, Senior, Sir Lionel Maddison, Sir Richard Bellasis, Sir George Vane, Christopher and Clement

Fulthorpe, James Clavering, Timothy Whittingham, George and Richard Lilburne, Nicholas Heath, Francis Wren and George Grey. Welford, *Records of the Committees*, p. 39; see also *Musgrave Muzled* (Newcastle, 1650), p. 17.

32. *C.J.*, III, pp. 561–2; Welford, *Records of the Committees*, p. 263.
33. *C.S.P., 1644–5*, p. 329.
34. Welford, *Records of the Committees*, pp. 276, 334.
35. *C.J.*, V, p. 239.
36. D.N.B.; D. Underdown, *The Reign of King Pym* (1941), pp. 5–6.
37. J. Lilburne, *A Just Reproof to Haberdashers' Hall*, (1651), p. 3.
38. Rushworth, *Historical Collections*, Vol. VI, p. 398; Vol. VII, p. 797, 949.
39. Newcastle Central Library, Newcastle Common Council Minute Book 1639–56, p. 83; J. Lilburne, *A Just Reproof*, p. 4. Lilburne's action was overruled by Parliament. *C.J.*, V, p. 638.
40. *C.J.*, V, pp. 436, 445, 448.
41. Welford, *Records of the Committees*, p. 75.
42. *Ibid.*, pp. 276–7.
43. *Musgrave Muzled*, p. 17.
44. Welford, *Records of the Committees*, p. 390.
45. John Hedworth, *The Oppressed Man's Out-cry*, (1651). Hedworth, Harraton's actual owner and original lessor, here sets out his own case and that of Primate, Grey and Lilburne.
46. This was his *A Just Reproof to Haberdashers' Hall.*
47. H. Brailsford, *The Levellers in the English Revolution* ed. C. Hill, (1961), p. 611.
48. J. Musgrave, *A True and Exact Relation of the Great and Heavy Pressures and Grievances the well-affected of the Northern bordering Counties lye under* (1650).
49. R. Surtees, *History and Antiquities of the County Palatine of Durham*, 4 Vols. (1816–40), Vol. I, p. CV (n.).
50. Saunders, *An Additionall Answer.*
51. *A True and Perfect Relation of a Great Victory obtained by the Parliament's Forces in Northumberland* (Jul. 1648). B.L., Thomason, E451 (22).
52. See the list of prisoners given in *A True and Perfect Relation.*
53. *Sir Arthur Haslerig's letter to the Lords and Commons at Derby House concerning the Revolt and Recovery of Tinmouth Castle*, (Aug. 1648), B.L., Thomason, E458 (26); *A Terrible and Bloudy Fight at Tinmouth Castle*, (Aug. 1648), B.L., Thomason, E459 (4).
54. *Ibid.*
55. *A Collection of the S(tate) P(apers of John) T(hurloe Esq.)*, ed. T. Birch, 7 Vols. (1742), Vol. I, p. 98.
56. B.L., Thomason, E417 (15).
57. *A True and Perfect Relation.*
58. J. Lilburne, *The Second Part of England's New-Chaines Discovered* (1649), p. 14.
59. *Memoirs of the Life of Mr Ambrose Barnes*, ed. W. H. D. Longstaffe, 50 (1867), p. 351–2.
60. *C.S.P., 1660–1*, p. 113.

61. John Lilburne, *A Preparative to a Hue and Cry after Sir Arthur Haslerig*, (1649), pp. 38–9.
62. *C.J.*, VI, pp. 386–8, 395–6.
63. Initially it comprised Thomas Delaval and Francis Wren, Haslerig's son Thomas and another Haslerig protégé – the St. Helens Auckland Quaker Anthony Pearson. Welford, *Records of the Committees*, p. 45.
64. Undated, but probably sent up in the latter part of 1649. P.R.O., SP 23/153/257.
65. *C.S.P., 1649–50*, p. 25.
66. *Liber Pacis*, P.R.O., C193/13/3.
67. J. Lilburne, *A Just Reproof*, p. 3.
68. D.C.R.O., Durham Quarter Session Order Books, Q/S/OB 4/177.
69. *S.P.T.*, Vol IV, 509; Vol. V, p. 296.
70. Fordyce, *History of Durham*, Vol. I, p. 570; Worcester College Library, Oxford, Clarke MS. LXXXXVI, Robert Lilburne's Letter-Book 1652–3.
71. A. C. Underwood, *A History of the English Baptists*, (1947), pp. 85, 92–3.
72. D.C.L., Allen MS. 7, f. 193; Randall, MS. 13, ff. 116–7.
73. *Calendar of the Proceedings of the Committee for the Advance of Money*, Vol. II, pp. 1082–4.
74. *S.P.T.*, Vol. V, pp. 296, 299, 349.
75. Ibid., Vol. IV, p. 283. When, in Sept. 1656, Sir Edward Hyde wrote seeking the names of loyal and discreet Royalists in the Northern counties Sir Marmaduke Langdale supplied him with three for Durham – Sir Richard Tempest of Stella, John Tempest of Old Durham, and Colonel John Forcer of Harbour House. *H.M.C., Various Coll.*, Vol. II, p. 352.
76. R. Howell, *Newcastle upon Tyne and the Puritan Revolution.* (1969), pp. 204–8.
77. *S.P.T.*, Vol. IV, p. 541.
78. G. E. Aylmer, *The State's Servants*, p. 314.
79. P.R.O., SP 29/7/59(1).
80. i.e Sir Arthur Haslerig.
81. *S.P.T.*, Vol. V, p. 296.
82. D.C.L., Randall MS. 13, ff. 116–7.
83. *S.P.T.*, Vol. V, p. 572; *C.S.P., 1661–2*, pp. 42, 313.
84. D.C.L., Randall MS. 13, f. 125.
85. D.C.L., Hunter MS. 24, ff. 2–8. Miles Stapleton, *A Printed Answer to the Five Reasons* (n.p., n.d.).
86. *C.J.*, IV, p. 410.
87. *C.S.P., 1655–6*, p. 262.
88. *Dairy of Thomas Burton*, ed. J. T. Rutt, 4 Vols. (1828), Vol. II, pp. 531–40. Significant absentees are Thomas Delaval, Francis Wren and George Lilburne.
89. *C.S.P., 1657–8*, pp. 78, 101.
90. Allen, *Allen Tracts*, 35a.
91. *S.P.T.*, Vol. VII, p. 434.
92. *Ibid.*, p. 411.
93. *Ibid.*, p. 436.
94. See Howell, *Newcastle in the Puritan Revolution*, p. 209 n.4 on this point.

95. Welford, *Records of the Committees*, p. 75.
96. *Ibid.*
97. Surtees, *History of Durham*, Vol. I, p. 258 n.(e).
98. P.R.O. SP 18/219/5.
99. *H.M.C. Leybourne Popham*, p. 159.
100. B. Whitelocke, *Memorials of English Affairs* (1853), p. 685.
101. *C.J.*, VIII, pp. 61, 66; *C.S.P., 1660–1*, p. 41.
102. *Ibid.*, p. 345.
103. *C.S.P., 1661–2*, p. 130.
104. *Calendar of State Papers, Venetian, 1659–61*, pp. 110, 173.
105. G. Burnet, *A History of my own Time*, 6 Vols. (1823), Vol. I, pp. 278, 280.
106. P.R.O., SP 29/7/59 – I.
107. Surtees, *History of Durham*, Vol. I, p. 258 n.(e).
108. D.U.L., Mickleton and Spearman MS. 31, f. 93.
109. J. D. Brearley, 'Discipline and Local Government in the diocese of Durham, 1660–72' (unpub. M. A. thesis, Durham Univ. 1974), appendix C.
110. *The Correspondence of John Cosin, Bishop of Durham*, ed. G. Ornsby, S.S., 2 Vols, 52, I, (1869), 55, II, (1872), II, p. 327.
111. Robson, *Antiquities of Sunderland*, 22, p. 122.
112. D.U.L., Mickleton and Spearman MS. 31, f. 73. The other was Francis Wren. *Ibid.* f. 81.
113. *C.S.P., 1660–1*, p. 113; Lambeth Palace Library, Ecclesiastical Records of the Commonwealth, Vol. XII, a/4 29.
114. *Correspondence of John Cosin, II*, pp. 3–4.
115. T. Shadforth, *Innocency modestly vindicated and truth impartially, though (but partly discovered) by Thomas Shadforth.* (n.d.) Huntingdon Library, San Marino, California.
116. P.R.O., SP 23/153/329–32. Lilburne's was one of three signatures on two warrants for the supply of horses from Darlington and Stockton wards to the Earl of Newcastle in Newcastle.
117. L. Stone, *Causes of the English Revolution* (1972), p. 34.

BIBLIOGRAPHY

The Bibliography comprises books, articles and pamphets referred to in the footnotes of the papers. It does not purport to be a comprehensive Bibliography of the region during the sixteenth and seventeenth centuries. Calendars have not been listed.

Acts of the Durham High Commission Court, ed. Longstaffe, Surtees Society, 34, 1858.

G. Allan, *Collectanea ad Statum Civilem et Ecclesiasticum Comitatus Dunelmensis* (1763–99).

G. Anstruther, *The Seminary Priests I, 1558–1603* (1968).

R. B. Armstrong, *History of Liddesdale, Eskdale, Wauchopdale and the Debateable Land* (1883).

G. E. Aylmer, *The King's Servants* (1961).

G. E. Aylmer, *The State's Servants* (1973).

R. Baddeley and J. Naylor, *Life of Dr. Thomas Morton, late Bishop of Duresme* (1669).

D. M. Barratt, 'The Condition of the Parish Clergy from the Reformation to 1660 with special reference to the Dioceses of Oxford, Gloucester and Worcester' (Oxford D. Phil. thesis, 1949).

J. M. V. Bean, *The Estates of the Percy Family* (1966).

W. Bean, *The Parliamentary Representation of the Six Northern Counties of England* (1890).

B. W. Beckingsale, 'The Characteristics of the Tudor North', *Northern History*, 5, 1969.

B. L. Beer, *Northumberland* (1973).

H. S. Bennett, *The Pastons and their England* (1979).

C. Hunter Blair, 'The Sheriffs of the County of Durham', *Archaeologia Aeliana*, 4th Series, 22, 1944.

C. Hunter Blair, 'Members of Parliament for Berwick-upon-Tweed and Morpeth, 1558–1831', *Archaeologia Aeliana*, 4th Series, 24, 1946.

C. Hunter Blair, 'Wardens and Deputy Wardens of the Marches', *Archaeologia Aeliana*, 4th Series, 28, 1950.

C. W. Boase, *Register of the University of Oxford* (1885).

R. Borland, *Border Raids and Reivers* (1895).

M. Bowker, *The Secular Clergy in the Diocese of Lincoln, 1495–1520* (1968).
H. Brailsford, *The Levellers in the English Revolution*, ed. Hill, (1961).
J. Brand, *History and Antiquities of Newcastle-upon-Tyne* (1789).
J. D. Brearley, 'Discipline and Local Government in the Diocese of Durham, 1660–72' (Durham M.A. thesis, 1974).
W. Brereton, *Travels in Holland, the United Provinces, England, Scotland and Ireland*, ed. Hawkins, Chetham Society, 1844.
W. M. Bryce, *The Scottish Greyfriars* (1909).
G. Burnet, *A History of My Own Time*, 6 Vols. (1823).
G. Burnet, *The History of the Reformation of the Church of England*, 2 Vols. (1850).
C. H. Cadogan, 'Brinkburn Priory Minister's Account of 1535/36', *Berwickshire Naturalists Club*, 12, 1887.
The Camden Miscellany, Vol. 9, ed. Simpson, Camden Society, New Series, 53, 1895.
The Canons of 1571, ed. Collins, Church Historical Society Tracts, 40, 1899.
J. Cannon, *Parliamentary Reform, 1640–1832* (1973).
R. Christophers, 'The Social and Educational Background of the Surrey Clergy, 1520–1620' (London Ph.D. thesis, 1975).
Churchwardens' Accounts for Pittington and other parishes in the Diocese of Durham, 1580–1700, ed. Barmby, Surtees Society, 84, 1888.
E. Coke, *The Fourth Part of the Institutes* (1648).
P. Collinson, 'The Puritan Classical Movement in the reign of Elizabeth', (London PhD. thesis, 1957).
P. Collinson, *Letters of Thomas Wood, Puritan*, Institute of Historical Reserch, Special Supplement, 5.
Commons Debates, 1621, ed. Notestein, Relf and Simpson, 7 Vols. (1935).
Commons Debates, 1629, ed. Notestein and Relf (1921).
Correspondence of Matthew Parker, ed. Bruce and Perowne, Parker Society, 1853.
The Correspondence of John Cosin, 1, ed. Ornsby, Surtees Society, 52, 1869.
The Correspondence of John Cosin II, ed. Ornsby, Surtees Society, 55, 1872.
J. H. Creham, 'The Return to Obedience: new judgement on Cardinal Pole', *The Month*, New Series, 14, 1955.
G. B. Crosby, 'Durham Cathedral's Liturgical Music Manuscripts, c.1620–1640', *Durham University Journal*, 66, 1973/4.
M. C. Cross, 'Berwick-on-Tweed and the neighbouring Parts of Northumberland on the eve of the Armada', *Archaeologia Aeliana*, 4th Series, 41, 1963.
M. C. Cross, *The Puritan Earl* (1966).
M. C. Cross, 'The Economic Problems of the See of York', in *Land, Church and People*, ed. Thirsk, Agricultural History Supplement, 1970.
G. J. Cumming, *The Anglicanism of John Cosin* (Durham Cathedral Lecture, 1975).
Depositions and Other Ecclesiastical Proceedings from the Courts of Durham, ed. Raine, Surtees Society, 21, 1845.
Diary of Thomas Burton, ed. Rutt, 4 Vols. (1828).
The Diary of Henry Machyn, 1550–63, ed. Nichols, Camden Society, 1847.

A. G. Dickens, *Lollards and Protestants in the Diocese of York, 1509–1558* (1959).

A. G. Dickens, *The English Reformation* (1966).

R. B. Dobson, *Durham Priory, 1400–1450* (1973).

M. H. Dodds, 'The Bishops' Boroughs', *Archaeologia Aeliana*, 3rd Series, 12, 1915.

M. H. and R. Dodds, *The Pilgrimage of Grace and the Exeter Conspiracy*, 2 Vols. (1915).

J. L. Drury, 'Durham Palatinate Forest Law and Administration, especially in Weardale up to 1440', *Archaeologia Aeliana*, 5th Series, 6, 1978.

J. L. Drury, 'Sir Arthur Hesilrige and the Weardale Chest', *Transactions of the Architectural and Antiquarian Society of Durham and Newcastle*, New Series, 5, 1980.

Durham Cathedral Statutes, ed. Thompson, Surtees Society, 143, 1929.

Durham Civic Memorials, ed. Whiting, Surtees Society, 160, 1952.

J. Dyer, *Reports of Cases* (ed. Vaillant), 3 Vols (1794).

D. E. Easson, 'The Reformation and the Monasteries in Scotland and England, some comparisons', *Transactions of the Scottish Ecclesiological Society*, 15 (1), 1957.

J. G. Edwards, *The Principality of Wales, 1267–1967*, Caernarvon Historical Society, (1969).

A. B. Emden, *A Biographical Register of the University of Oxford to A.D. 1500* (1957).

Essays on the Scottish Reformation, ed. McRoberts, (1962).

Fasti Dunelmenses, ed. Boutflower, Surtees Society, 139, 1926.

R. Fieldhouse and B. Jennings, *A History of Richmond and Swaledale* (1978).

A. J. Fletcher, *A County Community in Peace and War: Sussex, 1600–1660* (1975).

A. J. Fletcher, 'Factionalism in Town and Countryside: the significance of Puritanism and Arminianism', *Studies in Church History*, 16, 1979.

W. Fordyce, *History and Antiquities of the County Palatine of Durham* (1857).

A. Forster, 'Bishop Tunstall's Priests', *Recusant History*, 9, 1967/8.

A. Foster, 'The Function of a Bishop: the career of Richard Neile, 1562–1640', in *Continuity and Change*, ed. O'Day and Heal (1976).

A. Foster, 'A Biography of Archbishop Richard Neile, 1562–1640', (Oxford D. Phil. thesis, 1978).

G. M. Fraser, *The Steel Bonnets* (1971).

J. Freeman, 'The Parish Ministry in the Diocese of Durham, c.1570–1640' (Durham Ph.D. thesis, 1979).

C. H. Garrett, *The Marian Exiles* (1938).

W. S. Gibson, *The Monastery of Tynemouth*, 2 Vols. (1846–47).

I. M. Green, *The Re-Establishment of the Church of England, 1660–1663* (1978).

J. Gruenfelder, 'The Election to the Short Parliament', in *Early Stuart Studies*, ed. Reinmuth (1970).

C. Haigh, *Reformation and Resistance in Tudor Lancashire* (1975).

C. Haigh, 'Puritan Evangelism in the Reign of Elizabeth I', *English Historical Review*, 92, 1977.

S. M. Harrison, *The Pilgrimage of Grace in the Lace Counties, 1536–37*, Royal Historical Society Studies in History, 27, 1981.

Sir Arthur Haslerig's letter to the Lords and Commons at Derby House concerning the Revolt and Recovery of Tinmouth Castle (1648).
D. Hay, 'The Dissolution of the Monasteries in the Diocese of Durham', *Archaeologia Aeliana*, 4th Series, 15, 1938.
F. Heal, *Of Prelates and Princes* (1980).
J. Hedworth, *The Oppressed Man's Out-cry* (1651).
R. Hegg, *The Legend of St. Cuthbert, or the Historie of his Churches at Lindisfarne, Cynecascestre and Dunholm* (1663).
C. Hill, *Society and Puritanism in Pre-Revolutionary England* (1964).
D. Hirst, *The Representative of the People? Voters and Voting in England under the early Stuarts* (1975).
Historiae Dunelmensis Scriptores Tres, Surtees Society, 9, 1839.
Historical Collections of John Rushworth, ed. Rushworth, (1721).
J. F. Hodgson, 'The Church of St. Andrew Auckland', *Archaeologia Aeliana*, New Series, 20.
J. Hodgson and J. H. Hinde, *History of Northumberland*, 3 Vols. (1827–58).
J. G. Hoffman, 'John Cosin's Cure of Souls', *Durham University Journal*, 81, 1978.
C. Holmes, *Seventeenth Century Lincolnshire* (1980).
C. Holmes, 'The County Community in Stuart Historiography', *Journal of British Studies*, 19, 1980.
The House of Commons, 1558–1603, 3 Vols., ed. Hasler, (1981).
R. Howell, *Newcastle-upon-Tyne and the Puritan Revolution* (1967).
W. Hutchinson, *The History and Antiquities of the County Palatine of Durham*, 3 Vols, (1823).
The Injunctions and Other Ecclesiastical Proceedings of Richard Barnes, Bishop of Durham, ed. Raine, Surtees Society, 1845.
M. E. James, 'The Sixteenth and Seventeenth Centuries', in *Durham County* (British Association, 1970).
M. E. James, 'The Concept of Order and the Northern Rising of 1569', *Past and Present*, 60, 1973.
M. E James, *Family, Lineage and Civil Society* (1974).
S. M. Keeling, 'The Church and Religion in the Anglo-Scottish Border Counties, 1534–1572' (Durham Ph.D. thesis, 1975).
E. Le Roy Ladurie, *Montaillou* (1978).
P. Lake, 'Matthew Hutton: a Puritan Bishop?', *History*, 64, 1979.
W. M. Lamont, *Godly Rule: Politics and Religion, 1603–60* (1969).
G. T. Lapsley, *The County Palatine of Durham* (1900).
A. F. Leach, *English Schools at the Reformation, 1546–1548* (1972).
G. Lilburne, *A Most Lamentable Information of part of the Grievances of Mugleswick* (n.d.).
J. Lilburne, *The Resolved Man's Resolution* (1647).
J. Lilburne, *The Second Part of England's New-Chaines Discovered* (1649).
J. Lilburne, *A Preparative to a Hue and Cry after Sir Arthur Haslerig* (1649).
J. Lilburne, *A Just Reproof to Haberdashers' Hall* (1651).
D. M. Loades, 'The Last Years of Cuthbert Tunstall', Durham University Journal, 66 1973/74.
D. M. Loades, *The Oxford Martyrs* (1970).

D. M. Loades, *Politics and the Nation, 1450–1660* (1974).
D. M. Loades, *The Reign of Mary* (1979).
R. A. Lomas, 'Developments in land tenure on the Prior of Durham's estate in the late Middle Ages', *Northern History*, 13, 1977.
Lowther Family Estate Books, ed. Phillips, Surtees Society, 191, 1979.
A. A. Luxmoore, 'The Lieutenancy of County Durham', *Archaeologia Aeliana*, 4th Series, 30, 1952.
W. MacCaffrey, The Shaping of the Elizabethan Régime (1969).
E. Mackenzie and M. Ross, *The County Palatine of Durham* (1834).
D. Marcombe, 'The Dean and Chapter of Durham, 1558–1603' (Durham Ph.D. thesis, 1973).
D. Marcombe, 'The Durham Dean and Chapter: old abbey writ large?' in *Continuity and Change*, ed. O'Day and Heal, (1976).
D. Marcombe, 'Bernard Gilpin: anatomy of an Elizabethan Legend', *Northern History*, 16, 1980.
D. Marcombe, 'Church Leaseholders: the decline and fall of a rural elite', in *Princes and Paupers in the English Church*, ed. O'Day and Heal (1981).
'St. Mary the Virgin's Hospital, Newcastle', *Archaeologia Aeliana*, New Series, 7, 1876.
Memoirs of the Life of Mr. Ambrose Barnes, ed Longstaffe, Surtees Society, 80, 1867.
T. Moir, *The Addled Parliament of 1614* (1958).
J. A. Muller, *Stephen Gardiner and the Tudor Reaction* (1926).
J. Musgrave, *A True and Exact Relation of the Great and Heavy Pressures and Grievances the well-affected of the Northern bordering counties lye under* (1650).
Musgrave Muzled (1650).
P. Mussett, *Deans and Canons of Durham, 1541–1900* (1974).
Northumberland County History, 15 Vols, (1893–1940).
Notes of the Debates in the House of Lords officially taken by Henry Elsing, clerk of the Parliaments, 1621, ed. Gardiner, Camden Society, Old Series, 103, 1870.
Notes of the Debates in the House of Lords, 1624 and 1626, ed. Gardiner, Camden Society, New Series, 24, 1879.
R. O'Day, *The English Clergy* (1979).
T. Oldfield, *The Representative History of Great Britain and Ireland*, 6 Vols. (1816).
R. R. Orr, *Reason and Authority: the Thought of William Chillingworth* (1967).
D. M. Palliser, *The Reformation in York, 1534–1553* (1971).
Parliamentary Surveys of the Bishopric of Durham, 1, ed. Kirby, Surtees Society 183, 1968.
J. Patten, *English Towns, 1500–1700* (1978).
The Petition . . . by the Parishioners of Pont Island against Dr. Gray (1642).
N. Pevsner, *The Buildings of England: County Durham* (1953).
The Priory of Hexham, ed. Raine, Surtees Society, 40, 1864.
Proceedings in Parliament, 1610, ed. Foster, 2 Vols. (1966).
J. S. Purvis, 'The Literacy of the Later Tudor Clergy in Yorkshire', *Studies in Church History*, 5, 1969.

T. I. Rae, *The Administration of the Scottish Frontier* (1966).
A. L. Raimes, 'Shortflatt Tower and its owners', *Archaeologia Aeliana*, 4th Series, 32, 1954.
J. Raine, *Auckland Castle* (1852).
Records of the Committees for compounding with Delinquent Royalists in Durham and Northumberland, ed. Welford, Surtees Society, III, 1905.
J. Reed, *The Border Ballads* (1973).
The Register of Richard Fox, Lord Bishop of Durham, 1494–1501, ed. Howden, Surtees Society, 147, 1932.
The Registers of Cuthbert Tunstall, Bishop of Durham, 1530–1559, and James Pilkington, Bishop of Durham, 1561–1571, ed. Hinde, Surtees Society, 161, 1952.
R. R. Reid, 'The Rebellion of the Earls, 1569', *Transactions of the Royal Historical Society*, 2nd Series, 20, 1906.
R. R. Reid, *The King's Council in the North* (1921).
C. I. A. Ritchie, *The Ecclesiastical Courts of York* (1956).
The Rites of Durham, ed. Fowler, Surtees Society, 107, 1902.
H. L. Robson, 'George Lilburne, Mayor of Sunderland', *The Antiquities of Sunderland*, 22, 1960.
H. L. Robson, 'The Cosin Furniture in Durham Churches', *The Antiquities of Sunderland*, 24, 1969.
V. A. Rowe, *Sir Henry Vane the Younger: a Study in Political and Administrative History* (1970).
The Royal Visitation of 1559, ed. Kitching, Surtees Society, 187, 1975.
R. Ruigh, *The Parliament of 1624, Politics and Foreign Policy* (1971).
C. Russell, *Parliaments and English Politics, 1621–29* (1979).
J. Sainty, *Lieutenants of Counties, 1585–1642*, Bulletin of the Institute of Historical Research, Special Supplement 8, 1970.
T. Saunders, *An Additionall Answer to a Pamphlet called A Remonstrance written by Mr. George Lilburne*, (n.d.).
Sermons and Society, ed. Welsby (1970).
T. Shadforth, *Innocency modestly vindicated and truth impartially, though (but partly discovered) by Thomas Shadforth* (n.d.).
C. Sharp, *Memorials of the Rebellion of 1569* (1840).
S. Shepard, *The Committee Man Curried* (1647).
J. Simon, *Education and Society in Tudor England* (1966).
P. Smart, *A Briefe but True Historicall Narration of some Notorious Acts and Speeches of Mr. John Cosens and some other of his companions contracted into Articles* (n.d.).
P. Smart, *The Vanitie and Downe-fall of Superstitious Popish Ceremonies, or a Sermon preached in the Cathedrall Church of Durham by one Mr. Peter Smart, a Prebend There* (1628).
P. Smart, *A Short Treatise of Altars, Altar-Furniture, Altar-Cringing and Musick of all the Quire, Singing-Men and Choristers when the Holy Communion Was Administered in the Cathedrall Church of Durham, by Prebendaries and Petty-Canons in Glorious Copes Embroidered with Images* (1629).
W. H. Smith, *Walks in Weardale* (1885).
H. M. Smith, *Pre-Reformation England* (1938).

M. Spufford, *Contrasting Communities* (1974).
M. Stapleton, *A Pointed Answer to the Five Reasons* (n.d.).
J. W. Steel, *Early Friends in the North* (1905).
L. Stone, *The Causes of the English Revolution* (1972).
R. L. Storey, *Thomas Langley and the Bishopric of Durham*, 1406–1537 (1961).
J. Strype, *Ecclesiastical Memorials*, 3 Vols. (1822).
J. Strype, *The Life and Acts of Matthew Parker*, 3 Vols. (1821).
J. Strype, *The History of the Life and Acts of Edmund Grindal* (1821).
C. Sturge, *Cuthbert Tunstall* (1938).
R. Surtees, *The History and Antiquities of the County Palatine of Durham*, 4 Vols, (1816–1820).
G. Tate, *History of the Borough, Castle and Barony of Alnwick* (1866).
A Terrible and Bloody Fight at Tinmouth Castle (1648).
K. V. Thomas, *Religion and the Decline of Magic* (1971).
M. J. Tillbrook, 'Some Aspects of the Government and Society of County Durham, 1558–1642' (Liverpool Ph.D. thesis, 1981).
A True and Perfect Relation of a Great Victory obtained by the Parliament's Forces in Northumberland (1648).
T. H. Turner, 'Copy of a Commission for Church Livings in Northumberland', *Archaeologia Aeliana*, 1st Series, 3, 1844.
N. R. N. Tyacke, 'Arminianism in England in Religion and Politics, 1603–1640' (Oxford D. Phil. thesis, 1968).
N. R. N. Tyacke, 'Puritanism, Arminianism and Counter-Revolution' in *The Origins of the English Civil War*, ed. Russell (1973).
D. Underdown, *The Reign of King Pym* (1941).
A. C. Underwood, *A History of the English Baptists* (1947).
Valor Ecclesiasticus, ed. Caley, 6 Vols, (1810–34).
J. and J. A. Venn, *Alumni Cantabrigiensis . . . to 1751* (1922–27).
Victoria History of the County of Durham, ed. Page, 3 Vols, (1905–28).
S. J. Watts, 'Tenant-right in Early Seventeenth Century Northumberland', *Northern History*, 6, 1971.
S. J. Watts, *From Border to Middle Shire: Northumberland, 1586–1625* (1975).
R. Welford, *History of Newcastle and Gateshead*, 3 Vols, (1885–87).
P. A. Welsby, *Lancelot Andrewes, 1555–1625* (1958).
B. Whitelocke, *Memorials of English Affairs* (1853).
C. E. Whiting, *A History of Durham University* (1932).
Wills and Inventories I, ed. Raine, Surtees Society, 2, 1835.
Wills and Inventories II, ed. Greenwell, Surtees Society, 38, 1860.
Wills and Inventories III, ed. Hodgson, Surtees Society, 112, 1906.
B. Wilson, 'The Changes of the Reformation Period in Durham and Northumberland' (Durham Ph.D. thesis, 1939).
K. L. Wood-Legh, *Perpetual Chantries in Britain* (1965).
The Works of Bishop Pilkington, ed. Scholefield, Parker Society, 1842.
The Zurich Letters, 1558–79, ed. Robinson, Parker Society, 1842.

INDEX